The Art and Architecture of Academic Writing

The Art and Architecture of Academic Writing

Patricia Prinz
New York City College of Technology,
City University of New York

Birna Arnbjörnsdóttir
University of Iceland

John Benjamins Publishing Company
Amsterdam / Philadelphia

The paper used in this publication meets the minimum requirements of the American National Standard for Information Sciences – Permanence of Paper for Printed Library Materials, ANSI z39.48-1984.

DOI 10.1075/z.231

Cataloging-in-Publication Data available from Library of Congress:
LCCN 2020050367 (PRINT) / 2020050368 (E-BOOK)

ISBN 978 90 272 0752 4 (HB) / ISBN 978 90 272 0751 7 (PB)
ISBN 978 90 272 6077 2 (E-BOOK)

© 2021 – John Benjamins B.V.
No part of this book may be reproduced in any form, by print, photoprint, microfilm, or any other means, without written permission from the publisher.

John Benjamins Publishing Co. · https://benjamins.com

Table of contents

Part I. Developing your academic voice   1

CHAPTER 1
The art of academic writing   3
- A. The social context of writing   4
  1. Public and private writing   5
  2. Genres   6
- B. Writing for the academic discourse community   8
  1. Formal and informal language in writing   9
  2. Academic vocabulary   12
  3. The art of writing: Developing an academic voice   15
  4. Avoiding plagiarism   17
  5. Academic communication   19
- C. Expanding language   20

CHAPTER 2
The architecture of academic writing   23
- A. Examining expository writing contexts   24
  1. The architecture of the expository essay   24
  2. Expository thesis statements   26
  3. Body paragraphs and evidence   31
- B. Understanding an essay assignment   36
  1. Analyzing the instructions   36
  2. Writing: Following the instructions for a writing assignment   38
- C. Expanding language: Avoiding sentence fragments   39
  1. Sentence fragments: Subordinate phrases   39

CHAPTER 3
AWARE: A framework for thesis-driven writing   45
- A. Examining AWARE   45
- B. AWARE in practice   46
  1. AWARE: Arranging to write   46
  2. AWARE: Writing   53
  3. AWARE: Assessing   55

4. AWARE: Revising 59
5. AWARE: Editing 61
C. Expanding language 62
  1. Sentence fragments – subordinate clauses 62
  2. Recognizing and correcting adverbial and noun clause fragments 66
D. Summary of The AWARE Approach 68

CHAPTER 4
Description and narrative in thesis-driven writing 69
A. Examining description in thesis-driven writing 70
  1. Description: Illustration vs. explanation 70
  2. Precise language in description 71
B. AWARE: Writing a description to support a thesis 74
  1. AWARE: Arranging to write a description 75
  2. AWARE: Writing the description 76
  3. AWARE: Assessing a description to support a thesis 78
  4. AWARE: Revising a description 78
  5. AWARE: Editing commas 79
D. Examining narrative to support a thesis statement 80
  1. The building blocks of narrative 80
  2. Analyzing narrative 80
E. AWARE: Writing a narrative to support a thesis 82
  1. AWARE: Arranging to write a narrative 82
  2. AWARE: Writing a narrative 83
  3. AWARE: Assessing a narrative 83
  4. AWARE: Revising a narrative 84
  5. AWARE: Editing introductory words, phrases, clauses 84
F. Expanding language 86

CHAPTER 5
The body of the essay 89
A. The architecture of body paragraphs 89
  1. The building blocks of an essay: Body paragraphs 90
B. AWARE: Writing the body of an enumeration essay 97
  1. AWARE: Arranging to write 98
  2. AWARE: Writing 101
  3. AWARE: Assessing 101
  4. AWARE: Revising 102
  5. AWARE: Editing 105
C. Expanding language 107

CHAPTER 6
Compare/contrast and cause/effect   111
A. Compare and contrast   111
   1. Examining compare/contrast   111
   2. Compare/contrast thesis statements   112
   3. The architecture of a compare/contrast essay   113
B. AWARE writing: Compare/contrast essay   118
   1. AWARE: Arranging to write   118
   2. AWARE: Writing   120
   3. AWARE: Assessing   121
   4. AWARE: Revising   122
   5. AWARE: Editing   124
C. Expanding language: Comma splices   125
D. Cause and effect   127
   1. Examining cause and effect   127
   2. The architecture of cause and effect   127
E. AWARE writing: Cause and effect   131
   1. Arranging to write: Cause and effect   132
   2. AWARE writing: Cause and effect   134
   3. AWARE: Assessing   134
   4. AWARE: Revising   134
   5. AWARE: Editing   135

CHAPTER 7
Introductions and conclusions   137
A. Introductions   138
   1. Examining the introduction   138
   2. Strategies for writing the introduction   140
B. AWARE: Writing the introduction to a compare/contrast essay   144
   1. AWARE: Arranging to write the introduction   144
   2. AWARE: Writing the introduction   145
   3. AWARE: Assessing the introduction   146
   4. AWARE: Revising the introduction   146
   5. AWARE: Editing the introduction   146
C. Conclusions   146
   1. Examining the conclusion   146
   2. Strategies for writing conclusions   147
D. AWARE: Writing the conclusion   151
   1. AWARE: Arranging to write the conclusion   151
   2. AWARE: Writing the conclusion to a compare/contrast essay   151

3. AWARE: Assessing the conclusion   151
4. AWARE: Revising the conclusion   152
5. AWARE: Editing   152
E. Putting it together: Revising and editing a full essay   153
  1. AWARE: Revising the full essay   153
  2. AWARE: Editing the full essay   153
F. AWARE independent writing assignments – enumeration essay and cause/effect essay   155
  1. The architecture of the essays   155
  2. Essay instructions   155

Part II. Presenting the views of others

CHAPTER 8
Research to support a thesis   159
A. Examining academic research   160
  1. Quantitative research   160
  2. Qualitative research   160
  3. Conducting research   161
  4. Primary and secondary data sources   162
B. Examining and avoiding plagiarism   163
  1. Examining quotations   163
  2. Examining paraphrase   169
  3. Examining summary   173
C. AWARE: Writing   178
  1. Writing a summary   178
  2. AWARE: Revising   179
  3. AWARE: Editing   179

CHAPTER 9
Conducting research for a case study   181
A. Examining the case study   182
  1. Defining the case study assignment   182
  2. The building blocks of the case study   183
  3. Conducting research for a case study   183
B. AWARE: Writing a case study   199
  1. Arranging to write a case study   199

CHAPTER 10
Writing the case study 207
A. Writing the case study 207
    1. From research question to thesis statement 208
    2. Presenting case study research 209
    3. Citing sources in the case study – APA 216
    4. Writing the introduction to a case study 220
    5. Writing the conclusion for the case study 223
B. AWARE: Writing the case study document 226
    1. AWARE Arranging to write 226
    2. AWARE: Writing the draft of the case study 227
    3. AWARE: Assessing 229
    4. AWARE: Revising 230
    5. AWARE: Editing 231

CHAPTER 11
Conducting research for an academic paper 237
A. Examining the research paper 238
    1. The literature review 238
    2. Understanding the assignment 240
    3. Examining the new working thesis 241
    4. Developing a new working thesis 242
    5. Formatting the research paper 243
B. Examining published sources: A review of the literature 244
    1. Disciplinary literacy – academic genres 245
    2. Strategies for finding sources 246
    3. Identifying sources 247
    4. Strategies for choosing reliable and relevant secondary sources 248
    5. Evaluating sources 249
C. Reading and documenting selected sources 250
    1. Strategies for reading secondary sources 250
    2. Evaluating the relevance of selected sources 251
    3. Documenting selected sources 252
D. Taking notes while reading 254
    1. Annotation 255
    2. Quoting, paraphrasing and summarizing 256

E. Organizing sources for inclusion in the paper 259
   1. Strategies for organizing sources according to themes 260
   2. Organizing new information for inclusion in the research paper 263
   3. Reevaluating the strength and relevance of the new information 264
F. Expanding language 265

CHAPTER 12
Writing the research paper 267
A. Examining the thesis statement 267
   1. From working thesis to thesis statement 267
B. AWARE: Arranging to write the thesis statement and outline 269
   1. The thesis statement 269
   2. The detailed outline 270
C. Examining the body paragraphs of a research paper 272
   1. Synthesizing sources for body paragraphs 272
   2. A blueprint for incorporating synthesis into a research paper 277
D. AWARE: Arranging to write body paragraphs 278
E. AWARE: Writing the body paragraphs 279
F. Examining introductions to research papers 280
   1. Strategies for writing effective introductions to a research paper 280
G. AWARE: Arranging to write an introduction 282
H. AWARE: Writing an introduction 283
I. Examining conclusions to research papers 283
   1. Strategies for writing effective conclusions to research papers 283
J. AWARE: Arranging to write a conclusion 286
K. AWARE: Writing a conclusion to a research paper 286
L. AWARE: Assessing the research paper 287
M. AWARE: Revising 287
Checklist for revising and editing 289

References 293

Index 295

Part I

Developing your academic voice

Chapter 1

The art of academic writing

> L'art d'écrire est l'art de découvrir ce en quoi vous croyez.
> The art of writing is the art of discovering what you believe.
> Gustave Flaubert

The goal of this book is to help students become independent, autonomous writers with the confidence to express their ideas and beliefs clearly through the written word. Academic writing in English is challenging for native and non-native speakers alike. *The Art and Architecture of Academic Writing* has been created to address the specialized challenges of students whose first language is not English.

The book builds on the premise that becoming a writer is not unlike becoming an artist. In the same way that great artists must master the building blocks of line, color, shape, form, space, and texture before going on to create original styles of expression, writers need to master certain basic building blocks which serve as a foundation for communicating with creativity and authenticity in academic contexts. Like artists who follow processes for planning, gathering materials, creating, and refining a work of art, writers need a process that guides planning, research, crafting and revising a manuscript.

The authors recognize that academic writing requirements vary widely across disciplines. However, some fundamental elements of academic writing apply to all disciplines. This book will help students master core building blocks of academic writing which are used across most disciplines and will introduce the AWARE framework (Arranging to write, Writing, Assessing, Revising and Editing) that will guide students through the stages of academic writing from planning to the final draft. The book develops academic writing competencies from three perspectives:

- The architecture of academic writing focuses on the building blocks of academic writing – the required elements that create a strong foundation to support the writer's ideas. The architectural elements include a thesis statement, rhetorical patterns for organizing information, academic language, and appropriate stylistic conventions. All academic writers adhere closely to these architectural elements.
- The art of academic writing develops the aspects of writing that reflect the writer's unique style and message. Each writer makes choices with respect to vocabulary, sentence structure, grammar, topics, and focus. Together these combine to create a unique voice that distinguishes one writer from others. The writer's voice is as important as the architecture of writing. A sound structure is a necessary framework for presenting information, but it must never overshadow the writer's unique perspective on a topic.

- AWARE teaches a specialized framework that guides writers through the academic writing cycle from the beginning of an assignment to the final product. It provides step-by-step instruction for five stages of the academic writing cycle. AWARE demonstrates and practices a repertoire of strategies that students can use for each stage of writing. The process and strategies develop competent, independent writers who will be able to draw on AWARE as a foundation for writing throughout their academic careers.

The content of this book is presented in two parts. Part I develops the writer's voice by helping students analyze and communicate their thoughts about a topic effectively. To keep the focus on developing the writer's voice, the exercises and assignments in Part I do not require research. Part II focuses on writing that synthesizes and presents research from multiple sources.

This chapter will lay the groundwork for the rest of the book. In this chapter, students will:

- distinguish between private and public writing,
- recognize different writing genres,
- differentiate formal and informal language,
- identify the characteristics of academic language,
- expand their use of academic vocabulary,
- examine the role of voice in writing.

A. The social context of writing

All human communication and interaction are guided by social values and rules. Although writing is considered a solitary activity, it is essentially a social act initiated for the purpose of conveying a message to an audience. All writing is, therefore, guided by norms based on social purpose and the expectations of a community.

The term *discourse* is often used to refer to a set of language norms shared by a particular community in their communication. These norms include underlying rules for sentence structure, vocabulary, level of formality, and patterns for organizing sentences in extended speech or writing. All discourses evolve within a social context in order to serve specialized communication needs.

Most adults have learned to recognize different types of discourse in their own language. Readers are able to distinguish between a magazine article and a novel and have expectations for the type of language and content each will present. In fact, most people are proficient in multiple discourses; nevertheless, a majority of people find they are challenged to understand certain specialized discourses in their native language.

Effective writers identify their audience and follow the language norms of the corresponding discourse community. Understanding the discourse of academic writing is as important as proficiency in grammar and vocabulary. Although knowing grammar and vocabulary is necessary for writing in a second language, it is not sufficient. Second language writers must also follow the writing norms of the academic community and recognize how these norms differ from academic writing norms in their first language.

> *Reflection*
> *The discourse of the medical community, the legal profession, or even a sports club can be relatively difficult for the native speakers who are not involved in those communities. Can you give an example of a discourse that is challenging for you in your own language?*

1. Public and private writing

One way to examine writing is to situate it on a continuum that ranges from private to public communication. Private messages are usually intended for a designated audience that is known to the writer, often friends or family members. Examples of private writing include mobile text messages, diaries, private letters, and emails. In private written communication, the content as well as the context are familiar to both the writer and the reader. This shared knowledge makes private writing relatively easy for the reader to understand.

Public writing differs markedly in content and context from private writing. The writer may not know his audience personally and the audience often does not know the writer's intentions. Public communication may be intended for a small group of people or an audience of millions. In public writing, knowledge of the topic and context is not necessarily shared by writer and reader. Nor is the writer present or available to explain the written communication to the reader. Therefore, in public writing, the author must establish a shared context to communicate effectively with unknown readers.

Academic writing is public writing. One goal of this book is to help students meet the expectations of the academic audience by recognizing and mastering the types of writing most common to the academic community. In the case of academic writing, the audience (typically the instructor) expects the student to follow the writing norms of an academic discipline. Students are rarely aware of the differences across disciplines because they are not addressed in typical English courses.

> *Reflection*
> *The context of a tweet is clear to both writer and reader. They are familiar with the genre (the length limit, abbreviations, etc.) and thus know what to expect, which makes deciphering the message easier. Are tweets public or private writing?*

2. Genres

The concept of genre is fundamental to understanding public writing. A genre is a recognizable pattern of communication used to convey certain types of information to an identified audience. Genres evolve in response to the repeated demands for the same type of information for a defined social purpose (Hyland, 2007) or within a particular community of practice (Lave & Wenger, 1991). People distinguish the genres that they use in their personal, academic, and professional lives by their distinctive features.

A genre combines features of language, formality, organization, etc., in a unique configuration recognized by the writer and the reader. For instance, the genre of a technical or business report organizes and records factual information in a predicable format. The audience expects standardized features such as an abstract, an introduction, specific terminology, methods, tables or diagrams, appendices, and references to communicate information concisely. Since reports may be read by hundreds of people, the shared language and defined features provide a roadmap that facilitates both writing and reading.

Some scholars of English categorize public writing into two broad genres: literary and expository. Literary texts are generally fictional; their purpose is to entertain or engage the audience in an aesthetic or reflective experience. Expository text is non-fictional. Expository genres evolved to convey information and complex ideas for certain audiences. Literary and expository texts are structured differently and are characterized by different types of language.

a. Literary genres

Literary texts appeal to the readers' senses and imagination. This type of text is familiar to many students from their English as a foreign language classes where literature is part of the curriculum. Literary texts include:

- novels
- short stories
- poetry
- drama/plays

Literary texts are creative. They allow each reader to find personal meaning and interpret the text differently. This type of writing is taught in a creative writing program rather than an academic writing program.

b. Expository genres

This book focuses on expository genres that are typical of university writing assignments (Nesi & Gardner, 2012). Academic genres evolved to meet the communication needs of the academic community (Swales, 1990) and reflect the expectations of the academic audience. If a student wants to convey information, explain a problem, clarify an issue, or argue a point, she/he must adopt the appropriate genre.

The features of genres include ways of organizing information, vocabulary, levels of formality, and formatting. Genres vary from discipline to discipline. Some of the most frequently assigned student expository genres include:

- essays
- narratives
- reports
- case studies
- research papers

As students advance in their studies and enroll in increasingly more specialized subjects, the nature of writing tasks will become more complex. Each discipline has developed specialized genres that reflect the needs of that discipline. For example, biology students may write research reports and business students may write business proposals, while other students write primarily essays. Each of these is a genre which presents information in a specific way for a specific purpose.

While each of these expository writing genres has specialized requirements, they also share common characteristics: they are factual, require evidence to support the writer's point of view, use specific types of language, and organize ideas in predicable patterns. This book focuses on developing competency in these shared characteristics.

Reflection
Think about the types of writing you did in your English classes in secondary school. Would you consider them to be literary or expository texts? How prepared are you to write expository texts?

Practice: *Examining literary and expository genres*

Read the texts below and think about how they differ from one another.[1]

A. The Babe was laid in the Manger
    Between the gentle kine–
All safe from cold and danger–
    "But it was not so with mine,
        (With mine! With mine!)"
"Is it well with the child, is it well?"
    The waiting mother prayed.
"For I know not how he fell,
    And I know not where he is laid."

---

1. A. Rudyard Kipling, A Nativity 1914–1918.
   B. Jay Lalonde w/permission (2018)
   C. UI Dept. of Languages and Cultures. Self-evaluation report.
   D. Scott Fitzgerald. The Great Gatsby.

B. The Grotesque is by definition not a clear-cut and unambiguous term, and so it is not always apparent where the Grotesque ends and the Gothic – or, for example, the Horror – starts, as they are undoubtedly linked (Novak, 1979), and it might prove impossible to divide them perfectly.
C. It is a diverse faculty with a large number of departments, diverse specialization of staff and a variety of courses offered in different languages. This leads to small class sizes and close relations between faculty and students. However, the diversity complicates administration, places an extra burden on staff, and contributes to weak financial standing as opportunities for consolidation of courses are limited.
D. He didn't say any more but we've always been unusually communicative in a reserved way, and I understood that he meant a great deal more than that. In consequence I'm inclined to reserve all judgments, a habit that has opened up many curious natures to me and also made me the victim of not a few veteran bores.

1. For each text identify whether the text belongs to a literary or expository genre
2. Review the lists of literary and expository genres above. To which specific genre do you think the text belongs?

B. Writing for the academic discourse community

Upon entering university, students become members of an academic community. Like other communities, scholars share specific ways of interacting and a characteristic style of writing. Students become familiar with the norms of academic discourse through reading textbooks and journal articles, listening to lectures, and consulting academic sources.

Academic discourse differs markedly from the discourse of private communication. Most students have developed competence in the conversational discourse of private communication in English. However, developing proficiency in formal academic discourse is necessary for effective writing. Learning a new discourse is no more difficult, nor mysterious, than learning any other subject or skill. The next section of this chapter will introduce the key features of academic discourse.

Relevance
Academic writing plays an essential role in a successful university experience since the majority of assessment tasks include writing. Your instructor is your audience and your assessor. You will be able to communicate your knowledge most effectively by writing in an appropriate genre.

1. Formal and informal language in writing

Academic discourse is formal discourse. It differs markedly from the informal discourse of private conversations. Informal conversational language often includes sentence fragments and phrases, slang vocabulary, contractions, and is organized much like a narrative story which presents ideas in sequence. In contrast, the formal discourse of academic writing is characterized by an impersonal tone, full words instead of contractions, Standard English instead of colloquial language, grammatically complete sentences, and academic vocabulary.

Academic writing uses a wide range of words and phrases to link ideas and signal the nature of the relationship between ideas in sentences and paragraphs. In this book these are called *discourse connectors*. Adverbs are the most common discourse connectors. Examples of discourse connectors are *consequently*, *however*, and *despite*. Each of these clarifies the nature of the relationship between the two ideas they connect.

Second language writers tend to overuse certain discourse connectors such as "moreover" which have become characteristic of texts written in English as a second language. The book, therefore, explores a variety of discourse connectors appropriate for formal academic texts. All writers must learn to distinguish between formal and informal discourse connectors. For example, the phrase "last time I looked" is frequently used in conversation, while the formal connector, "in past experience" is more appropriate for academic writing.

> **Reflection**
> *Think about the formality of responses you have given to test questions and whether it may have affected the grade on the test. Why might the formality of the language affect the grade? What level of formality is the instructor likely to expect?*

Contrasting informal and formal text

INFORMAL TEXT EXAMPLES	FORMAL TEXT EXAMPLES
Formal text is generally impersonal; *it tends to avoid using the first person (I, me, my, we, us, etc.) and addressing the reader directly as "you." An acronym or abbreviation is spelled out within parenthesis the first time it is used in a text.*	
We found three types of system failures. (first person)	Analysis revealed three types of system failures.
I think that the characters in the story betray their values. (first person)	The characters in the story betray their values.
You will be surprised at the end of the film. (addresses reader as "you")	Viewers will be surprised at the end of the film.
Formal text tends to use full words; *it generally avoids the use of contractions and abbreviations (especially when first mentioned in the text).*	
She'll examine the results of the study again since they weren't conclusive. (contractions)	She will examine the results of the study again since they were not conclusive.
The use of ELF is becoming more widespread. (abbreviation)	The use of English as lingua franca (ELF) is becoming more widespread. ELF is used in business and academia across the world.

INFORMAL TEXT EXAMPLES	FORMAL TEXT EXAMPLES
Formal text uses only Standard English; *it usually avoids the use of informal and colloquial expressions.*	
The stock market crash (informal) led to a financial meltdown (informal). The government put a lot of money into education. (informal expression)	The sharp losses in the stock market resulted in an international financial crisis. The government invested heavily in education.
Formal text usually uses complete clauses with a subject and a verb; *it avoids fragments (stand-alone phrases missing subject or verb) and stand-alone subordinate clauses.*	
From the first experiment to the last. (phrase with no verb) When the election results were announced. (subordinate clause that must be attached to an independent clause)	The researchers followed the protocol from the first experiment to the last. When the election results were announced, Mr. Rodriguez was declared the winner.
Formal text uses precise and accurate vocabulary; *it avoids repetition and vague or imprecise words that can be interpreted in multiple ways.*	
Watching too much TV is bad for kids. ("too much" and "bad" are imprecise and open to interpretation by the reader) The room was full of useless stuff. (stuff is vague because it could refer to many things) Participants improved and their results showed that the program worked. ("improved" "showed", and "worked" are vague and open to interpretation)	Watching more than one hour of television daily is unhealthy for children's physical development. The room was full of unused medical equipment. Participants' scores increased by an average of 10 points, which indicates a positive gain on measures of reading comprehension.
Formal academic texts are generally based on expository genres with predicable organization patterns and explicit discourse connectors; *they avoid presenting information as a personal narrative.*	
I designed a study using questionnaire data. First, I prepared the questionnaire with 75 questions. Next, I identified 100 possible participants. After, I found that 40 participants didn't meet the criteria. At the end, I collected data from 60 participants. (This sample resembles a story. It uses the first person; discourse connectors that mark sequence rather than clarify the relationship of ideas to each other; the word "participants" is repeated; "at the end" is an informal discourse connector.)	The research design used a 75-item questionnaire based on the Chang inventory of cognitive functions. Initially, more than 100 participants applied for the study; however, 40 applicants did not meet the criteria for age and education level. Thus, the final data set consisted of 60 subjects. (In this sample, the underlined discourse connectors clearly signal how the ideas relate to each other.)

> **Relevance**
> Instructors often remark on students' use of informal conversational language in written assessments. Conversational language lacks the precision and accuracy needed to fully demonstrate understanding of complex and abstract thoughts.

Examining formal academic language

Below are examples of texts on the same topic written in formal academic language and informal language. The column on the left contains the original passage discussing the evolution of the art of Pablo Picasso. It relates the artist's changing art and his role in the development of abstract art.

The first column is a summary of the text written in formal language. It uses precise language appropriate for an academic text.

The second column is a student's summary of the text. Notice how the student uses an informal, conversational style to convey the information. This is too informal for an academic text.

Sample of formal and informal passage

A. Formal academic language	B. Informal language
1. Most of the legendary abstract artists of the 20th century were educated in traditional styles which represented objects, scenes, and people as they are in real life.	1. First, I think that Picasso is a great artist who changed styles and had an impact on other artists in the west.
2. The works of the celebrated artist Picasso illustrate the evolution from realistic painter to one of the most revolutionary artists in the history of western art.	2. He didn't paint abstract art at the beginning. He started as a great realistic painter.
3. In fact, Picasso excelled in depicting subjects with accuracy and precision, using a life-like color palette during his early career.	3. Then, his style slowly changed over his life and he developed Cubism. No longer painting real life pictures. He painted fragmented objects.
4. However, the artist moved progressively away from realism. He became the central figure in the development of Cubism, an artistic style that deconstructs objects to show all sides at once, creating a fragmented image.	4. His art changed a lot in 79 years and he used bold colors and simple forms that looked unreal and confusing when you saw them.
5. Over his 79-year career, Picasso embraced the use of bold colors and greater abstraction based on simplified, geometric forms with exaggerated features which were loosely related to real life images.	5. In the end, Picasso's great work was the start of abstract art. In abstract art it is difficult to recognize any figures at all.
6. Accordingly, Picasso is credited with establishing the foundation for modern abstract art in which recognizable figure forms are absent.	

Practice: Examining formal and informal language

Examine the text in the two columns above. Answer the following questions.
1. In column B the writer uses the adjective "great" repeatedly.
   - Underline any words that convey the concept of "great" in column A.
   - Explain the connotation of these words. How do these "synonyms" for "great" help you understand the subject?
2. In column B the writer uses the verb "change" repeatedly.
   - Underline any words or phrases that convey the concept of "change" in column A
   - Explain the connotation of these words.
   - How do these "synonyms" for "change" help you understand the subject?
3. The underlined discourse connectors, *for example, however, accordingly* in column A indicate a specific type of connection between one idea and the next.
   - Underline the discourse connecters that the writer uses in column B.
   - Do they indicate a specific type of relationship?
4. Did you notice any fragments in column B? Can you change these to full sentences?

2. Academic vocabulary

The vocabulary of academic discourse is distinct from the vocabulary of daily conversation. Although the English language is derived from Anglo Saxon, other languages such as Latin, Greek, and French have contributed to the vocabulary of Modern English. Although words and phrases derived from Anglo Saxon predominate in conversational English, vocabulary of Latin, Greek, and French origins are prominent in academic discourse. For instance, compare the informal words and phrases on the left with the formal equivalents on the right.

Formal and informal vocabulary

examine	test
receive	get
depart	go
require	need
purchase	buy
approximately	around
factor	thing

The important research of Coxhead (2000) led to the development of the well-known Academic Word List. Coxhead identified 60 general academic vocabulary words which appear most frequently in textbooks across multiple disciplines. The Academic Word List is a valuable resource for developing a general academic vocabulary which will contribute to formal tone and greater precision in word choice. Despite the fact that informal vocabulary is considered grammatically correct, it is inappropriate in academic discourse and diminishes the credibility of the writer.

Chapter 1. The art of academic writing

> **Relevance**
> Many students report that the terminology specific to their discipline is more familiar than general academic vocabulary. Understanding general academic vocabulary improves reading comprehension of academic texts in addition to supporting writing.

The list below shows 60 of the most common academic words found in textbooks according to Coxhead. Note that the word list is based on UK English while this textbook follows the spelling conventions of US English.

The 60 most common words in academic textbooks (Coxhead, 2000)

analyse	distribute	issue	section
approach	economy	labor	sector
area	environment	legal	significant
assess	establish	legislate	similar
assume	estimate	major	source
authority	evident	method	specific
available	export	occur	structure
benefit	factor	percent	theory
concept	finance	period	vary
consist	formula	policy	variables
constitute	function	principle	
context	identify	proceed	
contract	income	process	
create	indicate	require	
data	individual	research	
define	interpret	respond	
derive	involve	role	

> *Reflection*
> *Consider the following sentence:*
>
> *The new policy led to a big improvement in the standard of living among elderly citizens.*
> *What do you think "big" means? How great is the improvement?*
> *Substitute each of the synonyms below for "big" in the sentence.*
> *How does the meaning change?*
>   *important*
>   *significant*
>   *substantial*
>   *historic*
>   *monumental*

Practice: Substituting academic vocabulary for informal vocabulary

> A. Read the sentences below. The informal vocabulary that is not appropriate for academic writing is underlined in the first sentence.
> B. Rewrite the sentence using formal vocabulary from the list above or from other sources. You could also consult the synonyms feature on your writing program or a thesaurus.
>
> The first example is provided. In the second sample the informal words are underlined.
>
> 1. The digital age has caused a <u>big</u> transformation in professional communication.
>   The digital age has caused a <u>significant</u> transformation in professional communication.
> 2. When adjusted for inflation, factory workers' yearly <u>pay</u> declined.
>   When adjusted for inflation, factory workers' _____ declined.
> 3. The accident victim <u>needs</u> specialized medical treatment that is not available at the local hospital.
>   The accident victim _____ specialized medical treatment that is not available at the local hospital.
> 4. The United Nations <u>sent</u> food aid to urban and rural parts of the country.
>   The United Nations _____ food aid to urban and rural areas throughout the country.
> 5. The prime minister <u>gave</u> a public statement in which she denied the allegations against her party.
>   The prime minister _____ a public statement in which she denied the allegations against her party.
> 6. What are some of the <u>things</u> that affected the outcome of the study?
>   What are some of the _____ that affected the outcome of the study?

Practice: Examining texts in students' disciplines

> 1. Select 3 paragraphs from a textbook or article you have been assigned in your program of study. Read the paragraphs carefully. Can you find 3–4 words on the Academic Word List presented above in the paragraphs?
> 2. Underline 2–3 discourse connectors that signal transition between ideas in the paragraphs you chose. Look up their meaning and determine what they say about the relationship between the ideas they connect.

3. The art of writing: Developing an academic voice

A writer's voice is a unique set of characteristics that identifies a writer. In literature it is often possible to identify a writer or poet by his or her writing style. Similarly, works of film, art, music, and dance often reflect a creative signature style that audiences associate with the author.

As discussed previously, the academic audience has defined expectations for writing which include formal tone, academic vocabulary, and a genre appropriate to the task. Within those parameters, the writer may choose from an array of academic vocabulary, emphasize certain ideas, and use discourse connectors that highlight certain relationships. All of these choices combine to create a unique signature style – the writer's voice.

Writing in one's own voice adds authenticity and credibility to writing. Experienced writers present information from sources in their own words, integrating the sources into a unified message that reflects the writer's unique perspective. In contrast, writing by inexperienced writers may create the impression that the text is comprised of a series of disconnected ideas rather than a unified message. This often results when novice writers reproduce information from multiple sources with only minor changes in wording and present them in a linear sequence. The characteristics of writers who have not developed a voice include:

- uneven levels of formality,
- varying styles reflecting multiple authors' voices in a single text,
- shifts between varieties of English (British and American, for example),
- inconsistency in language and formatting related to sources from different genres.

Reflection
Did you ever feel like your essays at school were made up of a series of ideas that you strung together from others? When was that and were you pleased with your essay?

Practice: *Examining voice in writing*

One way to understand shifts in the writer's voice in response to task and audience is to retell a story from the viewpoints of different characters. Consider the story of Little Red Riding Hood summarized below. Little Red Riding Hood is a familiar fairy tale told in cultures around the world. Any story with an innocent character and an evil nemesis can be used for this exercise.

When you have finished the story, you will be asked to retell it from the perspective of two characters.

A little girl called Little Red Riding Hood is asked by her mother to take some food to her grandmother who lives in the woods. She is instructed to go straight to her grandmother's house and not to leave the path. Along the way, she encounters a wolf. He asks her where she is going and then rushes to the grandmother's house. By the time Little Red Riding Hood arrives, the wolf has already eaten the grandmother and is posing as the old woman in her bed.

When Little Red Riding Hood arrives, the wolf pretends to be the grandmother, but Little Red Riding Hood notices the size of her grandmother's arms, legs, ears, eyes, and teeth

> and remarks about how big each is. Little Red Riding Hood's last remark, "Grandmamma, what great teeth you have got!" was her last before the wolf responds with "That is to eat you up," and gobbles Red Riding Hood whole.
>
> A hunter comes by the house who witnesses events. He waits for the wolf to fall asleep and saves the grandmother and Little Red Riding Hood from the wolf's stomach and replaces them with stones. When the wolf wakes up, he rushes to a nearby stream, but as he leans down to drink, the rocks move in his stomach and he falls into the stream never to be heard or seen again.
>
> 1. Using the first person, write the story from the perspective of Little Red Riding Hood.
> 2. Using the first person, write the story from the perspective of the wolf.
> 3. Answer the following questions:
>   a. Did you use the same type of language for both characters?
>   b. Are you making a point or are you retelling a story?
>   c. Would you describe this as literary text or expository text?
> 4. Now write a short paragraph that explains the motivation for the behavior of either Little Red Riding Hood, the wolf, or the hunter.
>   a. In whose voice are you writing now?
>   b. Is there a difference between the language you used explaining the motivation compared to retelling the story?
>   c. Are you making a point or are you telling a story?
>   d. Would you describe your paragraph as literary text or expository text?
> 5. Which task was more difficult to complete and why?

Reflection
Think about writing in your native language. Do you always write in the same style? Do you vary the way you write according to the audience, and if so, how? What type of writing do you find most challenging in your first language?

4. Avoiding plagiarism

A strong writer's voice helps students avoid the appearance of plagiarism. Although students are expected to draw on course readings, research, and expert opinions in assignments and examination, students are always expected to use their own language to convey the ideas of others. Helping students develop a personal voice that enables them to express their ideas in their own words and style is a goal of this book.

Plagiarism is any reproduction of another's writing, lyrics, comments, or ideas without crediting the author through proper citation. Use of information from web pages, books, songs, films, personal correspondence, interviews, articles, artworks or any source without full attribution to the author is plagiarism. It is also considered plagiarism to reproduce the original idea of another person by changing the wording through paraphrase or summary without citing the source of the idea.

Whether intentional or unintentional, plagiarism is a serious breach of academic honesty and may result in disciplinary action for the student. To avoid the appearance of plagiarism, an assignment of any type must always give full credit to the original source of any creative or intellectual work used in writing. A citation gives credit to a source within the text of the document. References provide more detailed information about sources at the end of documents. The second part of this book examines the use of research and outside sources and develops skills in incorporating the ideas of others according to the norms of the academic community.

The exact information required in a citation or reference and the correct format depends on the citation style. Three of the most frequently used styles are:

- APA (American Psychological Association) style is generally used in education, psychology, and the natural sciences
- MLA (Modern Language Association) style is generally used in the humanities
- Chicago/Turabian style is generally used in business, history, and the fine arts

This book teaches APA as a reference style, but students should confer with their instructors about which style they require.

Most sources used in an academic writing assignment should be presented in the writer's own words. There are three ways to present ideas from others in academic writing: paraphrase, summary and quotations and they all require full APA, MLA, or Chicago citations and references.

Paraphrase
Paraphrase is typically used to reproduce a particular idea or a sentence from a source. A paraphrase replicates the meaning of the original source with minimal use of the original author's wording or structure. The length of a paraphrase is approximately the same as the original source.

Summary
A summary puts the main ideas from a source into your own words. It can include paraphrased ideas or sentences from the original text. Because a summary focuses on relating the author's main ideas, it is generally shorter than the original text. A general rule is that the length of a summary is about 25% of the original text. Summarizing strategies will be examined in Chapter 8.

Direct quotations
A quotation is a word-for-word reproduction of written or spoken text. It is always framed by quotation marks immediately preceding and after the quoted text. Usually, the writer is expected to summarize or paraphrase information from his sources and rarely uses direct quotations from original studies. They must be used sparingly and should be as brief as possible.

The Art and Architecture of Academic Writing

Practice: Avoiding plagiarism: Using paraphrase

This exercise asks you to write in your own voice. It practices two of the elements of academic writing discussed in this chapter: formal language and paraphrase. Remember that paraphrase reproduces the meaning of the statement while changing as much of the wording and structure as possible.

The list contains sentences with 10 of the most frequently used English idioms. The idioms are underlined.

1. Look up the meaning of the idiom if it is not familiar.
2. Paraphrase the sentence in your own words using formal language.

Sentence with informal idiom	Formal paraphrase
1. He usually tries to kill two birds with one stone.	1. He often attempts to solve two problems at the same time.
2. We should not judge a book by its cover.	2. We must avoid making judgments based on appearances.
3. My boss feels under the weather today.	
4. A good report will hit the nail on the head.	
5. He found the best of both worlds in his new job.	
6. By the end of the discussion, everyone could see eye to eye.	
7. Power failures take place once in a blue moon.	
8. The renovations cost an arm and a leg.	
9. Mr. Smith let the cat out of the bag when he was speaking to his team.	
10. Because the builders cut corners during construction, the roof leaks.	

5. Academic communication

As members of the academic community, students are expected to use formal academic discourse not only when writing assignments but also when corresponding with instructors, staff, and administrators. The use of informal colloquial language is not appropriate when speaking or writing about academic topics with an instructor. In fact, a student's voice and message may be lost when these norms of communication are violated.

The first example below is an email written by a student to an instructor in informal colloquial language. The second version is written in appropriate academic language based on the norms for formality and vocabulary examined in previous sections.

Example 1. Informal (and inappropriate) email

Hi Mr. Smith, your class is cool, but I think that grade you gave me on the last paper was way off. I totally worked my butt off on that paper and just got a pass. Nobody told me you couldn't copy things from the experts. I thought that was doing research. Can we please just talk? Where's your office?

Student X

Example 2. Alternative email written in formal language

Dear Professor Smith,

I really enjoy your class, but the grade I received on my last paper was very disappointing. I put a great deal of work into the paper and hoped to receive a better grade. I also did not realize that I could not use other people's words. I thought that was considered conducting research.

May I come to your office and discuss my work with you? I would like to understand how I can improve my writing and my grades in this class. If possible, I would like to make an appointment to meet with you?

The directory lists your office as Tower 17. Can you confirm the location?

Thank you,

Student X

Reflection

Examine the two emails. Which one is likely to lead to a positive outcome for the student? Which level of formality is the instructor likely to expect?

Practice: Formal communication

Consider all of the aspects of academic writing discussed in this chapter.
1. Write an email to the instructor of your class. The email should use formal discourse and include the following:
   – a greeting,
   – a request for an appointment to discuss your writing,
   – a description of two aspects of writing you find challenging.

Consult your instructor about how to submit this assignment.

Writing

Write 4–5 paragraphs that discuss your understanding of yourself as a writer.

Which aspects of writing do you enjoy? What aspects do you dislike?

Can you identify one or two areas of writing that you consider as strengths and one or two aspects of writing that you find challenging?

How are your writing processes different in English and your first language?

C. Expanding language

Word families

Expanding academic vocabulary is important in maintaining a formal style and expressing ideas with precision and accuracy. Studying academic word families and practicing the use of prefixes and suffixes will build academic vocabulary and support reading of academic texts.

A word family consists of all forms of a particular word. Each word in the family is a variation of the same word, modified with a prefix or suffix to create a different part of speech. Consider the word family for *create* from the Academic Word List above.

create	verb	Richard Thaler created an economic model that analyzes personal financial decision-making.
creation	noun	In 2017, Thaler was awarded the Nobel Prize for the creation of his economic theory.
creator	noun	As creator of behavioral economics, Thaler has changed the study of economics for future generations.
creating	noun (gerund)	By creating a bridge between economics and psychology, Thaler has expanded our insights into the factors that affect economic development.
creativity	noun	Thaler's creativity led to new ways of thinking about economic development.
creatively	adverb	Analyzing human financial behavior helps economists think creatively about the impact of public policy on ordinary citizens.
creative	adjective	Thaler has been recognized as one of the most creative spirits in modern economics.

> *Reflection*
> *There are four different noun forms for "create" in the table above.*
> *How do they differ in meaning?*
> *What is a gerund? How is it formed and how is it used?*

Although learning to use academic vocabulary effectively takes practice, it makes a noticeable improvement in a writer's tone and accuracy. Below are more examples of how different forms of the same word in a word family work to create meaning in different contexts.

Chapter 1. The art of academic writing

Practice: *Academic vocabulary*

> Place the appropriate form of the words (a)–(c) given in the lists 1–3 below in the gaps in the sentences. The forms of the first word on each list have been placed in the appropriate gaps.

1. The role of *technology* in increasing production is evident to the management of Delta Corporation. *Technological* advances have led to improved production. Delta has hired additional *technicians* to oversee production.

   technology (a) statistics (b) research (c) analysis

   (a) The role of _____ in increasing production is evident to the management of Delta Corporation. _____ advances have led to improved production. Delta has hired additional _____ to oversee production.

   (b) The role of _____ in increasing production is evident to the management of Delta Corporation. _____ advances have led to improved production. Delta has hired additional _____ to oversee production.

   (c) The role of _____ in increasing production is evident to the management of Delta Corporation. _____ advances have led to improved production. Delta has hired additional _____ to oversee production.

2. The legislature *created* a large fund for scholarships in the technical professions. The *creation* of a scholarship fund will facilitate international study for university faculty. By *creating* more scholarships, universities will support economic growth.

   create (a) distribute (b) establish (c) provide

   (a) The legislature _____ a large fund for scholarships in the technical professions. The _____ of a scholarship fund will facilitate international study for university faculty. By _____ more scholarships, universities will support economic growth.

   (b) The legislature _____ a large fund for scholarships in the technical professions. The _____ of a scholarship fund will facilitate international study for university faculty. By _____ more scholarships, universities will support economic growth.

   (c) The legislature _____ a large fund for scholarships in the technical professions. The _____ of a scholarship fund will facilitate international study for university faculty. By _____ more scholarships, universities will support economic growth.

3. *Investigating* the source of infectious disease is the responsibility of the Department of Health. The Department *investigated* the causes of the cholera epidemic last month. Based on their *investigation*, the city prevented the spread of the disease.

   investigate (a) determine (b) research (c) verify

   (a) _____ the source of infectious disease is the responsibility of the Department of Health. The Department _____ the causes of the cholera epidemic last month. Based on their _____, the city prevented the spread of the disease.

(b) _____the source of infectious disease is the responsibility of the Department of Health. The Department _____ the causes of the cholera epidemic last month. Based on their _____, the city prevented the spread of the disease.

(c) _____the source of infectious disease is the responsibility of the Department of Health. The Department _____the causes of the cholera epidemic last month. Based on their _____, the city prevented the spread of the disease.

Chapter 2

The architecture of academic writing

Chapter 1 explored the art of academic writing and the features that distinguish academic writing from other types of writing. It established that the primary purpose of academic writing is to communicate information, research, and opinions within a community of scholars, researchers, and professionals. Chapter 1 also presented the basic norms of academic discourse such as level of formality, types of vocabulary, and the use of expository genres. Finally, the chapter considered how the choices writers make with respect to topics, vocabulary, and style combine to create the author's personal academic voice.

Chapter 2 will explore the architecture of academic writing. The authors use the metaphor of architecture to describe the structural elements of academic writing. The most creative and innovative architecture must follow sound principles of design and construction or the structure will collapse. Similarly, academic writing must follow principles of organization and design to create a supportive structure for the writer's message. These structural elements are the building blocks of academic writing.

The expository essay genre is used to introduce the architecture of academic writing for two reasons. First, the essay is the most frequently assigned academic genre for student coursework. Since the assessment of content knowledge is often demonstrated through essay writing, it is important for students to master the genre. Next, the principles and structures of the expository essay apply to academic and professional genres such as case-studies, research papers, critiques, book reviews, reports, etc. Therefore, the essay is a gateway genre to the discipline-specific genres students will use as they advance in their programs of study (Nesi & Gardner, 2012).

In addition to examining the elements of the expository essay, the chapter provides supported practice in developing a thesis statement, structuring body paragraphs, and organizing ideas in an academic essay. It also analyzes sentence fragments, a common language error for many students, and provides strategies for avoiding sentence fragments in writing. By the end of the chapter, students will:

- be aware of cultural variations in presenting information in writing,
- recognize the building blocks of the English expository essay,
- examine thesis-driven writing as the underlying principle of academic writing,
- evaluate thesis statements through critical reading,

- write simple thesis statements,
- practice writing paragraphs to support a thesis,
- analyze instructions for writing assignments,
- understand sentence fragments and correct them.

A. Examining expository writing contexts

Writing may be logical, aesthetically pleasing, and effective in one cultural context but it may not make sense when read by someone from another culture. This is often related to variations in the ways cultures organize information. Native speakers learn to organize and present information in predicable rhetorical organization patterns that follow the norms of their own culture and language. When the writer and audience share knowledge of these rhetorical patterns, they follow a similar roadmap. Both understand the route and the destination.

> **Relevance**
> Students writing in English as a second language sometimes transfer the organizational patterns of their native language to English text. Even when language is grammatically correct and the sentences clear, the unfamiliar organization makes it difficult for the native English reader to understand the writer's message. Thus, understanding and learning to use the appropriate rhetorical organizational patterns is essential to conveying clear ideas in English.

Most academic writing is expository because its purpose is to share information among members of the academic community. In order for students to communicate effectively what they have learned about a subject, they need to understand and follow the norms for language, organization, and formatting.

1. The architecture of the expository essay

Awareness of the elements of an essay and how paragraphs are developed and organized is a prerequisite to academic writing. Moreover, research demonstrates that learning to recognize these textual elements improves reading comprehension.

An expository essay is a relatively short piece of writing with defined characteristics. A key characteristic of the academic essay is that it is thesis-driven: the content and organization is determined by a thesis statement.

In an effective academic essay, the student is expected to

- present thesis statement with a topic and point of view
- develop evidence to support the thesis statement
- organize the evidence in a pattern that aligns with the thesis statement.

The building blocks of the expository essay
The essay is structured in three parts: the introduction, the body paragraphs, and the conclusion, with all of the parts working together to support the thesis statement.

Introduction
The introduction to an essay presents general background information that the reader will need to understand the topic. An effective introduction also includes information that stimulates the reader's interest. A clear and concise thesis statement is usually presented at the end of the introductory paragraph.

Thesis statement
A thesis statement not only announces the topic of the essay, it also orients the reader to the line of reasoning that the writer will take in developing the essay. Since it is possible to examine any topic from many perspectives, the writer must make an informed choice about how to develop the content based on the audience and the topic. For example, the writer may use an essay to persuade, analyze, compare, describe, or explain.

Body
The body is the heart of the essay. In its simplest form, the expository essay has three body paragraphs. In longer essays there may be many more paragraphs. Each body paragraph develops evidence related to a single main idea. Evidence includes all types of factual information used to convince the reader about a specific point of view. All of the body paragraphs work together to develop sufficient support for the thesis statement. A topic sentence introduces the content of each body paragraph.

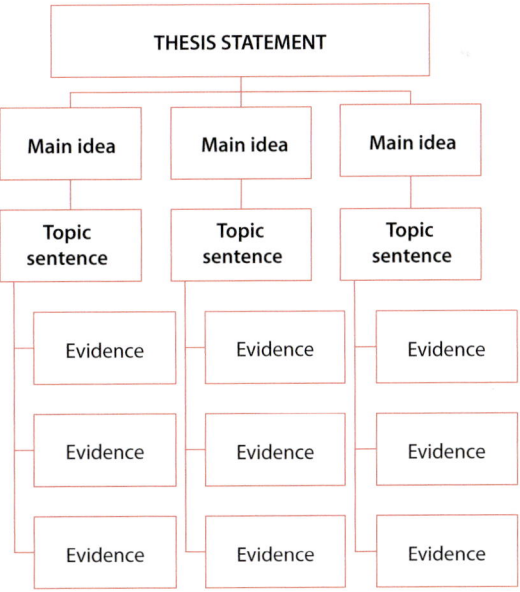

Conclusion
The conclusion returns the focus to the general topic and redirects the reader's attention to the thesis statement. It restates the thesis and summarizes the main ideas presented in the essay. <u>It does not introduce new information or new concepts</u>. A strong conclusion highlights the significance of the information and the strength of the author's case.

> **Relevance**
> Just as an artist masters the basics of drawing before moving on to expression, an academic writer must master the basics of the architecture common to most expository writing before moving on to expression.

2. Expository thesis statements

The thesis statement is truly the cornerstone of an essay since all of the content is selected, organized, and presented for the purpose of supporting the thesis statement. An effective thesis statement consists of two components: a topic and a point of view. The point of view in the thesis statement signals to the reader *how* the writer intends to develop the evidence.

For instance, for an assignment on the topic of "climate change" the writer could develop the essay from a wide range of viewpoints. The author might contrast the effects of climate change in two hemispheres, describe the effects on a community, or argue that climate change is not a real phenomenon, etc. Consider the thesis statement below:

<u>Signs of climate change</u> are found on every continent.
    Topic   Point of view

Based on the fact that the statement refers to "every continent," a reader is likely to expect that the essay will present instances of climate change for each continent. The reader would be confused if the essay explained signs of climate change on one continent only or compared signs of climate change in Africa and South America.

The point of view relates to the organizational pattern that the author will use to develop the essay. Some frequently used modes of exposition are: enumeration, description, narrative, compare/contrast, cause/effect, argument, and analysis. In each of these modes, the evidence to support the thesis statement is organized according to a distinct predictable pattern.

The seven thesis statements below present a different "point of view" on the topic of climate change. Each thesis statement corresponds to a specific type of exposition and suggests the nature of the evidence and the organization of the body paragraphs.

Enumeration: The writer presents a major idea and develops a list of facts or examples for support. The word "enumerates" means, "to name one by one, or to list."

> **Thesis statement:** Signs of climate change are found on every continent.

Description: The writer depicts the attributes of a person, place, object, or experience in a way that creates a clear image for the reader.

> **Thesis statement:** Scientists observe changes in the polar ice caps which they attribute to climate change.

Narrative (chronological recount or sequential order): The writer recounts an event chronologically or illustrates the sequence of events in a process.

> **Thesis statement**: The release of greenhouse gases warms the earth through a process of absorbing thermal radiation emitted from the earth's surface.

Compare/Contrast: The author provides evidence to show how two concepts are (1) similar to each other or (2) different from each other.

> (1) **Thesis statement** (compare): Both geothermal and wind energy reduce emissions of the greenhouse gases that cause climate change.
>
> (2) **Thesis statement** (contrast): Unlike the use of fossil fuels which releases destructive greenhouse gases, the use of geothermal energy for electricity production does not contribute to climate change.

Cause/Effect: The author illustrates (1) the causes of a phenomenon or event; or illustrates (2) the results of a phenomenon or event.

> (1) **Thesis statement** (cause): Certain human activities emit greenhouse gases which raise the temperature of the earth.
>
> (2) **Thesis statement** (effect): The rising temperature of the earth's surface has damaged important aspects of the polar bear's habitat.

Argument: The author makes a claim about a topic with which others might disagree and justifies the claim with evidence.

> **Thesis statement**: Unless human beings reduce greenhouse gas emissions significantly by 2030, the earth will become uninhabitable.

Analysis: The author evaluates an issue or idea by examining various aspects or parts of a topic. It breaks the issue or idea down into its component parts and presents evidence to support each component.

> **Thesis statement**: Warming ocean temperatures over the last two decades have increased the frequency and severity of extreme weather across the globe.

Reflection
Consider a time when you were reading and the text no longer made sense to you. This happens to all readers. Why might this happen even with text that uses grammar and vocabulary that you understand fully? How might your expectations have affected your comprehension of its content? What do you do when this happens?

Expository thesis and organizational patterns
Each mode of exposition corresponds to relatively predictable organization patterns for presenting information in an essay or research paper. The academic community relies on these organizational patterns to facilitate the exchange of ideas. The predicable nature of these organizational patterns helps both the reader and writer. They serve as a blueprint that guides the writer's presentation of the content and directs the reader from one idea to another.

> **Relevance**
> Recognizing the patterns in published texts improves reading comprehension and speed. To convey your message effectively, you must be aware of the specific view point you want to develop. Will you analyze, compare, describe? Each of these language functions organizes information in a specific way. Your reader will look for that organization. A mismatch between the reader's expectation and the way the material is presented often results in a communication failure.

The example below illustrates the relationship between the point of view in the thesis statement and the organization pattern for four types of expository essays: description, enumeration, compare/contrast, and cause/effect. Note the alignment between the point of view (underlined) and the organizational pattern.

Thesis statements and organizational patterns

Topic	Topic + Point of View	Organization Pattern/Types of Evidence
Health of children in a refugee camp	The officials observed <u>signs of healthy development</u> among the children in the Villa refugee camp.	Description: 4 body paragraphs. Each paragraph <u>describes</u> one aspect that indicates health. Main idea 1: normal body weight Main idea 2: good dental hygiene Main idea 3: daily school Main idea 4: engage socially with adults
Bicycles as transportation	The use of bicycles for commuting in urban settings <u>reduces numerous environmental problems associated with automobiles.</u>	Enumeration: 3 body paragraphs. Each paragraph develops one example of how bicycles reduce environmental problems. Main idea 1: traffic congestion Main idea 2: air pollution Main idea 3: noise pollution

Antibiotic use	Although antibiotics have reduced deaths from infectious disease, <u>their overuse has produced dangerous side effects.</u>	Compare/Contrast: 4 body paragraphs.
		   Two positive examples and
		   Two negative examples
		Main idea 1: positive – reduced infections
		Main idea 2: positive – contains epidemics
		Main idea 3: dangerous – resistant bacteria
		Main idea 4: dangerous – gastrointestinal

Topic	Topic + Point of View	Organization Pattern/Types of Evidence
Sugar consumption	High sugar consumption <u>resulted in an increase in chronic childhood diseases in the Republic of Sykra.</u>	Cause and effect: 3 body paragraphs. Each presents one effect of sugar consumption. Main idea 1: effect – obesity Main idea 2: effect – diabetes Main idea 3: effect – depression

All the thesis statements in the practice exercise below are for essays on the topic of climate change. However, <u>each thesis indicates that the writer will examine climate change from a different point of view.</u> In this exercise, you will analyze the thesis statement and make a prediction about the type of evidence the author could use to support it and thus which organizational pattern is most appropriate.

Practice: Thesis statements and organizational patterns

Read the thesis statements. Each statement presents the topic and states the author's point of view on the topic.

1. Circle the author's point of view.
2. Make a prediction about the types of evidence the author might present to support each thesis statement.

EXAMPLE:
Enumeration: The writer presents a major idea and develops a list of facts or examples for support.

1.

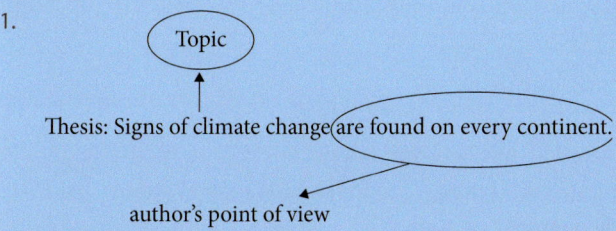

The author's point of view is that evidence of climate change exists on every continent. Based on this, we might expect the author to develop a list of facts or examples to prove this point. We do NOT expect the author to compare continents or focus on explaining the causes of global warming. Based on this we may expect the following:

2. <u>Prediction: The author will present evidence of examples of climate change for multiple continent such as:</u>
   a. Melting of ice in Antarctica
   b. The number and strength of hurricanes in Asia
   c. Increase in severity of droughts in Africa.

1. **Description:** The writer depicts the attributes of a person, place, object, or experience in a way that creates a clear image for the reader.

   Thesis statement (description): Scientists observe alarming changes in the polar ice caps which they attribute to climate change.

   The author might describe
   _____
   _____

2. **Narrative:** (chronological recount or sequential order): The writer recounts an event chronologically or illustrates the sequence of events in a process.

   Thesis statement (sequential order): The release of greenhouse gases warms the earth through a process of absorbing thermal radiation emitted from the earth's surface.

   The author might present evidence that
   _____
   _____

3. **Compare and contrast:** The author provides evidence to show how two concepts are similar to each other or different from each other.

   Thesis statement (contrast): Unlike the use of fossil fuels which releases destructive greenhouse gases, the use of geothermal energy for electricity production does not contribute to climate change.

   The author might present evidence that
   _____
   _____

   Thesis statement (compare): Both geothermal and wind energy reduce emissions of the greenhouse gases that cause climate change.

   The author might present evidence that
   _____
   _____

4. **Cause/effect:** The author illustrates (1) the causes of a phenomenon or event; or illustrates (2) the results of a phenomenon or event.

   Thesis statement (cause): Many human activities emit greenhouse gases which raise the temperature of the earth.

   The author might present evidence that
   _____
   _____

   Thesis statement (effect): The rising temperature of the earth's surface has damaged important aspects of the polar bear's habitat.

   The author might present evidence that
   _____
   _____

5. **Argument:** The author makes a claim about a topic with which others might disagree and justifies the claim with evidence.

    Thesis statement (argument): Unless human beings reduce greenhouse gas emissions significantly by 2030, the earth will become uninhabitable.

    The author might present evidence that

    _____
    _____

6. **Analysis:** The author evaluates an issue or idea by examining various aspects or parts of a topic. It breaks the issue or idea down into its component parts and presents evidence to support each component.

    Thesis statement (analysis): Warming ocean temperatures over the last two decades have increased the frequency and severity of extreme weather across the globe.

    The author might present evidence that

    _____
    _____

3. Body paragraphs and evidence

Evidence for the thesis statement is developed and presented in the body paragraphs. Evidence, as we have seen, is reliable information, facts, statistics, expert opinions, or research used to establish the credibility of the thesis statement. Multiple sources of reliable evidence are essential to support a thesis statement. Each body paragraph focuses on evidence related to only a <u>single main idea.</u> The main idea for the paragraph is stated in a topic sentence which supports the thesis statement directly.

Like a thesis statement, a topic sentence is constructed in two parts. It consists of the topic + the focus. The sample topic sentence relates to the thesis statement for the compare/contrast organization pattern on antibiotic use from above.

Antibiotic use	Although antibiotics have reduced deaths from infectious disease, <u>their overuse has produced harmful side effects.</u>	Compare/contrast. 4 body paragraphs: 2 provide positive examples and 2 provide negative examples Main idea 1: reduced deaths – infections Main idea 2: reduced deaths – control epidemics Main idea 3: harmful – resistant bacteria Main idea 4: harmful – gastrointestinal

Notice that the topic sentence below introduces the main idea for body paragraph 3 by establishing a harmful effect of antibiotic use.

Overuse of antibiotics results in the emergence of antibiotic resistant bacteria.

      ↓   ↓

Topic   +   focus   = main/controlling idea

This main idea controls the content of the paragraph: all sentences present evidence to explain, illustrate, or exemplify antibiotic resistant bacteria. The main ideas work together to develop sufficient evidence to support the thesis statement.

> *Reflection*
> *Multiple sources work together to demonstrate your knowledge of a topic or to show that you have conducted thorough research.*
> *Think about an instance when someone was successful or unsuccessful in his or her attempt to convince you about something. How did the quantity and quality of the evidence affect your view?*

Part 1 of the exercise below develops awareness of the role of a sound thesis statement in previewing the topic and the writer's intent. Part 2 analyzes the body paragraphs in relation to the thesis statement.

The essay is an example of an enumeration essay. In an enumeration essay, each paragraph names a main idea in a linear progression. The enumeration essay, like other expository essays in English, contains an introduction, a series of body paragraphs, and a conclusion. In the simplest terms, the writer states what they are going to say (introduction), presents the information (body paragraphs), then summarizes the significance of that information (conclusion).

Practice: Reading to write: Analyzing evidence in thesis-driven text (Science)

Part 1: Examining thesis statements

Read the introduction (1) to the essay *The Truth about Organic Food* below. Before you continue on to read the body paragraphs (2)–(5), answer the following questions:

What is the thesis statement?

Based on the thesis statement, what do you expect the essay to discuss?

Has the author said anything that stimulates your interest? What?

Based on the introduction, do you believe the author is for or against organic farming?

The Truth about Organic Food

(1) Many consumers question whether they should care about agricultural techniques if an organically cultivated green pepper looks identical to a conventionally grown pepper. Many people are aware that food grown according to organic principles is free from exposure to harmful herbicides and pesticides, but that is only one small aspect of organic agriculture. A core value of organic farming, preserving the health of the soil, is relevant to everyone because it affects the quality of our food and our ecosystems.

(2) Unlike synthetic chemicals (such as herbicides, pesticides, and/or inorganic fertilizers) that interrupt or destroy the micro-biotic activity in the soil, organic farming maintains the micro-biotic activity of the soil. Once the micro-biotic activity in the soil has stopped, the soil becomes merely an anchor for plant material. In this conventional method of agriculture, plants receive only air, water, and sunlight from their environment – everything else must be distributed to plants by farmers. Plants are commonly fed only the most basic elements of plant life and so are dependent on the farmer to fight nature's challenges, e.g. pests, disease, and drought.

(3) As a consequence, an organically cultivated pepper is more nutritious than a conventionally cultivated pepper. When a pepper grows in a living soil where micro-biotic activity breaks down organic matter and minerals into nutrients, the pepper is nurtured constantly. An organically cultivated plant always has exactly what it needs to grow and the plant will be healthier throughout its lifespan than a conventionally grown plant. This results in a pepper full of micro-nutrients and trace minerals that are important for human nutrition.

(4) Flavor is another benefit of healthy plants growing in a living soil. Flavor results from a mixture of many different and complex molecules. Healthy, living soil provides a constant and more complex mixture of these molecules, which results in more flavor. It is no surprise that chefs working in the highest caliber restaurants prefer organic ingredients to conventionally grown ingredients.

(5) Synthetic pesticides and herbicides not only kill soil microbes and leave toxic residues on food, they also threaten the health of farm workers and disrupt natural ecosystems around the farm. By purchasing locally grown, organic produce, the consumer also supports sustainable methods of land use that result in far less pollution and topsoil loss than conventional agriculture does. Chemical fertilizers pollute lakes, ponds, rivers, and groundwater.

(6) When considering the pros and cons of organic produce, the consumer should consider that organic farming does more than eliminate toxic chemicals from our food. Organic farming improves the quality of food and the ecosystem by maintaining healthy soil. While synthetic chemicals harm the micro-biotic activity of the soil, organically farmed soils preserve nutrients that grow healthier and more flavorful produce. In the long run, organically grown food benefits everyone by preserving soil fertility and natural ecosystem.

Adapted from: The Maine Organic Farmers and Gardeners Association
<http://www.mofga.org/tabid/166/Default.aspx>

Reflection
After reading the essay, did you feel that the content of the essay and the author's position met the expectations created in the introduction? Do you think that the thesis was effective at orienting you to the content of the essay? How?

Part 2: Examining body paragraphs (2–5)

1. Answer the questions from memory.
2. Then go back to the essay and complete the answers.

Read the entire essay *The Truth about Organic Food* above and answer the questions below. The paragraphs have been numbered to help you answer questions.

1. What is the main idea for each of the four body paragraphs?
2. What evidence does the author provide for the main idea in each body paragraph?

Main idea	Supporting evidence facts, examples, quotes, and statistics.
1. Synthetic chemicals destroy micro-biotic activity	1. Soil acts as an anchor only 2. Only air, light, water from environment 3. Plant totally dependent on farmer
2.	1. 2. 3.
3.	1. 2. 3.
4.	1. 2. 3.

Conclusion (6)
The conclusion redirects the reader's attention to the thesis statement and summarizes the main ideas presented in the essay.

a. How does the author restate the thesis? Copy the statement and compare it to the original statement.
b. Which sentences in the conclusion summarize each of the main ideas in the essay?

Main idea of body paragraph	In the conclusion this is stated as:
1. Synthetic chemicals destroy micro-biotic activity	1. Synthetic chemicals harm the micro-biotic activity of the soil.
2.	2.
3.	3.
4.	4.

Practice: Evidence to support a thesis (Social Science)

In this guided writing exercise, you will practice writing body paragraphs to support a thesis statement on a topic that is well known to most people. The introduction and the thesis statement have been developed and are presented below.

Write from your own knowledge, observations, and experience. Do not conduct research. Instead, focus on developing what you know about the subject.

1. Read the introduction to the essay. The thesis statement is underlined.

   Introduction
   Today's fathers are much more involved in parenting children than previous generations. In the US, fathers have nearly tripled their time spent in child care. Despite this progress, mothers in two-parent households who are employed outside of the home work four hours more per day than their husbands. <u>Working mothers report more stress than their husbands as a result of often taking on more parenting responsibilities.</u>

   Yavorsky, J. E., Dush, C. M., & Schoppe-Sullivan, S. J. (2015)

2. Select two or more main ideas for evidence from the outline below or develop your own main ideas.
3. List as much evidence as you can to support your main idea.
4. Write at least two body paragraphs that support the thesis statement.

Include a topic sentence.

Body paragraph/Main idea	Supporting evidence such as facts, examples, quotes, and statistics.
Managing children's activities	1. organize play dates 2. transport to programmed activities 3. supervise homework
Taking care of sick children	1. 2. 3.
School or child-care related	1. 2. 3.
Household chores	1. 2. 3.

Your essay

1. Copy the introduction above.
2. Write two or more body paragraphs to support the thesis statement.

B. Understanding an essay assignment

We have seen that purposeful information on a topic can be presented from multiple perspectives using different organizational structures. The thesis statement and organizational structure for the writing assignments flow directly from the instructor's directions. Therefore, the first step in any writing assignment is to understand the purpose of the assignment and the instructor's expectations.

1. Analyzing the instructions

Instructors convey what they expect from a writing assignment in different ways. Below are some guidelines for analyzing instructions for an assignment. Students should always consult the instructor when they have questions or concerns about instructions for a writing assignment.

Background information for the assignment
Assignment instructions may refer to major themes or course concepts as a background for the task. When instructions do not provide a thematic or conceptual context for the writing task, consider that most assignments assess how well the student is able to apply course concepts or skills. As you chose your topic, reflect on how well it relates to the content of the course.

Directives
The use of specific directive verbs helps the student understand the instructor's expectations. The instructor may use informational directives such as "define" or "compare" to ask the student to demonstrate what she or he knows about the topic using evidence in the form of examples, principles, definitions, or concepts from class or research.

On the other hand, instructors may use directive verbs such as "discuss," "examine," "explain", "comment" and "explore" which require interpretation or clarification on the part of the student. In the context of a written assignment at university, verbs such as "discuss" or "examine" are generally asking the student for purposeful and careful presentation of evidence that leads to a better understanding of an aspect of the topic.

> **Relevance**
> Directive verbs as writing prompts define the instructor's expectations and tell the student the organizational pattern the student needs to use. Notice how some of these directives relate to the expository organizational patterns.

Informational directives

Informational directives ask students to demonstrate their knowledge about the topic using evidence in the form of examples, principles, definitions, or concepts from class or research. Notice how informational directives relate to the expository organizational patterns examined in previous sections. Examples of informational directives are:

Compare/Contrast: Present the similarities and differences between two subjects by identifying points of comparison and presenting evidence.
Define: Present special characteristics that delineate a concept, thing, event from others in its class.
Describe: Present detailed characteristics that create a visual image of an object, action, place, or person.
Explain: Present facts, reasons, or information that clarifies a subject, event, results, etc.
Relate: Present evidence to show the connections among ideas, events, causes, etc.
Recount: Narrate a past event chronologically including details about who, what, where, when, and why.
Review: Give an overview or summary, identifying main issues and commenting on them.
Summarize: Present the main points or essential facts in a concise and abbreviated way, omitting details, examples, and explanations.
Trace: Present the progression of events, ideas, trends, etc.

Interpretative directives

Interpretive directives ask students to state an opinion and support that opinion with examples, principles, definitions, or concepts from class or research. Examples of interpretive directives are:

Analyze: Identify specific aspects of a subject, event, or creative work to show how they relate to each other and affect the whole.
Argue: Establish validity by using factual evidence, examples, statistics, etc.
Assess: Present the factors that determine the significance or value of something.
Critique: Present a judgment about the value or the validity of something using evidence to support your position.
Discuss: Investigate and present the different aspects of a problem or subject, usually in support of a position or argument.
Evaluate: Use explicit criteria to judge the significance or value of an idea, event, or statement.

2. Writing: Following the instructions for a writing assignment

This guided writing practice will help you respond to informational directives for two short writing assignments. Both are based on the photograph below. Before you begin to write, review the explanations for "describe" and "recount" directives above.

Photograph of girl waiting for bus. Arnar Baldvinsson, 2019. Used with permission.

1. Instructions for a description assignment

Describe the photograph above in no more than 6–8 sentences based on what you observe. Create a visual image with your words. Describe only what you see in the photograph. Do not explain your feelings, impressions, connotations or memories. Avoid phrases such as "reminds me of …", "looks like …", or "could be …".

2. Instructions for a narrative recount assignment

Invent a story about the girl in the photograph and recount it in a paragraph of 6–8 sentences. Recount the events that took place from the time the girl got up in the morning until she stood in front of the bus. Use words and phrases such as "this morning", "after", "when", and "finally" to mark the chronological sequence.

Reflection
Read your paragraphs. What is the difference between a description and a narrative recount? How do your paragraphs differ? Which did you find more difficult to write? Why?

C. Expanding language: Avoiding sentence fragments

The use of incomplete sentences, called sentence fragments, is one of the characteristics of informal language that was discussed in Chapter 1. While sentence fragments are used in informal conversations, they are never acceptable in formal written communication.

Sentence fragments appear in the writing of many novice writers, especially those who write in English as a second language. A sentence fragment is a serious grammatical error that interferes with communication. The most frequent causes of sentence fragments are:

- a missing subject,
- a missing verb (or predicate),
- a subordinate phrase or a subordinate clause that is not connected to a sentence (prepositional phrases, verbal phrases, and subordinate clauses).

As writers develop greater fluency, they use more complex sentences that include subordinate clauses and subordinate phrases. Subordinate clauses and phrases are groups of words that function as a unit of meaning but are not complete sentences. Sentence fragments are easily overlooked in long complex sentences with multiple parts.

This chapter focuses on recognizing and correcting sentence fragments related to subordinate phrases. Chapter 3 will continue the examination of sentence fragments by examining subordinate clauses.

1. Sentence fragments: Subordinate phrases

A **phrase** is a word group that is used as a single part of speech. A phrase does not contain a subject and verb; consequently, it cannot stand alone and must always be part of a complete sentence.

a. *Avoiding sentence fragments: Prepositional phrases*

A prepositional phrase is a word group that begins with a preposition and is followed by an object or objects. This object may be a pronoun, gerund, or even a clause.

> In the tropics = (preposition + noun)
> Without them = (preposition + pronoun)
> By protecting = (preposition + gerund)
> Near where we live = (preposition + clause)

A prepositional phrase that is not part of a sentence is a fragment. In the example below, the prepositional phrase is punctuated with a period as if it were a full sentence. It is corrected by attaching the prepositional phrase to the sentence where it becomes an introductory phrase. <u>A comma is usually used to separate an introductory phrase from the main part of a sentence.</u>

Fragment:	After working many years. The factory workers received the same wage as when they started.
Correction:	After working many years, the factory workers received the same wage as when they started.

Common prepositions that introduce phrases					
after	about	above	across	before	behind
along	among	around	at	beyond	by
below	beneath	beside	between	for	from
despite	down	during	except	of	off
in	inside	into	near	through	to
on	outside	over	past	with	without
under	until	up	upon	against	

When multiple prepositional phrases follow each other, inexperienced writers often treat them as sentences and punctuate them with a period. The word groups below consist of several prepositional phrases but they are not sentences. To create a grammatically correct sentence, the word group must be connected to a complete sentence. Notice that each of the fragments is made up of three or more phrases introduced by a preposition.

Fragment:	Despite serving the government for many years inside the Ministry of Education.
Correction:	Despite serving the government for many years inside the Ministry of Education, Dr. Lopez did not improve the schools.
	Dr. Lopez did not improve the schools despite serving the government for many years as Minister of Education.
Fragment:	By working with experts in the field of infectious diseases.
Correction:	By working with experts in the field of infectious diseases, the regional government was able to prevent an epidemic.

Practice: Avoiding fragments with prepositional phrases

> Each of the following word groups is a fragment beginning with a prepositional phrase. Correct the fragment by creating a sentence that completes the thought. Remember to change the period to a comma in each sentence.

> *Examples:*
> After returning the equipment to the laboratory, *the student wrote a draft of her report.*
> *She has worked in the laboratory* since entering university.
> 1. By starting the project early.
> 2. Before meeting with the professor.
> 3. Along with her classmates.
> 4. Without help from colleagues.
> 5. Over the next four years.
> 6. Until graduation.
> 7. Upon completing university studies.

b. *Avoiding sentence fragments: Verbal phrases*

Verbal phrases are another common source of sentence fragments. The term verbal refers to words that are formed from verbs but function as nouns, adjective, or adverbs. A verbal phrase consists of a verb and any objects or modifiers. It is important to remember that a verbal phrase does not perform the function of a true verb. Consequently, a verbal phrase must be connected to a sentence or it is a fragment.

Two common types of verbal phrases are gerunds and infinitives. Gerund phrases and infinitive phrases frequently appear as fragments in writing, especially when the phrase begins a sentence.

Gerund phrases

A gerund is a verb ending in -ing which functions as a noun. In the sentence below "studying" functions as a noun and is the subject of the sentence.

   Studying at university was his lifelong goal.

When gerunds are part of a longer verb phrase, they may be incorrectly punctuated as a full sentence.

Gerund (-ing) phrase fragments	Gerund fragment connected to sentence
Earning a university degree in a second language	Earning a university degree in a second language is a remarkable accomplishment for anyone.
	The speaker stated that earning a university degree in a second language is a remarkable accomplishment for anyone.
Winning the 2018 Nobel Prize in Medicine for the development of new cancer treatments	Winning the 2018 Nobel Prize in Medicine for the development of new cancer treatments helped James P. Allison and Tasuku Honjo fund future research.

Infinitive phrases

An infinitive is derived from to + simple form of the verb. Infinitives may function as adjectives, adverbs, or nouns. An infinitive phrase is a word group made up of the infinitive + any objects + any adjectives or adverbs.

> "To be or not to be" is quite possibly the most famous phrase in English literature. (functions as noun)
> The United Nations sent troops to protect the refugees from harm. (functions as adjective)
> To finish the project on budget and on time, the crew worked on weekends. (functions as adverb)

To correct an infinitive phrase fragment you will need to make it part of a complete sentence. A comma is required when an infinitive phrase functions as an adverb at the beginning of a sentence.

Infinitive (to + verb) phrase fragments	Infinitive fragment correction
To earn a university degree in a second language	To earn a university degree in a second language is a remarkable accomplishment for anyone.
	I think that to earn a university degree in a second language is a remarkable accomplishment for anyone.
To win the 2018 Nobel Prize in Medicine for the development of new cancer treatments	To win the 2018 Nobel Prize in Medicine for the development of new cancer treatments was an honor for James P. Allison and Tasuku Honjo.
	To win the the 2018 Nobel Prize in Medicine for the development of new cancer treatments, James P. Allison and Tasuku Honjo conducted years of research.

Practice: Avoiding fragments with verbal phrases

Below are some sentence fragments. Indicate whether each fragment contains a gerund or infinitive phrase. Then correct the fragment by

(a) making the fragment into a sentence, or
(b) connecting the fragment to a sentence.

Remember to add commas where necessary.

Example 1. Protecting the public against identify theft. Gerund phrase

(a) *We are* protecting the public against identify theft.
(b) Protecting the public against identify theft *must be a priority for governments.*

> *Example 2.* To protect against identity theft. Infinitive phrase
> (a) *My office shreds old mail* to protect against identify theft.
> (b) To protect against identity theft, *shred documents with personal information before putting them in the trash.*
> 1. To ensure the safety of credit card information.
> 2. Subscribing to identity theft protection services.
> 3. Reviewing bank account records monthly.
> 4. To secure home internet access.
> 5. To prevent hackers from accessing email accounts.
> 6. Refusing to give personal information over the phone.

The list below summarizes the type of sentence fragments that we examined in the sections above. Please review it before completing the exercise below.

Fragment	Sentence
Missing a verb	**Correction – add verb**
A tropical ecologist about the relationships between the living and nonliving parts of the tropical environment. **What** is the action of a tropical ecologist?	A tropical ecologist **studies** the relationships between the living and nonliving parts of the tropical environment.
Missing a subject	**Correction – add subject**
Studies tropical habitats, especially those with high annual rainfall. Who or what is the subject?	**Dr. Chan** studies tropical habitats, especially those with high annual rainfall.
Prepositional phrase	**Correction – connect to full sentence**
Beyond studying the flora and fauna. "after" introduces a propositional phrase consisting of a proposition and a gerund. It is not a complete sentence.	Beyond studying the flora and fauna, Dr. Chan **documents species that are in danger of extinction.**
Gerund phrase	**Correction – connect to full sentence**
Analyzing data from research projects in four tropical regions. The gerund phrase is not a complete sentence.	Analyzing data from research projects in four tropical regions, **scientists reported similar problems in all regions.**
Infinitive phrase	**Correction – connect to full sentence**
To ensure the quality of his data collection procedures and the accuracy of his data analysis. The infinitive phrase is not a complete sentence.	To ensure the quality of his data collection procedure and the accuracy of his data analysis, **Dr. Chan asked a colleague to review his findings.**

Practice: *Recognizing and correcting sentence fragments*

Review the common sources of fragments above.
Each statement below is either a full sentence or a fragment.

- Mark full sentences with S.
- Mark fragments with F. If it is a fragment, correct the problem by adding the missing element.

Example 1. During the second set of experiments. (F) Correction: During the second set of experiments, *many of the subjects dropped out of the study*.

Example 2. The research report was submitted after the semester ended. (S) No correction needed.

1. Food that decomposes quickly.
2. The down-stroke of the piston compresses the air in the cylinder.
3. The first half of the nineteenth century was prosperous throughout Europe.
4. Witnessing a scene of chaos with overturned furniture.
5. Atoms of different elements dissimilar from each other.
6. To understand the mechanics of a compression engine.
7. Identifying the causes of extreme poverty.
8. To collect business and personal taxes throughout the country.

Chapter 3

AWARE

A framework for thesis-driven writing

Most academic writing tasks are thesis-driven. Thesis-driven writing means that a claim or assertion is made, often in the introduction, and then supported by evidence presented in the text. AWARE is a framework that has been developed to make the cycle of thesis-driven academic writing transparent and clear for novice writers. The framework leads students through five stages of academic writing from beginning to final editing. AWARE adapts a process-oriented approach, familiar to many students, to the specialized needs of academic writers.

This chapter describes the AWARE approach and applies to all the chapters in this book. The chapter examines AWARE in relationship to essay writing. As discussed in the previous chapter, the essay is a genre that provides a gateway to developing knowledge and skills to the specialized genres used in academic and professional writing. For example, some genres may include a literature review, a summary of findings, or recommendations section. These sections are previewed in this chapter. The structure of each of these sections is similar to an essay: an introduction, a central thesis or question, and paragraphs with supporting evidence. Later chapters in this book will explore in more detail how to use AWARE for research papers.

In this chapter, students will:

- become familiar with the AWARE writing cycle,
- examine the nature of the different stages of writing,
- practice strategies for each stage of writing,
- recognize the importance of rewriting.

A. Examining AWARE

The purpose of AWARE is to make the academic writing cycle transparent and easy to follow. The five stages of AWARE writing are:

- **A**rranging to write
- **W**riting
- **A**ssessing
- **R**evising
- **E**diting

AWARE supports students in becoming autonomous writers by teaching writing strategies for each of the five stages. Learning to use a repertoire of academic writing strategies contributes significantly to becoming a confident, independent author. Strategies are tactics people apply *consciously* to help them accomplish an unfamiliar task. Successful writers are usually not aware of the multiple cognitive strategies involved in developing a thesis statement, creating a strong introduction, or producing cohesive text.

Many students apply the same strategies they use for informal writing tasks such as a personal journal, a tweet, or an email to a friend, to academic writing assignments. This is especially true when writing in a second language. With sufficient practice a new strategy becomes a skill that the writer uses automatically and unconsciously.

Part I of this book, *Developing your academic voice*, applies the AWARE cycle and strategies to writing essays based on what students know. The ability to recall, organize, and write about information learned though reading, study, and coursework is an important exam-taking skill and a foundation for other types of writing. Part II of this book, *Presenting the views of others*, applies AWARE to writing a case study and a research paper. The following sections examine the AWARE cycle as applied to the academic essay. They mention the use of secondary sources only as a general preview to the AWARE program and to assignments in the second part of the book.

B. AWARE in practice

1. **AWARE: Arranging to write**

Taking a piece of writing from concept to finished product requires planning and focus. The first task is to analyze the instructions for the assignment and know what the instructor expects. (Chapter 2). Next, the Arranging-to-write stage prepares students for the actual writing task: selecting a topic, creating a working thesis statement, conducting research, and organizing the presentation of the information.

a. *Choosing a writing topic*

Finding a topic, or narrowing an assigned topic for a writing assignment, is challenging for all writers. Essentially, the writer needs to limit a topic to a point of view that can be examined within the parameters of the assignment.

Brainstorming refers to the use of strategies and techniques that help the writer generate a range of potential ideas for narrowing the focus of the topic. The writer begins the brainstorming with a broad topic and generates as many related ideas, aspects, features, and characteristics as possible.

There are many approaches to brainstorming. Each writer finds brainstorming techniques that suit his or her writing voice and task. Writers need to be familiar with multiple techniques to stimulate thinking, make connections, and narrow the topic to arrive at a viable thesis statement.

Some of the most well-known are:

Listing	Listing is a process of noting down all the ideas that come to mind about the topic, in random order, as fast as possible.
Free writing	Writing about a topic as quickly as possible without stopping, editing, or revising for 5–15 minutes is called free writing. The uninterrupted flow of writing often reveals unconscious connections and associations that help the writer narrow the topic.
Clustering	Clustering, or mind mapping, is a non-linear process that begins with a circled word or phrase representing an idea related to the topic. The writer creates additional clusters of concepts by adding circles around the center. The resulting "web" or "cluster" provides a visual map that reveals connections among concepts which can help the writer narrow a topic and identify potential areas for research.

In the mind map below, the author adds a circle for each association that comes to mind. The general topic is sugar.

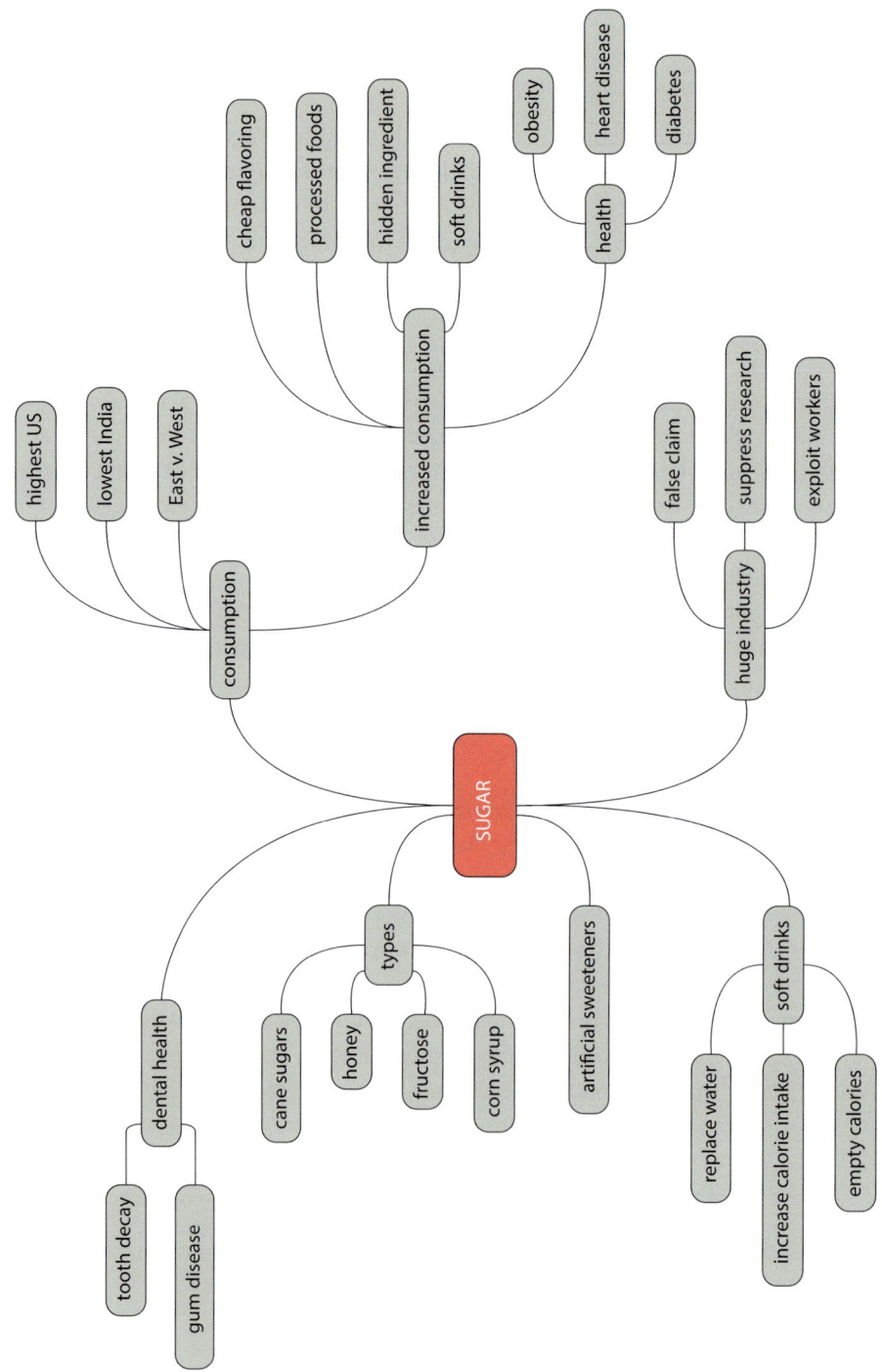

Practice: Brainstorming

> Brainstorm one of the topics in the writing prompts below. You can use one of the methods above or an alternative method to generate ideas on your chosen topic.
> - Examine the effects of increased sugar consumption.
> - Assess the bicycle as a mode of transportation.
> - Discuss the treatment of infectious diseases.

> *Reflection*
> *What additional modes of brainstorming have you encountered? Were they effective in helping you explore the range of possibilities for a writing topic? Do you know what works for you?*

b. *Developing a working thesis*

Understanding the nature of a working thesis can lessen the pressure to find the "right thesis statement" before writing. Most novice writers find it difficult to formulate a thesis statement. A working thesis is expected to evolve into a final thesis statement as it is shaped by new insights, evidence, or sources that emerge during the research and drafting stages.

The time and effort needed to explore a topic fully when formulating a thesis statement is a good investment. A thoughtfully crafted working thesis steers the writing of the first draft and still provides flexibility to alter the direction of the writing as needed. Successful writers make many modifications to the thesis statement and supporting evidence during the research and writing cycle.

Thesis statements are based on two elements:

1. A topic or subject
2. The point of view the author will use to examine the topic.

The process of developing a thesis statement begins with a broad general topic as illustrated below.

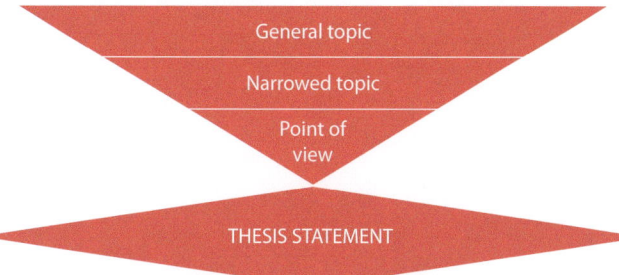

The examples below relate to the brainstorming topics in the practice exercise above and show the process of moving from general topic, to narrowed topic, to point of view for the topics below.

General Topic	Increased sugar consumption
Narrowed topic	Effects on health of children
Point of view	Growth in debilitating diseases
Working thesis statement	The increase in sugar consumption among children has contributed to the growth of a number of chronic diseases such as obesity, diabetes, and depression.
General Topic	Prevention and treatment of infectious diseases
Narrowed topic	The use of antibiotics to treat infections
Point of view	Negative and positive effects
Working thesis statement	Although antibiotics have revolutionized the treatment of life-threatening infections, their use also creates harmful side effects.
General Topic	Bicycles as transportation
Narrowed topic	Bicycles as transportation in urban environments
Point of view	Improves the living environment
Working thesis statement	The use of bicycles for commuting in urban settings improves the quality of life for citizens.

Practice: Developing a working thesis statement

For each of the topics below

- brainstorm the topic using one of the methods above
- narrow the topic to a specific aspect
- propose a point of view for examining the topic
- create a working thesis

General Topic	Free access to the internet
Narrowed topic	
Point of view	
Thesis statement	
General Topic	Solar energy
Narrowed topic	
Point of view	
Thesis statement	
General Topic	Driverless car technology
Narrowed topic	
Point of view	
Thesis statement	

Alternative general topics:	Censorship and the arts Video games and violence Privacy and the internet Social media and relationships Literary topics

Reflection
Effective authors prepare before they begin to write.
Think about how you prepare to write. What you do before you begin a writing assignment? What writing strategies have you used? Why might it be useful to try out a new strategy?

c. *Establishing the evidence*

All thesis-driven writing requires evidence to support the thesis statement. Academic writing assignments often require students to develop evidence based on either their own investigation as in the case study or reading other people's research articles as in Part II of this book. Both are covered in the AWARE program. The use of other people's writing is presented below as a general preview and will be revisited in Part II of the book for assignments requiring a literature review.

Conducting effective and appropriate research includes making decisions about the quantity and quality of the sources.

In AWARE, the following key principles guide the academic research process:

- The quality of the sources is as important as the quantity.
- Sources must be appropriate for the type of assignment and the instructor's expectation, for example:
  - **Expert sources** are written by academics or practitioners whose expertise has been established through affiliations with reputable universities or professional organizations. The most highly valued sources are disseminated through peer reviewed, scholarly publications;
  - **Facts** containing verifiable measurements, dates, scores, and statistics;
  - **Examples** containing references to historical events or current events, or examples from a literary work;
  - Sources referring to **common knowledge** or (in some types of writing) **personal knowledge**. This sort of information is usually found only in the introduction.
- Conducting research is not a linear process. It usually starts with a search for sources related to the thesis statement. However, the direction of the research, and the thesis statement, often evolves or changes in response to new information that emerges through the process.
- Strong academic writing incorporates *only research* that relates directly to the thesis statement.

> **Reflection**
> *What are your reactions when you are asked to write on a topic that requires you to investigate the topic? How do you begin the process?*

> **Relevance**
> Successful papers include only the most relevant evidence to support the thesis.

d. *Organizing the evidence*

Outlining is a traditional way for the writer to select and organize ideas that will provide the evidence for an assignment. However, the traditional outline format with headings and subheadings is not effective for all writing styles.

Throughout this program we will explore alternative forms of outlining. Visual and kinesthetic learners often find graphic outlines much more productive than traditional outlines because they provide a visual representation of the structure of the essay and the evidence. The visual image makes the writer aware of how the parts of an essay or research paper fit together and helps the author identify missing information before writing begins.

> **Relevance**
> Most students have had instruction in outlining, yet most students report that they do not use outlines. Research shows that mapping the content prior to writing leads to a more successful outcome. Thus, finding a strategy that helps you map the order and content of your paragraphs will make your writing stronger.

Examining a two-column graphic organizer

Additional graphic organizers that correspond to specific modes of exposition will be presented in subsequent chapters.

Below is an example of a partially filled out two-column graphic organizer that helps the writer visualize the flow of information in an essay.

Thesis statement: The use of bicycles for commuting in urban settings improves the quality of life for citizens.

Main idea	Supporting evidence
A. Traffic congestion	1. Small size takes up less road space
	2. Alternate routes avoid streets.
	3. Parking lanes can be used for travel
B. Decreases noise pollution	1. No combustion engine
	2. No honking horns
	3.

Main idea	Supporting evidence
C. Traffic deaths	1. 2. 3.
D. Environmental pollution	1. Uses no fossil fuels 2. No emissions 3. Less energy and fewer resources to build
E. Healthy lifestyle	1. 2. 3.

Practice: *Organizing the writing task*

1. Choose a topic from the list below or another assigned by your instructor.
   Free access to the internet
   Cigarette smoking
   Driverless car technology
   Censorship and the arts
   Video games and violence
   Privacy and the internet
   Social media and relationships
   Literary topic
2. Write a working thesis
3. Brainstorm main ideas for at least 2–3 body paragraphs
4. List potential evidence to support each main idea.

Your working thesis:

Main idea	Supporting evidence
A.	
B.	
C.	

2. AWARE: Writing

In the Writing phase of the AWARE cycle, the primary focus is on drafting the body of essay or paper. Understanding and embracing the concept of "draft" frees the writer to concentrate on expressing ideas. Drafts are early, unfinished versions of the final product. They are created as the author begins to translate ideas from the outline into written form.

A common misconception held by inexperienced writers is that the assignment is complete when the first draft has been written. Experienced writers view the initial draft as the start of the writing phase and understand that they will compose multiple drafts.

Writing the draft

With a working thesis as a starting point and the outline as a map, the writer is now ready to draft the body paragraphs that will support the thesis statement. The writer creates a topic sentence for each point on the outline and develops the evidence to support it. Writing the draft may open up new connections or ideas which deserve further exploration. It is best to make notes of new ideas to review later and stay focused on drafting the content of the outline.

The first draft of the body paragraph does not necessarily include the introduction. In fact, it is an effective strategy to wait until the body paragraphs have been completed to write the introduction. When the final content is in place, the writer can create a context to prepare the readers for the key points.

Practice: Drafting body paragraphs to support a thesis

1. Reread the thesis statement below. Underline the topic and double underline the point of view.
2. List supporting evidence for each main idea below from your own knowledge of the topic.
3. Choose two to three main ideas to develop into paragraphs. The topic sentence is provided for each main idea. Each topic sentence relates to the point of view.
4. Compose two to three draft paragraphs that support the main ideas you have chosen. Begin each paragraph with the topic sentence.

Working thesis statement:
The use of bicycles for commuting in urban settings improves the quality of life for citizens.

Main idea/topic sentence (support for thesis statement)	Supporting evidence
A. Traffic congestion *Substituting bicycles for automobiles during rush hour reduces traffic congestion.*	
B. Noise pollution *Unlike automobiles, bicycles do not produce noise pollution.*	
C. Traffic deaths *Automobiles cause many types of fatalities in crowded cities.*	

> D. Environmental pollution
> *Bicycles use fewer industrial resources to operate and manufacture.*
>
> E. Healthy lifestyle
> *Bicycles contribute to a healthy lifestyle.*
>
> Your paragraphs.
> Begin each with the topic sentence.

Once the first draft has been written, the author needs to step back and assess the quality and quantity of evidence for the working thesis. Time away from the draft will allow the author to a take a fresh, and more objective look at the draft.

3.   AWARE: Assessing

Before reading this section, review the section above about appropriate evidence. The measure of success in academic writing is how well the author supports his thesis with evidence. Once the first draft is finished, the writer needs to step back and assess whether there is sufficient evidence to support the thesis and whether the quality of the evidence is acceptable. <u>This applies to all assignments regardless of whether they use expert sources, facts, examples, or common or personal knowledge.</u>

The writer needs to determine if:

a. the *quantity* of ideas is sufficient to create strong evidence,
b. the *quality* of the ideas is appropriate and reliable,
c. the evidence validates the point of view in the working thesis.

a.   *Quality of evidence*

The success of academic writing always relates to the quality of the evidence used. The purpose of most academic writing is to explore new perspectives on a topic. Novice writers who conduct research using popular publications and web pages will not produce a strong paper. Likewise, overreliance on personal or common knowledge as evidence creates the impression that the topic is under-researched or the author's knowledge is superficial.

In addition to the quality of the sources, credible evidence depends on factors such as the expectations of the instructor, the purpose of the writing task, and the academic discipline. For example, papers on climate change require scientific evidence; analysis of a piece of literature must include textual evidence from the work that is being studied; a reflection assignment may credibly include the student's personal experience. Specific details and practice assessing the quantity and quality of evidence will be examined fully in later chapters on research papers.

> **Relevance**
> In academic writing certain sources are considered more convincing and reputable than others. While writers use a variety of evidence, most academic assignments expect the writer to draw on high-quality sources to support the thesis statement.

b. *Quantity of sources*

The amount of evidence required to support a thesis depends on the assignment. For a traditional academic essay, at least three paragraphs of credible evidence are the norm. Each of the paragraphs should develop sufficient, high-quality evidence to convince the reader of the validity of the topic sentence. Each paragraph may present evidence from a single source or from multiple sources.

<u>Single source</u> body paragraphs usually provide a summary of an expert source such as a research study, an expert opinion, an official document, or a detailed example. Relying on several single source body paragraphs is an appropriate approach for an essay or literature review based on three or more expert sources. The evidence in the sample paragraph below is based on a single source.

Practice: Assessing evidence – Single expert source body paragraphs

> The following paragraph relies on examples from a single expert source for evidence to support an essay with the thesis statement "Sleep deprivation is as debilitating as intoxication."
>
> *According to researchers Dement and Vaughn (2011), sleep deprivation was a major contributing factor in some of the great disasters in modern history. Sleep debt was cited as the cause of the environmental disaster of 1989 when the Exxon Valdez oil tanker spilled millions of gallons of crude oil into the waters of Alaska. The third mate who was piloting the tanker had slept fewer than 6 hours in the previous 48. The authors note similar conclusions from a year-long investigation of the 1986 space shuttle Challenger disaster. The report found sleep deprivation contributed to errors in judgment on the part of the managers who decided to launch the shuttle despite the lack of evidence that it was safe in cold temperatures.*
>
> 1. Read the paragraph above.
> 2. Underline the topic sentence.
> 3. How many sources is the information taken from?
> 4. How many examples does the writer include for the topic sentence? Does the writer provide an explanation for the examples?
> 5. Do you think that the author provides convincing evidence for the topic sentence?

<u>Multiple source body paragraphs.</u> Multiple source paragraphs combine several examples, expert sources, and facts to support a topic sentence. When using multiple sources or pieces of evidence, it is important to ensure that all of the sources provide evidence that directly supports the focus of the topic sentence. It weakens the paragraph to include information that is not specifically related to the focus.

Chapter 3. AWARE: A framework for thesis-driven writing

The general topic of the example paragraph below is antibiotics. However, the focus is on antibiotic-resistant bacteria only. Notice that all of the sources provide evidence that relates specifically to antibiotic resistance.

Practice: *Assessing evidence – Multiple source body paragraphs*

1. Read the paragraph on antibiotic-resistant bacteria below.
2. Underline the topic sentence.
3. Read the passage carefully.
4. Examine the source of the evidence and indicate what type of source is used to support the topic sentence (example, fact/statistic, expert source).

The practice of overprescribing certain antibiotics has contributed to a potential global health crisis caused by antibiotic-resistant bacteria. The World Health Organization reports a worldwide increase in levels of bacteria that have gradually become resistant to drugs that killed them in the past. A growing number of physicians observe that bacteria which cause life-threatening diseases such as pneumonia, meningitis and tuberculosis are resistant to commonly prescribed antibiotics. The Centers for Disease Control estimate that in the United States alone, 23,000 people die each year from infections caused by antibiotic-resistant bacteria. Despite ample warnings of the public health dangers of antibiotic-resistant bacteria, the Centers estimate that approximately 30% of antibiotic prescriptions are unnecessary.

Evidence	Type of source
The World Health Organization reports that bacteria have gradually become resistant to drugs that killed them in the past.	Expert Source
A growing number of physicians observe that bacteria which cause life-threatening diseases such as pneumonia, meningitis and tuberculosis are resistant to commonly prescribed antibiotics.	
The federal government estimates that in United States alone, 23,000 people die each year from infections caused by antibiotic-resistant bacteria.	
Despite ample warnings of the public health dangers of antibiotic-resistant bacteria, the Centers for Disease Control estimates that approximately 30% of antibiotic prescriptions are unnecessary.	

Reflection
What was your reaction to single source versus multiple sources of evidence in the body paragraphs? What are the advantages and disadvantages of both approaches?

c. *Assessment checklist*

Before the revision stage, the author needs to systematically assess how effectively the evidence and organization support the working thesis. It may be necessary to conduct further research or delete some ineffective evidence during revision. The chart below will serve as a guide.

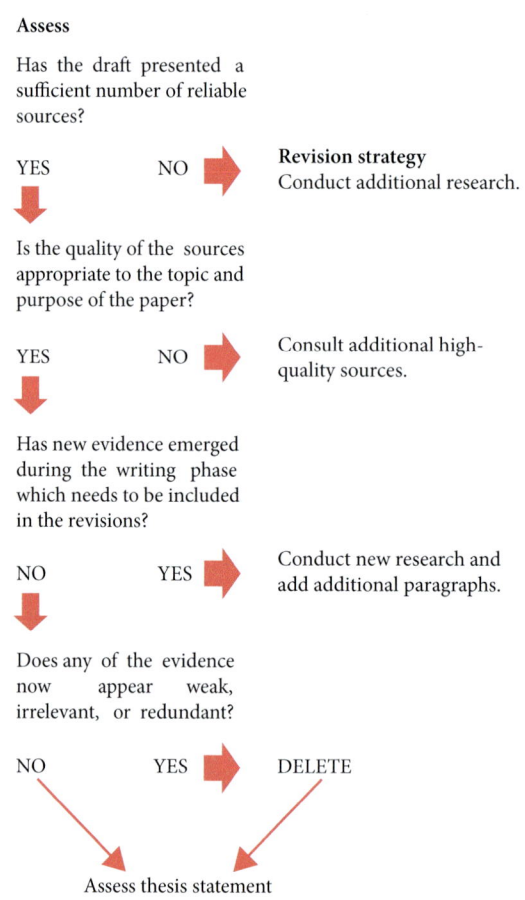

Steps in assessing evidence and thesis statement

> **Reflection**
> All successful writers find they cannot possibly use all their sources. They must assess the quality and quantity of their evidence and decide what to keep and what to discard.
>
> Think about your experience with academic writing assignments in your first language. How do you determine what to keep and what to eliminate?

d. *Assessing the working thesis statement*

The writer's point of view on the topic usually evolves or changes during the drafting stage. During the assessment stage, the writer may realize that evidence is stronger for a different point of view than the one in the thesis statement. The writer can modify or change the thesis statement at any time during the writing process to reflect the available evidence or a new perspective. What appears to be credible evidence to support the thesis may not hold up when paragraphs are developed.

It is essential for the writer to make a formal assessment to see how well the evidence aligns with the thesis statement before beginning revisions. Based on this assessment, the writer can modify the thesis statement and decide whether or not more research is needed.

4. AWARE: Revising

In the revision stage, an author makes changes to a draft based on their assessment and reflection. Revising focuses on strengthening the building blocks of academic writing such as organization, content, and evidence. Revision is followed by editing which ensures that writing adheres to the appropriate rules for language and academic style.

Novice writers often confuse editing, the process of checking for grammatical accuracy, conventions, and formatting, with revising. Novice writers and experienced writers tend to view the process of writing differently as illustrated in the table below.

Novice Writers	Experienced Writers
Maintain the structure and content of the first draft in the final draft	Understand that major changes are part of the revision process
Consider revising as a single step during the final stage of writing	Revise in stages and use multiple strategies
Focus revisions on local changes and editing	Make local changes as well as global revisions (reorganization, deleting expanding, or adding material)

AWARE views revising as indispensable to successful writing. AWARE considers two aspects of the revision process. The first looks at the architecture of writing. The second looks at the art of writing. Each of the following sections will explain and provide practice in one aspect of revising. By the end of the chapter, students will have developed a repertoire of strategies that they can use to evaluate and revise their writing.

> **Reflection**
> *"The best writing is rewriting"* (E. B. White)
> *Do you revise? How do you feel about rewriting multiple drafts?*

Revising the architectural elements of academic writing
The architecture of the paper is what holds the paper together. It provides a structure for what the author wants to say. The architecture includes the building blocks of academic writing: the thesis statement, the organizational pattern, and the body paragraphs with evidence.

Revise for evidence/content and organization
The writer adds additional research, deletes information, or changes the order in which the material is presented based on the assessment stage.
a. Evidence
   - Delete any information identified as redundant or irrelevant during the assessment stage.
   - Add additional information to fill in gaps identified in the assessment stage.
   - Add new evidence found during the research process.
b. Organization. Reorder the paragraphs if necessary, to ensure that related information is grouped together, that ideas flow into each other, and that the materials are presented in an order which makes sense to the reader.

Revise the working thesis
Make any changes in the thesis statement that may be needed to reflect new information uncovered during research. In conducting research, new ideas and information that relate to the thesis usually emerge. At the same time, ideas that informed your initial thesis may lack evidence.

Practice: *Revising*

> Reread each of the paragraphs you wrote above on the use of bicycles for commuting in urban settings.
>
> 1. Does the paragraph contain sufficient evidence to support the topic sentence?
> 2. Does the paragraph provide convincing evidence for the topic sentence?
> 3. Is the paragraph strong enough to include in an essay or should you develop another point?
>
> Where needed, add, delete, or reorder the information to create stronger support for the topic sentence.

5. AWARE: Editing

Editing is the final phase of the AWARE cycle. Until this point, the focus has been on the evidence and organization to support the thesis statement. Editing focuses on making sure that the writing adheres to the appropriate rules for academic style. These include grammatical accuracy, conventions, and formatting (margins, font, citations, bibliography, etc.).

Editing: Non-count nouns

A typical challenge for new writers, especially those writing in English as a second language is the correct use of non-count nouns. Non-count nouns refer to items, qualities, or concepts that cannot be counted and generally do not have a plural form. Non-count nouns are used frequently in academic writing. This chapter has examined the concepts of evidence, information, and research. These three words belong to the category of non-count nouns.

Commonly used non-count nouns				
advertising	advice	assistance	damage	equipment
energy	editing	feedback	furniture	gravity
software	homework	pollution	jewelry	debris
rubbish/trash	sunshine	traffic	violence	water
evidence	information	knowledge	research	terminology

Practice: Editing

In each sentence, substitute the underlined word with the non-count word in parenthesis. Make any necessary changes to verbs, quantifiers, or demonstrative adjectives.

Example:
These studies present information to support his theory. (research)
This research presents information to support his theory.

1. Because there are so many accidents on the highway, he does not drive after dark. (traffic)
2. These new computer applications make it easier to find information. (software)
3. Too many facts confuse the reader and lead to misinterpretation. (information)
4. Although the instructions were very clear, they were too long to follow. (feedback)
5. With so many prisoners in the building, the city increased the number of policy on duty. (violence)
6. The proposal failed because too few resources were available. (equipment)
7. Too many plastic bottles in the river harm fish and kill river animals. (pollution)
8. The city found that few volunteers were available on Sundays. (assistance)

> **Reflection**
>
> Many students expect the teacher to correct all the errors in their writing. What are the advantages and disadvantages of this expectation for students?

C. Expanding language

Avoiding sentence fragments: Subordinate clauses

This chapter will continue the discussion of sentence fragments. Chapter 2 focused on recognizing and correcting sentence fragments related to subordinate phrases. Chapter 3 examines fragments related to subordinate clauses.

In Chapter 2 we saw that the most frequent causes of sentence fragments are:

- a missing subject,
- a missing verb (or predicate), or
- a subordinate phrase or a subordinate clause that is not connected to a sentence. These include prepositional phrases, verbal phrases, and subordinate clauses.

> **Relevance**
>
> Grammatical accuracy is the backbone of making a clear and persuasive argument about the topic you are discussing in your essay. Acceptable grammar in a second or foreign language is key to credibility in writing.

1. Sentence fragments – subordinate clauses

Clauses are groups of words that function as a unit. Clauses contain both a subject and a verb. There are two main types of clauses: (a) independent clauses, which can function independently as sentences, and (b) subordinate clauses, which must be connected to an *independent* clause to form a sentence.

An independent clause is a simple sentence. It can stand on its own and expresses a complete thought.

Example:

> *The professor gave an interesting lecture.*
> *The newspapers reported the accident.*

In contrast, a *subordinate* clause functions to modify or clarify the main sentence. A subordinate clause may be mistaken for a sentence but usually does not express a complete thought and cannot stand alone. Two types of subordinate clauses frequently appear as fragments in writing: adverbial clauses and noun clauses.

a. *Avoiding sentence fragments with adverbial clauses*

An adverbial clause is a subordinate clause that functions as an adverb within a sentence by adding extra information to clarify the predicate of the main sentence. An adverbial clause begins with a subordinating conjunction (see chart below) which indicates the relationship between the subordinate and main clause. When it is not part of sentence, an adverbial clause is a fragment and needs to be corrected.

The most common position for an adverbial clause is at the beginning of a sentence followed by a comma. Adverbial clauses are sometimes placed after the main clause. In this case they do not require a comma.

Relates to	Common subordinating conjunctions	Examples
Time	after, as soon as, as long as, before, once, still, until, when, whenever, while	The children complained to parents <u>as soon as</u> the schools removed fast food from the lunch menu.
Concession	although, as though, even though	<u>Although</u> fast food is more popular than ever, most adults recognize that is not healthy.
Comparison/contrast	just as, though, whereas, while	<u>Whereas</u> fruits and vegetable provide vitamins and fiber, fast food is mostly fat and salt.
Cause/reason	as, because, in order that, since, so that	Parents need to prepare healthy meals at home <u>in order that</u> children develop good eating habits.
Condition	even if, if, in case, provided that, unless	<u>Unless</u> adults restrict unhealthy foods, children consume too much fat, salt, and sugar.
Place	where, wherever, whereas	<u>Wherever</u> they eat, children should have alternatives to junk food.

In the sentence below, the adverbial clause clarifies the main part of the sentence. It cannot stand alone because it is not a full sentence; thus, to be grammatically correct it must be connected to a sentence. As noted above, when an adverbial clause begins a sentence, it is punctuated with a comma.

Fragment (adverbial clause) Although the corporation's profits increased dramatically
Correction (Connect to a sentence) Although the corporation's profits increased dramatically, *the salaries of the factory workers remained unchanged.*
or
The salaries of the factory workers remained unchanged although the corporation's profits increased dramatically.

Practice: Correcting adverbial clause fragments

Each of the items below contains a fragment and sentence.
a. Correct the fragment by joining it to the sentence.
b. Make any necessary changes in punctuation.
c. Indicate in parenthesis the relationship indicated by the subordinating conjunction.

Examples:

Fragment: Although the novel *Nineteen Eighty-Four* was published in 1949. The story resonates with contemporary readers.

Correction: Although the novel *Nineteen Eighty-Four* was published in 1949, the story resonates with contemporary readers. **(concession)**

Fragment: Dr. Rodriguez saw injured people waiting outside. As soon as he arrived at the hospital.

Correction: Dr. Rodriguez saw injured people waiting outside **as** soon as he arrived at the hospital. **(time)**

1. Although the prime minister knew the agreement was a mistake. He would not admit it in public. (...................)
2. The damage will be greatest. Where Monsoon flood waters recede slowly. (...................)
3. Unless the tourists always wear hats and sunglasses. The danger of heatstroke is high. (...................)
4. Whereas drought is a problem in the Southwest. Rising water levels threaten coastal cities. (...................)
5. Since he is a very wealthy man. He is able to donate a lot of money to charity. (Cause/reason)
6. Even though the new drug performed well in clinical trials. It was not approved. (...................)
7. Because China is the largest manufacturing economy in the world. It plays a prominent role in world trade. (...................)
8. Even though Millennials are viewed as selfish and apathetic. The generation cares deeply about global issues. (...................)
9. The poor are getting poorer. While the rich are getting richer. (...................)
10. Wherever disease prevention is inadequate. Death rates are highest. (...................)

b. *Avoiding sentence fragments with noun clauses*

A noun clause is a type of phrase with a subject and a verb (often with an object or adjective) which acts as a subject in a sentence. Because noun clauses contain a subject and a verb they are often mistaken for sentences. A noun clause that stands alone is a fragment.

In the examples below the noun clauses are fragments.

Noun Clause as a fragment: *Whoever encouraged the workers to strike for higher pay and more vacation*

Noun Clause as a fragment: *How the company will respond to the workers' demands*

To correct a fragment, make the noun clause the subject or the object of a verb.

Fragment	Correction: Subject of a verb	Correction: Object of a verb
Whoever encouraged the workers to strike for higher pay and more vacation	Whoever encouraged the workers to strike for higher pay and more vacation *is the true hero*	*The true hero* is whoever encouraged the workers to strike for higher pay and more vacation
How the company will respond to the workers' demands	How the company will respond to the workers' demands *is unclear*	*It is unclear* how the company will respond to the workers' demands

The chart below presents some of the commonly used relative pronouns

Relative pronouns that often introduce subordinate noun clauses					
that	which	who	whose		
whether	what(ever)	where(ever)	when(ever)		whom(ever)

Practice: Correcting fragments with a noun clause

Each of the word groups below contains a fragment with a noun clause. Correct each fragment by connecting it to an independent clause as either a subject or an object of the sentence

Fragment	Subject of a verb	Object of a verb
Whoever encouraged the workers to strike for higher pay and more vacation	Whoever encouraged the workers to strike for higher pay and more vacation *is the true hero.*	*The true hero is* whoever encouraged the workers to strike for higher pay and more vacation
How the company will respond to the workers' demands	How the company will respond to the workers' demands *is predicable.*	*It is unclear* how the company will respond to the workers' demands
How the union leaders will respond to the company's offer		
What the company plans do with the current workers		
Why the company plans to relocate after the strike		
Whichever city the company chooses for its corporate offices		
Who declares victory		

2. Recognizing and correcting adverbial and noun clause fragments

Fragment	Correction
Subordinate adverbial clause Because rapid deforestation, agriculture, and climate change are leading to a reduction of its habitat. *"Because" introduces a subordinate adverbial clause which must be attached to an independent clause to complete the thought.*	*Connect to full sentence* Because rapid deforestation, agriculture, and climate change are leading to a reduction of its habitat, scientists are working to protect the Golden Lion Tamarin Monkey of Brazil. Because rapid deforestation, agriculture, and climate change are leading to a reduction of its habitat, the Golden Lion Tamarin Monkey of Brazil is an endangered species.
Subordinate noun clause Whatever happens to the Golden Lion Monkey population in the next decade. *The entire clause functions as a noun. It is not a sentence because it is missing the verb.*	*Make the phrase a subject or an object of a verb* Whatever happens to the Golden Lion Monkey population in the next decade depends on the environmental regulations. (Subject of the sentence) Scientists will record whatever happens to the Golden Lion Monkey population in the next decade. (Object of the sentence)

Practice: *Adverbial and noun clause fragments*

The word groups below are adverbial or noun clauses.
a. Determine whether the fragment is an adverbial or noun clause.
b. Make each into a full sentence by attaching it to a sentence.

Examples:

Fragment: before the plane took off – (adverbial clause)
Correction: *The passengers waited for three hours* before the plane took off.
Fragment: Whoever wished to leave the aircraft – (noun clause)
Correction: Whoever wished to leave the aircraft *was allowed to return to the terminal*.

1. So that passengers would stay calm (clause)
2. As soon as the jet took off from the airport (clause)
3. What happened next (clause)
4. Although the captain assured the passengers that all was well (clause)
5. What caused the problem (clause)
6. Because the plane was still close to the airport (clause)

D. Summary of The AWARE Approach

	Stage	Strategy
A	Arrange	Analyze the assignment
		Brainstorm topic, audience
		Create working thesis
		Conduct research
W	Write	Architecture
		– Structure (organizational pattern)
		– Content
		– Paragraph unity
		Art
		– Language
		– Cohesion
A	Assess	Working thesis
		Evidence (quantity, quality)
		Organization
R	Revise	Architecture
		– Finalize thesis
		– Reorganize
		– Coherence and cohesion.
		Art
		– Voice (sharpen language, point of view, cohesion)
		– Audience (tone, register)
E	Edit	Accuracy
		– Conventions
		– Format
		– Language

> **Relevance**
> AWARE is a simple but powerful acronym (a type of abbreviation) for a process that will guide you through the stages of writing an academic paper.

Chapter 4

Description and narrative in thesis-driven writing

Chapter 4 examines the role of narrative and description in expository writing. Although description and narration are most often associated with creative writing and storytelling, these patterns are also used in academic writing. Description and narrative are used in thesis-driven writing in most fields of study. They are incorporated into expository essays, research papers, and reports to illustrate points and as examples to support the thesis statement.

Narratives and descriptions are often familiar to students when they enter university since description and storytelling are part of our everyday lives. Thus, description and narrative provide a good foundation for developing a personal writing voice, distinguishing different organizational structures, and expanding vocabulary.

In this chapter the student will:

- examine the structure, characteristics and purpose of a description and a narrative,
- recognize the relevance of description and narrative to thesis-driven writing,
- use strategies while arranging to write a description and a narrative,
- practice writing description and narrative,
- examine the use of discourse connectors in description and narrative,
- practice strategies for assessing, revising and editing descriptions and narratives.

> **Relevance**
> Writing in familiar genres on familiar topics gives students an opportunity to focus on developing their own voice in writing.

A. Examining description in thesis-driven writing

Many fields of study use description as evidence in thesis-driven texts. In natural science and social science, some types of research are based on systematic observation and detailed description. Science research studies often include rich descriptions of subjects and their behavior. Consider the research of the primatologist Jane Goodall in Tanzania. She recorded detailed descriptions of chimpanzees in the wild which created a body of evidence to support her theories.

> **Relevance**
> Description is often incorporated into essays and research papers in all disciplines to support the thesis; therefore, learning to use descriptive language is fundamental to strong academic writing in any field of study.

Description has specific characteristics that distinguish it from other types of text. In writing a description, the writer's task is to generate a mental image of a person, a place, a thing, or an event in the mind of the reader. The use of precise, descriptive vocabulary plays an important role in painting a vibrant mental picture.

1. Description: Illustration vs. explanation

Description "illustrates" the scene by engaging the reader through sensory experiences of sight, smell, taste, texture, and sound. On the other hand, explanation "tells about" a scene using general vocabulary that helps the reader understand the scene rather than experience it.

Description:	Explanation:
– paints a picture of a person, place, or event	– tells about a person, place, or event
– evokes a sensory impression	– states the situation
– shows attributes	– presents information
– uses precise vocabulary	– uses general vocabulary

Practice: Description vs. explanation

> The two texts below recount the same scene.
> 1. Read text A. Then close your eyes and imagine the scene.
>   A. *The doctor's reception room was shabby. It had an unpleasant smell. The hallway leading to the office had a creaky, grimy wood floor. The office at the end of the hall was sunny but the windows were dirty.*
> 2. Read text B. Then close your eyes and imagine the scene.
>   B. *The air of the reception room reminded the visitor of old socks and moldy plaster. The floor creaked as Jose walked along the gritty grey path worn into the wood. Opening the door to the examining room, he was surprised by the stripes of sunlight falling on stacks of papers on the doctor's desk.*

3. Which text created the most vivid image for you?
4. Do both texts portray an unpleasantly dirty, shabby, and smelly office?
5. How do you know the office in text A is shabby, smelly, and dirty?
6. How do you know the office in text B is shabby, smelly, and dirty?
7. Which text is more descriptive?

2. Precise language in description

Vocabulary plays an especially prominent role in description since the writer's intent is to illustrate the scene in vivid detail. Effective writers choose precise words that convey subtle differences in meaning. A description the writer paints is only as clear and vivid as the vocabulary. Even words that are considered synonyms have distinct connotations and shades of meaning. The word groups below are listed as synonyms in a thesaurus and yet each conveys a different impression. Imagine a place or object and then add each of the adjectives below. Can you see each in your mind's eye? Can you see the difference depending on the adjective?

blue – azure – navy – cobalt
big – large – huge – gigantic
magnificent – superb – splendid – wonderful

Changing a single word can create a very different image and impression. Most concepts can be expressed in many ways and good writers draw upon a large vocabulary to express subtle differences in meaning. For instance, the colors pink and fuchsia are related. Each word creates a distinct impression in the following sentences:

The mother dressed the newborn baby in a pink hat and matching mittens.
The mother dressed the newborn baby in a fuchsia hat and matching mittens.

Reflection: Visualization strategy
Visualize a newborn baby wearing a pink hat and mittens.
What does the image of a pink hat and mittens suggest to you?
Visualize a newborn baby wearing a fuchsia hat and mittens.
What does the image of a fuchsia hat and mittens suggest?
Why do the words pink and fuchsia create different impressions for you?

Practice: Precise vocabulary

> This exercise will help you explore variations in words with similar meanings. It will help expand your vocabulary. Read the example first and then do the exercise.
>
> We have chosen to examine the word "difficult" used in the sentence below:
>
> > *The professor's assignments became more* difficult *as the semester progressed.*
>
> Words with similar meaning to "difficult" are: hard, challenging, impossible, tough, demanding, unmanageable, thought-provoking, and taxing.
>
> The chart shows them arranged based on least to most difficult
>
> | thought-provoking | difficult/ hard | challenging/ taxing | demanding | unmanageable | impossible |
> |---|---|---|---|---|---|
>
> Remember that everyone brings a slightly different understanding to each word. The meanings are on a relative continuum and the differences between some words are slight.
>
> 1. Write a sentence using two of these words: fun, beautiful, cold, interesting, and similar.
> 2. List as many synonyms as you can for each word.
> 3. Organize the synonyms on a continuum from least to most intense.

> **Reflection**
> *How many synonyms were you able to generate? Compare your list with a classmate. What did you learn through this activity?*

Reading and writing are interactive processes. *Visualization* is a powerful strategy that supports both reading and writing. The strategy translates the words on a page into a vibrant image of a person, place, or thing for the reader; for the writer, it helps create a vivid image that serves as the basis for a description.

Below is an exercise to help you visualize an image in your mind. The passage uses precise vocabulary that creates pictorial images and sensory impressions for the reader.

Practice: Reading to write – Visualization as a reading strategy

> This exercise is based on passages from *The Adventures of Tom Sawyer* by Mark Twain. It includes a description of a haunted house.
>
> A haunted house is a building that people believe is inhabited by ghosts. The myth of the haunted house appears in western storytelling, holiday traditions, and films. Haunted houses are often depicted as old, broken down buildings which create an impression of fear.
>
> Read the descriptive paragraphs below and answer the questions at the end.
>
> *There in the middle of the moonlit valley below them stood the "haunted" house, utterly isolated, its fences gone long ago, rank weeds smothering the very doorsteps, the chimney crumbled to ruin, the window-sashes vacant, a corner of the roof caved in. The boys gazed awhile, half expecting to see a blue light flit past a window.*

> Then they crept to the door and took a trembling peep. They saw (…) an ancient fireplace, vacant windows, a ruinous staircase; and here, there, and everywhere hung ragged and abandoned cobwebs. They presently entered, softly, with quickened pulses, talking in whispers, ears alert to catch the slightest sound, and muscles tense and ready for instant retreat.
>
> 1. What time of day was it? What language "shows" you the time?
> 2. What was the physical condition of the building? What language "shows" you the condition of the building?
> 3. How do the boys feel? Does the author tell the reader how the boys feel? What words create this sensory impression?
> 4. How would you feel about entering this building?

The practice below will lead you through the process of writing a short description of a haunted house. It will use visualization as a writing strategy.

Practice: Using visualization as a writing strategy

> What do you know about haunted houses?
>
> What are the characteristics of a haunted house and what is it like to visit one? Some of the elements that come to mind are the building, its interior, furniture, sights, sounds, smells, and your reactions.
>
> The map below presents some descriptive language that relates to these elements. Add at least three descriptive words to each category.
>
>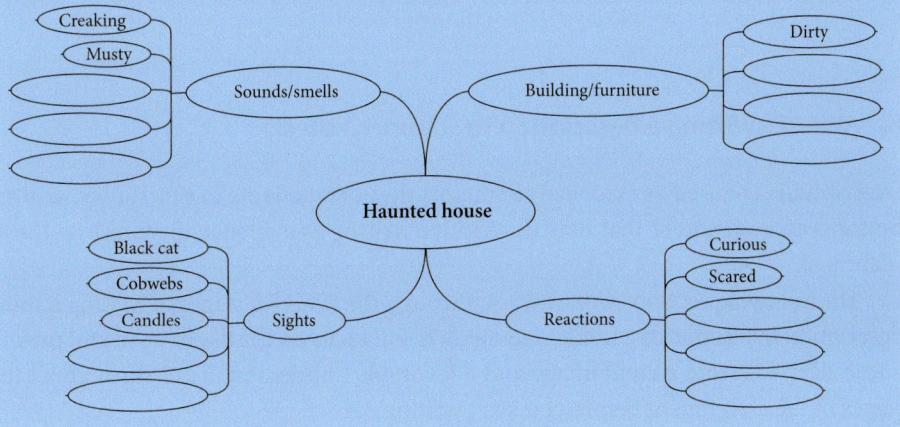

> Visualize your answer to the questions below. Write a response immediately after each question. Do not skip a line or leave a space. The answers will fit together to create a single description.
>
> Picture in your mind a house that is haunted. Imagine as a child you visited this house. Describe what you saw and what you experienced.
>
> 1. Visualize the image of a haunted house in your mind. Describe its location, the front door, the time of day.
> 2. Open the front door. What do you see, hear, smell? How do you feel?
> 3. As your eyes adjust to the light, you see a tall staircase. Walk up the staircase. What do you see, hear, smell, or feel?
> 4. When you reach the last step, you see a mystery room. Describe your walk to the mystery room.
> 5. Enter the mystery room. What do you encounter in the room?
> 6. You know you must escape as quickly as possible. Describe your escape.
> 7. Write a concluding sentence.
>
> Which of the following sentences or thesis statements best describes the content of your paragraph?
>
> a. The concept of a haunted house is based on images that frighten children.
> b. Creaking staircases are a characteristic of haunted houses.
> c. As a child, my imagination created frightening images that I remember as if they are real.
>
> What evidence can you find in the descriptive paragraph to support the thesis statement you chose?
>
> Adapted from Link, F. & Almquist, S. (1988)

B. AWARE: Writing a description to support a thesis

Descriptions are used as evidence to support thesis statements in expository writing. Below is an assignment that uses descriptive writing as evidence to support a thesis statement.

The following sections will lead you through the AWARE stages of writing a short description that supports a thesis statement. It will focus on the use of vivid and precise vocabulary to create a vivid image and a favorable impression. Read through all the stages of the assignment before you start writing.

1. AWARE: Arranging to write a description

a. *Understanding the assignment*

As discussed in Chapter 3, the first stage in the writing cycle is to understand the assignment and the instructor's expectations. Read the assignment before you follow the stages below.

The assignment: Selling property

> You are a real estate agent who has been asked to find a property for a wealthy family. You have found the ideal home (country house, city flat/apartment, vacation cottage, etc.). You write an email to convince the client that this property meets all of their needs.
>
> The email contains an introduction plus at least two body paragraphs.
>
> - The introduction includes a sentence that functions as a thesis by clearly stating the type of house and why it is ideal for the buyer.
> - The two body paragraphs present evidence of two features that support your view that the house is an exceptional choice for your clients.

b. *Generating ideas and brainstorming*

What type of home will be the subject of your email? Make a list of all of the types of homes that you can think of, such as a country house, semi-detached home, flat, seaside cottage, bungalow, ski lodge, etc. Add any other types of homes that you are familiar with. Remember that you must have a clear picture in your mind's eye in order to write a vivid description of the outstanding features of the home. Choose a home type that sparks your interest.

Visualize this ideal house in your mind. Brainstorm all of the features that you think make this house exceptional. Using one of the brainstorming approaches such as listing, free writing, or mapping, brainstorm any ideas and language related to the house. When you have finished your brainstorm, choose the two to three selling points that are most vivid in your mind. Focus on features that you want your client to <u>see</u> through your description.

Possible categories of features include, but are not limited to:

- the exterior of the house (color/architectural style/size),
- condition of the house interior/exterior,
- the living area (kitchen, living room etc.),
- the bedrooms and bathrooms,
- location/landscaping/gardens,
- views.

c. *Working thesis statement*

Create a thesis statement that states the type of house (topic) and why this house is an exceptional choice for your clients. You can use the template in the instructions below:

Introduction:

I am very pleased to write to tell you that I have located a home that meets all of the criteria that you have requested. The____ is an ideal property for your family with _____

or create your own.

For example:

The *bungalow* is an ideal property for your family <u>*with original architectural features*</u>.

The *flat* is a rare find which has <u>*extraordinary views and a convenient location*</u>.

The *large detached home* is beautifully constructed <u>*with high-end materials in the bathrooms and kitchen*</u>.

> **Relevance**
> Many novice writers believe that brainstorming is a waste of time. Experienced writers have learned that spending time arranging to write and having a clear idea of what the content of the essay will be before writing saves time in the long run.

2. AWARE: Writing the description

As you write your draft paragraphs, remember that you have already stated that the house meets all of the client's requirements. The descriptive paragraphs should create an appealing image in the mind's eye of the exceptional features of this property. Use descriptive language and avoid explanation.

Remember that there is a difference between an explanation and a description. Notice how the explanation below is a basic narrative that lists the features and their function. The description includes descriptive words that help the reader 'see' the room and even create a 'feel' for it.

A. <u>Explanation</u>: The house contains many original features and a working fireplace. The cozy library is a great place for the family to spend winter afternoons. The large windows look out on the garden. The built-in bookcases provide plenty of room for your book collection.

B. Description: In the library, the sunlight floods the room through three tall windows creating a glow in the white marble of the fireplace. The light warms the golden oak of the floor-to-ceiling bookcases on the opposite wall. As the visitor takes in the gleaming marble fireplace, warm oak paneling, and the views of the garden, visions of a family sitting around a fire on a chilly winter evening come to mind.

Reflection
Compare the language in the two passages above. Passage A states that the library is "cozy". Passage B does not use the word cozy. What language does B use to create the sensory experience of a cozy room for the reader?

Writing Practice: Selling a property

You are a real estate agent who has been asked to find a property for a wealthy family. You have found the ideal home (country house, city flat/apartment, vacation cottage, etc.). You will write an email to convince the client that this property meets all of their needs.

The email contains an introduction plus at least two body paragraphs.

- The introduction includes a sentence that functions as a thesis by clearly stating the type of house and why.
- The two body paragraphs present evidence of two features that support your view that the house an exceptional choice for your clients.

1. Use formal language. Begin with a salutation such as Dear….
2. Introduction:
   I am very pleased to write to tell you that I have located a home that meets all of the criteria that you have requested. The____ is an ideal property for your family with _____
3. Body paragraphs:

   Write 2 or more paragraphs that describe the unique features that make this property an exceptional choice for your clients. To sell the property and earn a commission, you must create a favorable impression through a vivid description. Describe at least 2 features that make this property exceptional.

Reflection
You have finished the first draft of a description!
Was the process of writing the description easier or more difficult than you expected? In what way/s?
Did the brainstorming help? If yes, how did it help? If no, why do you think it didn't help?
Does it help to spend time arranging to write before starting the actual writing? If yes, how? If no, why?

3. AWARE: Assessing a description to support a thesis

Success in academic writing is how well the author supports his thesis with evidence. Once the first draft is finished, the writer needs to assess how effective the description is in illustrating the thesis.

Practice: Assessing

> The body paragraphs in the email supports your thesis statement by describing the unique features that make this property an exceptional choice for your clients. The instructions were to include at least two features as evidence.
>
> 1. Do your paragraphs describe at least two distinct features? What two features did you describe? If you wrote two paragraphs about the same feature, you did not meet the requirements for the assignment. Add a description of at least one more feature.
> 2. How do the descriptions support the thesis statement? What evidence do they present to convince the reader that the property is worth considering?

4. AWARE: Revising a description

In revising, the author re "visions" his or her writing based on assessment. Experienced writers recognize that most writing is rewriting. If your description is not as vivid as it could be, now is the time to make the necessary changes so the piece of writing reflects your intention by examining the precise meaning of some of the words you have used.

Strategies for revising: Visualization and word precision

1. Close your eye and visualize each the descriptive paragraphs in your mind. Can you create a mental picture?
2. Underline any sentences that "explain" rather than describe. Rewrite these sentences to create an image in your mind.
3. Underline the words and phrases that do not create a vivid picture or impression.
   - Use an online dictionary or the synonym feature in your writing program to examine different shades of meaning and choose the most appropriate word for your description.
   - Make sure you understand the exact meaning of the words you choose. You may need to look up their precise meaning and use.

Checklist for revising:

As you read your descriptions, keep the following in mind:

1. Formality of language (see Chapter 1).
2. Accuracy and precision in vocabulary.

5. AWARE: Editing commas

One aspect of editing that challenges most writers is the correct use of the comma. This is especially true when English uses different norms for punctuation from the writer's first language. Another complicating factor is variations in rules for comma usage among the formatting styles discussed in Chapter 1 (APA, MLA, and Chicago). Below are three basic rules for comma use according to the APA style.

Comma usage

Commas are used to indicate a natural pause in the flow of the text, to separate elements in a sentence, or to distinguish a subordinate idea from the main clause.

Use a comma

- to separate the elements in a series or list, or to punctuate multiple adjectives presented in a series,

Example: *The house is majestic, well maintained, and perfectly located.*

- to separate clauses in compound sentences that are joined using conjunctions such as *and, but, for, or, nor, yet,*

Example: *The home is in a residential neighborhood, but not far from the downtown area.*

- after introductory (a) clauses, (b) phrases, or (c) words that come before the main clause. (For a review see the sections on fragments in Chapters 2 and 3.)

Examples:

Because the building is located near a park, it is quiet at night. (clause)
As soon as he entered the room, he felt completely at home. (phrase)
Tomorrow, demolition of the old buildings begins. (word)
Finally, the project came to a successful end. (word)

Check your paragraphs for fragments and correct use of commas. It might be helpful to read through for one feature at a time. With practice, editing several features at a time will become easier.

Editing Checklist:

1. Fragments (Chapter 2, 3)
2. Comma usage.

D. Examining narrative to support a thesis statement

A narrative tells a story. Stories entertain, instruct, inform, and relate events. The type and complexity of narrative structures are extensive and vary from complex novels to the straightforward narration of journalists or historians. A simple narrative moves events though time chronologically. The basic elements of the narrative genre are: the setting (when and where the events take place), the protagonists (the agents who carry out the events), the events (the incidents that take place), the climax, and the conclusion (what the story teaches or illustrates).

1. The building blocks of narrative

The architecture of a narrative consists of the following building blocks:
- the elements of setting, characters, a series of events, climax, and conclusion,
- a chronological organizational pattern for events,
- a signaling of the sequence of events using discourse connectors.

Discourse connectors are used in narratives to help the reader follow the progress of events and are, therefore, an integral part of this text type. The following discourse connectors signal the sequence of events.

Discourse connectors that signal progression in a narrative			
after	afterward	as soon as	before
during	finally	first	following
immediately	initially	later	meanwhile
next	not long after	now	on (date)
preceding	second	soon	then
third	today	until	when
(days, weeks, etc.) ago			

Relevance
The ability to write good narrative text is a skill that supports other forms of academic writing. Short sections of narrative are often embedded within other expository patterns and research papers to support the thesis. This type of embedded narrative can be used to report, clarify, explain, link theory to real-life experience, or summarize relevant parts of fiction in literary analysis.

2. Analyzing narrative

In addition to telling stories that entertain, narratives can instruct and inform. A narrative can be used to chronicle a series of events that supports a thesis statement. The passage that follows is an example of a short narrative that could be embedded into an expository essay or paper as an example. It is adapted from a chapter in an economics book, *The Age of Big Business, A Chronicle of the Captains of Industry*, written in 1919. The author, Burton J. Hendricks, uses the narrative as an example to support his economic theory.

> *At the beginning of the 20th century, an English manufacturer, seeking the explanation of America's ability to produce an excellent car so cheaply, made an interesting experiment. Initially, he obtained three American automobiles, all of the same "standardized" make, and gave them a long and racking tour over English highways. Workmen then took apart the three cars and threw the disjointed remains into a promiscuous heap. Every bolt, bar, gas tank, motor, wheel, and tire was taken from its accustomed place and piled up, a hideous mass of rubbish. Workmen then painstakingly put together three cars from these disordered elements. As soon as they were assembled, three chauffeurs jumped on these cars, and they immediately started down the road and made a long journey just as acceptably as before. The Englishman had learned the secret of American success with automobiles. The one word "standardization" explained the mystery.*

Practice: Reading to write – The elements of a narrative

Use the graphic organizer below to identify all the elements of Hendricks's narrative, then complete the points and answer questions at the end.

Subject:

Protagonists	Time and place

Events

1.

2.

3.

Climax (the turning point of the story)

Conclusion (what the narrative illustrates)

1. Underline the topic sentence.
2. According to the topic sentence, what is the author seeking?
3. Underline the discourse connectors that the author uses to show the progression of the narrative.
4. What conclusion does the author reach?
   How does the conclusion relate to the topic sentence?
5. What do you imagine that the topic of the chapter might be?
   Write a hypothetical thesis statement for the chapter.

E. AWARE: Writing a narrative to support a thesis

Narratives, like descriptions, are used as evidence to support thesis statements in expository writing. The following sections will lead you through the AWARE stages of writing narratives that support a thesis statement.

1. AWARE: Arranging to write a narrative

In this assignment you will write a short narrative paragraph that might serve as evidence in a longer essay with the thesis statement "Preparation is the key to success." Read through the entire assignment before you start writing.

a. Understanding the assignment

> "Before anything else, preparation is the key to success."   Alexander Graham Bell
>
> Write a short narrative of no more than 250 words. The paragraph will be used as evidence to support the thesis statement "Preparation is the key to success." The purpose of the narrative is to illustrate the role of preparation in navigating life's events. The topic should directly support the thesis statement.
>
> The narrative will present a <u>single event</u> or experience that illustrates the consequence of preparation or lack of preparation. Tell the story in chronological order and use appropriate discourse connectors from the table above.
>
> Choose an event that is familiar to you or one that was significant for you or someone you know.

b. Brainstorming

Make a list of events or experiences where preparation, or lack of preparation, clearly influenced an outcome. What did you learn from each experience that you can share with others?

c. Opening statement

Develop an opening statement that explains the type of experience (topic) and the lesson it teaches (focus). This serves as the topic sentence. Your narrative will illustrate an event or experience that supports the topic sentence.

> *I learned that for a successful job interview, preparing to ask questions is as important as preparing to answer them.*
>
> *Locating the nearest exit increases the chance of a successful escape in an emergency.*
>
> *Hikers who are fully prepared for the terrain and conditions will usually survive even if they get lost.*
>
> *Being in the right place at the right time is sometimes as important as preparation.*

Practice: Planning the narrative

Use the graphic organizer below to outline the narrative paragraph you will use to support the thesis statement. Remember to write from personal knowledge or experience.

Thesis Statement: Preparation is the key to success.

Opening statement: Type of experience and what you learned

Protagonist(s)	Time and setting

Events
1.
2.
3.

Climax

Conclusion (What the narrative illustrates)

2. AWARE: Writing a narrative

Following the outline above, write the draft of your paragraph. Include an opening statement and a conclusion.

3. AWARE: Assessing a narrative

Below are guidelines for assessing the narrative assignment:

1. Does your narrative fit into the 250-word limit?
2. Have you included an opening statement? Does it state the topic and the aspect of the topic that will be examined?
3. Does the introductory sentence support the thesis "Preparation is the key to success?"
4. Does the narrative include a setting, protagonists, events, and climax?
5. Have you included a conclusion that states what the narrative illustrates?

4. AWARE: Revising a narrative

Once you have assessed your writing, it is time to revise the narrative essay.

1. Do your discourse connectors advance the narrative? Do you repeat the same discourse connectors? Would any of the connectors in the table above be a better choice?
2. Does your conclusion relate to the introductory statement?

Checklist for revising:

As you read your narrative, keep the following elements in mind:
- formality of language (see Chapter 1),
- accuracy and precision of word choice,
- discourse connectors and the relationship between words and sentences.

5. AWARE: Editing introductory words, phrases, clauses

Narratives rely on discourse connectors (words or phrases) to clarify the sequence of events and the time that they took place. Narrative discourse connectors are often placed at the beginning of a sentence as words, phrases, or clauses. Care should be taken not to overuse discourse connectors and to evaluate carefully when they are necessary to indicate progression.

As we saw above, a comma is required after introductory (a) clauses, (b) phrases, or (c) words that come before the main clause. (For a review of phrases and clauses, see the sections on fragments in Chapters 2 and 3.)

Practice: Add a comma where required in the sentences below

> Before the end of the 20th century man had travelled to the moon.
>
> On July 20th 1969 images from the Apollo mission were broadcast from the moon.
>
> The next day Neil Armstrong descended from the spacecraft to become the first man to set foot on the lunar surface.
>
> After 19 minutes Buzz Aldrin joined Armstrong
>
> As soon as the images of the astronauts appeared on television people claimed that they were not authentic.
>
> Immediately scientists attested to the authenticity of the photos and the space mission.
>
> Now most people consider the Apollo 11 mission as a historical achievement for all mankind.

Editing Checklist

Remember to check for one feature at a time. Check paragraphs for:
- fragments (Chapter 2, 3),
- correct use of non-count nouns,
- comma usage after introductory words or phrases.

Practice: Revisiting and revising narrative and descriptive paragraphs

> In Chapter 2, you were asked to write a descriptive paragraph and a narrative paragraph based on the photograph below.
> Reread your paragraphs.
> How would you critique your paragraphs based on what you learned in this chapter?
> How well did your paragraphs meet the requirements for "narrative" and "description"?
> Revise your paragraphs and resubmit if assigned by your instructor.
> The instructions are repeated below:
>
> 1. Instructions for a description assignment.
>   Describe the photograph above in no more than 6–8 sentences based on what you observe. Create a visual image with your words. Describe only what you see in the photograph. Do not explain your feelings, impressions, connotations or memories. Avoid phrases such as, "reminds me of …", "looks like …", or "could be …".
> 2. Instructions for a narrative recount assignment:
>   Invent a story about the girl in the photograph and recount it in a paragraph of 6–8 sentences. Recount the events that took place from the time the girl got up in the morning until she stood in front of the bus. Use discourse connecters such as "this morning", "after", "when", and "finally" to mark the chronological sequence.

Photograph of girl waiting for bus. Arnar Baldvinsson, 2019. Used with permission.

F. Expanding language

Spelling: UK and US

Students must check spelling and punctuation carefully. It is important to become familiar with the difference among spelling rules in different English-speaking countries. Check with your instructor to ensure that you are using the required version. Whichever spelling rules are used, it is important to be consistent throughout the entire document.

The spell checker in the Word processing program is an important tool that students should use for every assignment. Before using it, confirm that the spell checker is set for the version of English that your instructor requires. The most frequently used settings are *English (United States)* or *English (United Kingdom)*.

Below are charts with differences in US and UK spelling patterns and words that students must learn to identify.

DIFFERENCES IN SPELLING PATTERNS			
UK		**US**	
VERB ENDINGS			
ise	industrialise	ize	industrialize
yse	analyse	yze	analyze
NOUN ENDINGS			
isation	*organisation*	ization	organization
	globalisation		globalization
WORDS ENDING IN RE/ER			
tre	centre	ter	center
	metre		meter

DIFFERENCES IN WORD SPELLING	
UK	**US**
aeroplane	airplane
analogue	analog
behaviour	behavior
catalogue	catalog
centre	center
colour	color
defence	defense
endeavour	endeavor
encyclopaedia	encyclopedia
fibre	fiber

foetus	fetus
instalment	installment
labour	labor
paediatric	pediatric
plough	plow
programme	program
rigour	rigor
sceptical	skeptical
skilful	skillful
travelled	traveled

Practice: UK and US spelling

> The following narrative contains a number of words that use UK spelling. Read it carefully. Underline the words using UK spelling. Rewrite the paragraph using US spelling.
>
> *The jewelry store robberies became famous once the story was aired on a local television programme. The employees in each of the seven stores reported similarities in the speech and in the behaviour of the robbers. Within days, the public questioned the rigour of the original investigations. As a result, detectives from various towns sent fibres from the robber's clothing to be analysed at the National Crime Research Centre. Scientists recognised that the fibres from all the crime scenes were an exact match in colour and composition. The labour of professionals in multiple organisations finally led to the arrest of the criminals.*

Chapter 5

The body of the essay

The focus of Chapter 5 is developing body paragraphs that present clear and convincing evidence for the thesis sentence. Mastering body paragraphs is the foundation of effective academic writing across all genres. Previous chapters introduced the general characteristics of body paragraphs. This chapter examines specific features of body paragraphs and provides guided practice in effective strategies for constructing them.

In this chapter students will:

- examine the structure of body paragraphs,
- develop a working thesis statement,
- explore the relationship between thesis statements and the organizational patterns of the essay,
- study paragraph unity,
- write topic sentences for each paragraph,
- evaluate the evidence to support topic sentences,
- write concluding sentences for each paragraph,
- examine discourse connectors that indicate the relationship between evidence within and between paragraphs.

A. The architecture of body paragraphs

Chapter 2 introduced thesis statements that reflected various ways of developing evidence: enumeration, compare/contrast, cause/effect, narration, argument, and analysis. Enumeration organizes a series of body paragraphs, each focused on a single main idea, into a linear series as depicted below. Therefore, the enumeration essay serves as an uncomplicated platform for learning the components of effective body paragraphs.

Introduction	
Thesis statement	
Main Idea 1	Evidence
Topic Sentence	Evidence
	Evidence
Main Idea 2	Evidence
Topic Sentence	Evidence
	Evidence
Main Idea 3	Evidence
Topic Sentence	Evidence
	Evidence

1. The building blocks of an essay: Body paragraphs

Body paragraphs are the building blocks of all academic genres. The format and organization of essays, reports, research papers, and case studies will vary. Yet, they all depend on a network of strong interconnected body paragraphs to support the thesis statement or research question. The building blocks of effective body paragraphs are:

- a topic sentence that states the main idea and the focus of the paragraph,
- evidence (factual information, expert sources, examples) to support the topic sentence, and
- clear connections between new and previous information.

The sections below will examine each of these characteristics.

a. *Examining topic sentences*

A topic sentence informs the reader of what to expect in the paragraph. It states the subject and also indicates what aspect of the subject will be the focus of the paragraph. Together, the subject + focus create the main idea. All the information in the body paragraph must relate directly to this main idea. Any information without a direct connection to the main idea weakens the paragraph.

The topic sentence below indicates the content of the paragraph by stating both the topic and the focus.

The practice of overprescribing antibiotics has contributed to an increase in ear infections in young children.

The practice of over-prescribing antibiotics	*has contributed to an increase in ear infections in young children*	
↓	↓	
Topic +	focus	= main idea

Effective topic sentences do **all** of the following:	Ineffective topic sentences may have one of the following:
– clearly state the subject of the paragraph – signal a focus of the topic – support the thesis statement directly	– a vague subject or topic – unclear or missing focus for the topic – unclear support for the thesis statement

The characteristics of topic sentences

The following principles apply to developing strong topic sentences.

1. A topic sentence states the subject and signals the focus it will develop.
    Which of these sentences is more effective?
    (a) Music affects hearing in many ways.
    (b) Loud music often leads to permanent hearing loss by damaging multiple parts of the ear.

    Sentence a is ineffective. The subject is vague and there is no clear focus. It does not tell the reader the type of evidence the paragraph will examine.
    Sentence b is more effective. It has a defined subject and a clear focus. It tells the reader to expect evidence related to the parts of the ear that are damaged by loud music.

2. A topic sentence shows a clear relationship between the subject and the focus.
    Here are two sentences about studying literature at university.
    (a) Studying literature courses at university is important.
    (b) Studying literature at university develops insights into human nature that support interpersonal skills in the professions.

    Sentence a is ineffective. It states the subject, literature courses, and focuses on their importance. However, the sentence does not show how the subject and focus relate.
    Sentence b is more effective. It indicates the nature of the relationship between literature and education. The reader will look for information that explains how literature creates an understanding of human nature.

3. A topic sentence should avoid statements such as "I think" or "in my opinion". The reader will assume that the writer is stating their opinion.
    Read the following sentences:
    (a) I believe more research is needed on the emotional impact of unemployment on families.
    (b) Studies have not addressed the emotional impact of unemployment on their families.

Sentence a is less effective. Writing always presents the author's perspective on a topic. It is not necessary to state it.

Sentence b is more effective. It focuses on the gap in the research rather than the writer's opinion. It tells the reader to expect evidence to show the need for research in this area.

4. Avoid questions as topic sentences.

Which of these sentences is more effective?

(a) How can we reduce sugar consumption?
(b) A number of countries have been successful in reducing sugar consumption with a sugar tax.

Sentence a is less effective. The purpose of the topic sentence is to inform the reader what to expect in the paragraph, not to raise a question

Sentence b is more effective. It signals that it will provide examples of countries that have used a sugar tax to reduce sugar consumption.

b. *Developing evidence to support a topic sentence*

Chapter 3 examined several types of acceptable evidence for student writing: facts, examples, common knowledge and expert sources. Body paragraphs may support the thesis by:

- developing one piece of evidence through examples and explanation, or
- including multiple types of evidence.

Regardless of the number or types of evidence, every sentence in the paragraph must relate directly to the main idea (subject + focus) in the topic sentence. Information not directly related to the controlling idea weakens the evidence and does not belong in a body paragraph.

Practice: Reading to write – Examining evidence (body paragraphs)

Read the body paragraph below on the the topic of antibiotic resistant bacteria. It uses multiple types of evidence from common knowledge to one expert source to support the topic sentence. The topic sentence is highlighted.

One of the most urgent threats to public health is the growth in antibiotic-resistant bacteria. The practice of overprescribing certain antibiotics has contributed to a growing global health crisis. There has been a world-wide increase in levels of bacteria that have gradually become resistant to drugs that killed them in the past. In fact, according to the World Health Organization, doctors in most countries report that life-threatening diseases such as pneumonia, meningitis and tuberculosis are resistant to commonly prescribed antibiotics. People die each year from infections caused by antibiotic-resistant bacteria. Most people know of someone whose infection resisted treatment by common antibiotics. Despite ample warnings of the public health dangers of antibiotic-resistant bacteria, the CDC estimates that approximately 30% of antibiotic prescriptions are unnecessary.

Notice the following:

1. The topic sentence is highlighted. It presents the main idea (subject +focus)
   - the topic "the practice of overprescribing certain antibiotics";
   - the focus "contributed to a growing global health crisis".
2. The paragraph uses three types of evidence to support the topic sentence. Find an example of each type of evidence in the paragraph.
   - A. Expert source
   - B. Common knowledge
   - C. Factual information

Practice: Examining the enumeration essay

Following is an example of a short enumeration essay on the subject of sleep deprivation. Each body paragraph adds another type of evidence to that presented in previous paragraphs. The body paragraphs use the types of evidence (see Chapter 3): expert sources, facts, examples, and common knowledge.

The first paragraphs are examples.

The thesis sentence is underlined in the introductory paragraph.

   a. Read through the essay.
   b. Answer the questions in the left hand column.
   c. Mark the type of evidence in the paragraphs.

   A. Facts
   B. Expert source
   C. Examples
   D. Common knowledge

Introduction	Underline or highlight the thesis statement for the essay.	More than two centuries ago Benjamin Franklin recognized the importance of sleep to a happy and healthy life. When Franklin said "Early to bed and early to rise makes a man healthy, wealthy, and wise," he anticipated the findings of modern science. Science has helped us understand the process of sleep and the effects of sleep, or sleep deprivation, on human wellbeing and safety. <u>In fact, sleep deprivation is a significant factor in transportation-related tragedies.</u>
Body Paragraph 1	1. Highlight the topic sentence. - What is the topic? Answer: Expert views on sleep processes.	A comprehensive overview of published research on the sleep process highlights the deadly consequence of sleep deprivation for drivers. **A** Findings from a 2006 study conducted by the Institute of Medicine of the National Academy of Sciences revealed

	– What is the focus? Answer: Consequences of sleep deprivation. 1. Put a letter next to each source of evidence in the paragraph. 2. Indicate the type of source. A. Factual knowledge B. Expert source	that driver sleepiness was a factor in about 20% of all serious car accidents and 57% of fatal accidents. **B** Research (Epstein, 2011) has demonstrated that the effects of sleep deprivation on hand-eye coordination and reaction time is similar to being intoxicated. It could be argued that public safety is linked to adequate sleep for drivers and pilots.
Body Paragraph 2	1. Highlight the topic sentence – What is the topic? – What is the focus? 1. Put a letter next to each source of evidence in the paragraph. 2. Indicate the type of source.	According to Dement and Vaughn (2011) sleep deprivation was also a major contributing factor in some of the great disasters in modern history. For example, sleep deprivation was cited as the cause of the Exxon Valdez disaster of 1989 when an oil tanker ran aground and spilled millions of gallons of crude oil into Prince William Sound in Alaska. The person piloting the ship had slept fewer than six hours in the previous 48. Findings from a year-long investigation of the 1986 space shuttle Challenger disaster found sleep deprivation contributed to errors in judgment. The managers made the decision to launch the shuttle despite the lack of evidence that it was safe in cold temperatures. In both cases, adequate sleep may have prevented the disasters.
Body Paragraph 3	1. Highlight the topic sentence. – What is the topic? – What is the focus? 1. Put a letter next to each source of evidence in the paragraph. 2. Indicate the type of source.	Finally, a neighbor's tragedy illustrates how sleep deprivation brings heartbreak and tragedy into the lives of many people. Her 20-year old son fell asleep at the wheel of his car on the way home from class on a rainy night. The young man died of his injuries the next day in the hospital. His mother explained that he had not gone to sleep the night before in order to complete an assignment for his course. The tragedy is a warning for everyone who skips sleep in order to meet a deadline.

Conclusion	1. The restated thesis statement is highlighted.	The safety of our transportation systems depends upon adequate sleep for those who operate equipment. It is obvious that sleep debt has a negative impact on the skills required to navigate a vehicle safely. The Exxon Valdez and Challenger disasters illustrate that even the functioning of highly trained professionals is impaired by a lack of sleep. Public safety depends on a good night's sleep.

Reflection
Use what you have learned about the architecture of academic text while reading. How will it help you with reading and writing academic text?

c. *Discourse connectors for enumeration*

The term cohesion refers to clarity in the relationships among ideas in a text and among the sentences in a paragraph. Creating cohesion is a challenge in academic writing assignments where multiple sources of information are used to build a strong case for the thesis statement. However, cohesion is necessary to help the reader see how multiple sources work in unison to validate the thesis statement.

One of the ways that academic writing creates cohesion is through the use of discourse connectors. Discourse connectors are the words and phrases that signal to the reader the explicit relationships among ideas and focus the reader's attention on key information. When a discourse connector is placed in a sentence, it creates an explicit link with information in preceding and following sentences. Discourse connectors should be used only when they are important to the meaning of the text. Second language writers of English have a tendency to overuse certain discourse connectors such as "moreover" and "furthermore". Below are some alternatives.

Discourse connectors for enumeration most often signal when the author is adding new information, emphasizing the importance of information, or providing an example to illustrate or clarify. The table below contains some of the most frequently used connectors in an enumerative essay. They can be used at the beginning or end of a sentence as well as within sentences.

Discourse connectors for enumeration

Addition connectors signal new information or evidence	Emphasis connectors signal or highlight relevance	Exemplification connectors signal examples to illustrate or clarify
in addition to	actually	for example
additionally	to illustrate	for instance
another	obviously	namely
also	convincingly	specifically
besides	most convincing	characteristically
furthermore	clearly	in this way
moreover	indeed	typically
that	in fact	
finally	as a rule	
not only…but also		

Practice: Reading to write – Examining discourse connectors

Read through the body paragraphs for the essay on Sleep Deprivation again. In this second reading, highlight or underline all of the discourse connectors you find. In the column on the right indicate whether the connector signals addition, emphasis, or exemplification. The first paragraph has been completed.

A comprehensive overview of published research on the sleep process highlights the deadly consequence of sleep deprivation on drivers. For instance, findings from a 2006 study conducted by the Institute of Medicine of the National Academy of Sciences revealed that driver sleepiness was a factor in about 20% of all serious car accidents and 57% of fatal accidents. Also, research (Epstein, 2011) has demonstrated that the effects of sleep deprivation on hand-eye coordination and reaction time is similar to being intoxicated. Additionally, it could be argued that public safety is linked to adequate sleep for drivers and pilots.	exemplification addition addition

According to Dement and Vaughn (2011) sleep deprivation was also a major contributing factor in some of the great disasters in modern history. For example, sleep deprivation was cited as the cause of the Exxon Valdez disaster of 1989 when an oil tanker ran aground and spilled millions of gallons of crude oil into Prince William Sound in Alaska. The third mate who was piloting the ship had slept fewer than six hours in the previous 48. Moreover, findings from a year-long investigation of the 1986 space shuttle Challenger disaster found sleep deprivation contributed to errors in judgment. The managers made the decision to launch the shuttle despite the lack of evidence that it was safe in cold temperatures. In both cases, adequate sleep may have prevented the disasters.

> Finally, a neighbor's tragedy illustrates how sleep deprivation brings heartbreak and tragedy into the lives of many people. Her 20-year old son fell asleep at the wheel of his car on the way home from class on a rainy night. The young man died of his injuries the next day in the hospital. His mother explained that he had not gone to sleep the night before in order to complete an assignment for his course. The tragedy is a warning for everyone who skips sleep in order to meet a deadline.
>
> The safety of our transportation systems depends upon adequate sleep for those who operate equipment. Research shows convincingly that sleep debt has a negative impact on the skills required to navigate a vehicle safely. The Exxon Valdez and Challenge disasters illustrate that even the functioning of highly trained professionals is impaired by a lack of sleep. Public safety depends on a good night's sleep.

B. AWARE: Writing the body of an enumeration essay

The following section is a step by step guide to writing body paragraphs for an enumeration essay on the following topic:

1. "Downloading music from the internet: The consumer perspective", or
2. "Downloading music from the internet: The music industry perspective".

When finished with all of the steps you will have the first draft of the body of your essay. You will complete the essay in Chapter 7 with the addition of the introduction and the conclusion for the essay.

This essay does not require the use of expert sources. The purpose of this exercise is to develop confidence in your ability to write in your own voice and express your own knowledge on a topic. The evidence that you provide will be from your own knowledge and experience, common knowledge or general facts rather than other peoples' writing or research.

> **Relevance**
> Essay examinations ask students to present evidence to support a thesis statement from established facts, expert sources, and personal observations and experiences. It is important for students to develop confidence in their ability to express what they know.

1. **AWARE: Arranging to write**

   a. *Generating ideas*

   This section applies the brainstorming strategies discussed in Chapter 3 to the topic of "Downloading music from the internet"

   Practice: Generating ideas

   A. Listing. List all the ideas that come to mind related to downloading music from the internet. Think broadly. The music industry includes artists, production companies, shipping, packaging, and advertising among others. Consumer issues include access, costs, availability, censorship, parental controls, tax revenues for governments, etc.
      - Analyze your list. Indicate which ideas relate to the industry and which to the consumer. Do you have more ideas related to the consumer perspective or the music industry perspective?
      - Choose one perspective for the free writing activity.
   B. Clustering or mind mapping. Put either consumer or music industry in the center circle.
      - Add clusters for three to four subjects that emerged from Listing
      - Add sub clusters to subjects with potential evidence.

   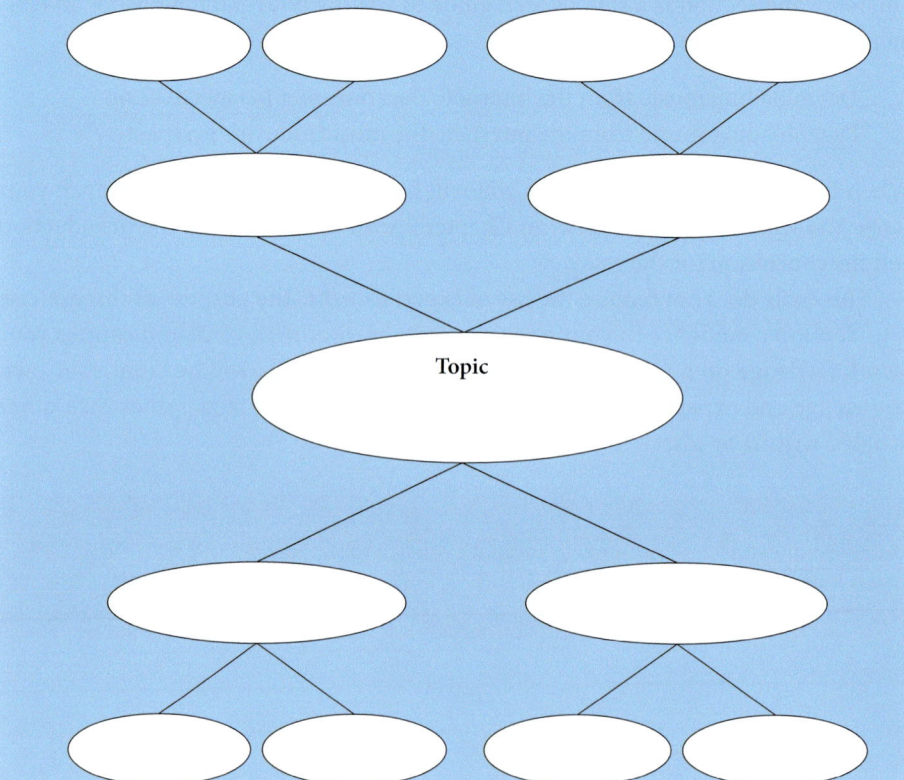

b. *Strategy: Developing a working thesis statement*

A working thesis is a preliminary statement that guides the initial process of research and writing. Because research and writing are processes of discovery, research often changes the writer's understanding of the topic. In this case, the writer needs to modify the working thesis statement to reflect the new information.

The working thesis contains the key elements of a thesis statement that were examined in Chapter 2: topic + point of view. The steps to developing a working thesis statement are:

1. Analyze the ideas generated during brainstorming.
2. Narrow the topic.
3. Identify a point of view.

For example, the topic of "downloading music" has been narrowed to two perspectives, the consumer or the music industry. Either perspective may be examined through the lens of a specific viewpoint such as the impact on the finance, creativity, parental controls, and copyright laws, etc.

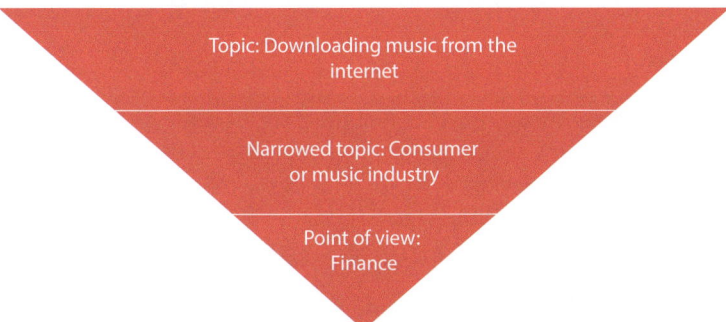

General topic	Downloading music from the internet	Downloading music from the internet
Narrowed topic	The consumer perspective	The music industry perspective
Point of view	Positive economic impact for consumers	Negative economic impact for artist
Working thesis statement	Paid digital music streaming services offer consumers low-cost alternatives to purchasing albums.	Illegal downloading of music from the internet is a form of piracy that steals royalties from artists.

Practice: Developing a working thesis

From the ideas you generated in the listing, clustering, and free writing exercises, develop a working thesis statement on the topic of downloading music. This working thesis statement will guide the first draft of your essay. Use the example presented in the previous section to guide you.

General Topic

Narrowed topic

Point of view

c. Strategy: Outlining

Outlining is a well-known prewriting activity. The T chart is a simplified outline format used for generating ideas and creating a visual representation of the relationships between supporting ideas and evidence. It consists of two columns, where the writer notes the supporting concepts and the corresponding evidence. It does not create a detailed outline for the essay, but it assists the writer in evaluating the quantity and quality of evidence, developing topic sentences, and organizing the supporting ideas.

Practice: Outlining

The following exercise will guide you in transforming the ideas you generated above into structured body paragraphs. It is based on the listing and clustering above for "Downloading music from the internet: advantages for the consumer" or "Downloading music from the internet: disadvantages for the artist".

When finished you will have an outline for the first draft of the body of your essay.

You will develop an introduction and conclusion later.

Follow the instructions on the left hand side of the chart and fill in the blanks on the right hand side of the chart to create your draft.

Introduction

| Copy the working thesis for downloading music from the internet. | Thesis statement: |

Body Paragraphs

Choose the three main ideas from your prewriting that provide the strongest support for your thesis statement. Write a topic sentence for each main idea.

The topic sentence:

- provides direct support for the thesis statement
- informs the reader of the subject
- signals a focus for the subject

Topic sentence for main idea 1:

- supporting evidence:
- supporting evidence:
- supporting evidence:

Transition:

Write a sentence by each bullet that shows the reader how each fact, example, statistic, quote, etc. is evidence in support of the validity of the topic sentence.	Topic sentence for main idea 2: – supporting evidence: – supporting evidence: – supporting evidence: *Transition:*
Provide transition words to connect the paragraphs and signal their relationship to one another.	Topic sentence for main idea 3: – supporting evidence: – supporting evidence: – supporting evidence: *Transition:*
Conclusion Rephrase your thesis using different language but conserve the original meaning. The restated thesis helps the reader reconnect the content of the body paragraphs with the original thesis.	Restated thesis:

2. AWARE: Writing

Following the outline above, write drafts for each of the three body paragraphs on downloading music.
   Each body paragraph will:

- develop a single main idea,
- state the main idea in a topic sentence,
- present explanation or evidence (factual information, expert sources, examples, personal observations, etc.) for the topic sentence,
- signal relationships between and among ideas using discourse connectors, and
- support the thesis statement clearly and directly.

3. AWARE: Assessing

Once the first draft is complete, the writer needs to assess the evidence.

- Do the topics provide sufficient support for the thesis statement?
- Is there sufficient evidence or explanation in each paragraph to support the body paragraphs?

Assessing strategy: Reverse outline
A useful strategy for assessing whether the topics provide adequate and logical support for the statement is to create a reverse outline. In this strategy, the writer copies the thesis

statement and each topic sentence into a single paragraph. Since the topic sentences state the points that the writer will make to support the thesis statement, together they should create a logical summary of the types of evidence that will be developed. This allows the writer to see how directly the topic sentences relate to the thesis statement.

To use the reverse outline strategy to assess your evidence, create a single paragraph by:

a. copying the thesis statement in full,
b. adding the topic sentences for each paragraph.

Here is this strategy applied to the essay on "Sleep Deprivation" above.

Thesis statement + topic sentences for each paragraph	In fact, sleep deprivation is a significant factor in transportation-related tragedies. A comprehensive overview of published research on the sleep process highlights the deadly results of sleep deprivation on drivers. According to Dement and Vaughn (2011) sleep deprivation was a major contributing factor in some of the great disasters in modern history. Finally, a neighbor's tragedy illustrates how sleep deprivation brings heartbreak and tragedy into the lives of many people.

Practice: Assessing strategy: Reverse outline

1. To create a reverse outline summary, copy the thesis statement + topic sentences for each paragraph from your draft paragraphs on downloading music.
2. Does the reverse outline present a logical summary?
   Does it contain three separate topic sentences that support the thesis statement directly?
3. If any of the topic sentences do not support the thesis statement directly, the paragraph needs revision.

Relevance
Reverse outlining is also a good note-taking strategy. Try to use reverse outlining to identify and remember key ideas when reading textbooks.

4. AWARE: Revising

Paragraph unity is essential to building a strong network of support for the thesis statement. Paragraph unity occurs when all of the information in a paragraph has a direct relationship to the controlling idea in the topic sentence. Every sentence explains, presents supporting detail, or clarifies concepts related to the topic sentence.

Revising strategy: Paragraph unity
In the initial stages of arranging to write, interesting ideas emerge from research and brainstorming. Writers instinctively include most of the noteworthy facts and

information in the early drafts. As the writer develops and refines the final thesis statement, some of the evidence no longer provides direct support for the controlling idea in the topic sentence. Any information that does not relate directly to the controlling idea in the topic sentence is considered irrelevant. Irrelevant information weakens the paragraph and needs to be cut out regardless of how interesting or noteworthy it is.

Practice: Revising paragraph unity

The paragraph below contains irrelevant information that weakens paragraph unity. The irrelevant information relates to the topic of antibiotics in general but does not provide support for the main idea (overprescribing + global health) in the topic sentence. Read and analyze the paragraph. Then respond to the following points.

1. What is the paragraph's main controlling idea?
2. Underline or highlight the topic sentence.
3. Does each sentence in the paragraph directly develop or explain the topic sentence?
4. Cross out any sentences that do not relate directly to the topic sentence.

Example:
Controlling idea: Antibiotic resistant bacteria are a problem.
One of the most urgent threats to public health is the growth in antibiotic resistant bacteria. **The practice of overprescribing certain antibiotics has contributed to a growing global health crisis.** The World Health Organization reports a worldwide increase in levels of bacteria that have gradually become resistant to drugs that killed them in the past. ~~The development of new antibiotic drugs takes many years and is costly.~~ A growing number of physicians observe that bacteria which cause life-threatening diseases such as pneumonia, meningitis and tuberculosis are resistant to commonly prescribe antibiotics. ~~Fortunately, frequent and complete hand washing helps avoid the spread of bacteria that cause infectious diseases. The rising cost of antibiotics makes them unavailable to many who need them.~~ The Centers of Disease Control estimate that in United States alone, 23,000 people die each year from infections caused by antibiotic-resistant bacteria. Despite ample warnings of the public health dangers of antibiotic-resistant bacteria, the Center estimates that approximately 30% of antibiotic prescriptions are unnecessary. ~~It is well known that diseases caused by viruses do not respond to antibiotics.~~

Adapted from: <https://www.cdc.gov/features/antibioticuse/index.html> <https://amr-review.org/> <https://www.who.int/mediacentre/news/releases/2018/antibiotic-resistance-found/en/>

Practice: Revising paragraph unity

Read and analyze the paragraphs. Then respond to the following points.

1. What is the paragraph's main controlling idea?
2. Underline or highlight the topic sentence.
3. Does each sentence in the paragraph directly develop or explain the topic sentence?

Cross out any sentences that do not relate directly to the topic sentence.

- Self-driving cars or trucks that will be operated safely without the direct control of human drivers will soon be a reality. Automakers and researchers such as Uber, Tesla, Nissan, and Google are developing self-driving systems based on sensors and software that will control, navigate, and steer vehicles and safeguard riders. Millions of professional drivers could be displaced by the extensive growth in the use of driverless vehicles. Technologies such as radar, laser beams, and high powered cameras can map the environs with a high degree of accuracy and reliability. Vehicles currently use autonomous systems such as cruise control or automatic braking which are controlled by the car rather than the driver. The data from these technologies are inputs which allow the software to chart a route and command the vehicle's acceleration, braking, and steering. The software will process other input from algorithms, predictive modeling, and object discrimination programs to ensure that self-driving vehicles will follow traffic laws and avoid obstacles. The automobile industry is investing in safe self-driving vehicles as the future of personal and commercial transportation.

- The benefits and cost of driverless cars on society and the economy are still hypothetical. As the technology develops, scientists have begun to consider potential effects of driverless vehicles on the environment. The manufacture of safe and affordable self-driving cars could lead to an increase in the total number of miles driven in a year. The elderly or disabled who are unable to drive themselves could benefit from driverless vehicles which would increase their mobility. Increases in any vehicles using gasoline-powered engines will raise dangerous carbon emissions which would contribute to climate change. On the other hand, the use of electric-powered self-driving cars and trucks are friendly to the environment. They have the potential to reduce the total of transportation-related emissions released into the atmosphere. Automobile manufacturers expect significant increases in sales when the driverless cars become lawful.   Adapted from: <https://www.ucsusa.org/clean-vehicles/how-self-driving-cars-work>

- Magic realism is a literary genre that incorporates magical or supernatural elements into a real world setting and plot. Although magical realism is well represented in English literature, many critics consider it to be a primarily Hispanic genre. In fact, the term "magic realism" is said to have originated with a German art critic who used it to describe a type of painting in 1925. Magical realism and Latin America are firmly linked because the most iconic work in the genre, *One Hundred Years of Solitude*, is the creation of Columbian author Gabriel Garcia Márquez. Márquez was awarded the Nobel Prize for Literature in 1982. The fame of other Latin American authors such as the Chilean Isabel Allende, the Argentinian Jorge Luis Borges, and the Mexican Laura Esquivel add strength to the popular belief that magic realism is primarily a Latin American genre. Yet, the Russian Mikhail Bulgakov used magic realism in his subversive novel penned during the Stalin era.   <https://bookriot.com/2017/04/25/the-10-best-books-to-introduce-you-to-magical-realism/>

- Literary scholars such as Bowers (2004) increasingly recognize the influence of American and British authors on the genre of magical realism. English-speaking writers have contributed some of the world's most celebrated works of fiction to the genre of magical realism. Haruki Murakami's mesmerizing magical realist tale, *The Wind-Up Bird Chronicle*,

> was translated from Japanese to English in 1998. British novelist Salman Rushdie was awarded the Booker Prize for his fantastical novel, *Midnight's Children*, a work of magic realism set in India. Rushdie gained international fame when he received death threats after the publication of *The Satanic Verses*. American author Toni Morrison won the Pulitzer prize for *Beloved*, the tale of a freed slave whose new home is haunted by the ghost of her deceased baby. The success of the Harry Potter novels along with J. K. Rowling's numerous awards for children's literature reflects the appeal of magical realism to readers of all ages. J. K. Rowling is one of the richest authors in the world today. The phenomenal success of these authors suggests that magical realist literature is as much a part of the English literary tradition as the Hispanic tradition.   Adapted from: Bowers, M. (2004). *Magic(al) realism: The new critical idiom*. Routledge.

5. AWARE: Editing

This stage focuses on proofreading for surface errors such as grammar, spelling, mechanics, and style. Novice writers often give minimal attention to this final stage. However, editing is especially important when writing in a second language. Too many surface errors distract the reader's attention from the content and make it hard to follow the development of ideas in the paper.

Strategy: Punctuation for discourse connectors

The discourse connectors below improve the cohesion of text. They make ideas more explicit by signaling how ideas relate. These words and phrases are bridges between ideas, sentences, and paragraphs. Below are examples of conjunctive adverbs that serve as discourse connectors.

accordingly	however	nonetheless
also	indeed	otherwise
besides	instead	similarly
consequently	likewise	still
conversely	meanwhile	subsequently
finally	moreover	then
furthermore	nevertheless	therefore
hence	next	thus

Discourse connectors are usually separated from the rest of the sentence with commas. They are frequently placed at the beginning of a clause. They perform two functions at the beginning of a clause:

(a) They can join two independent clauses and create a compound sentence.

The correct punctuation is:
- place a semicolon at the end of the first clause,
- place the conjunctive adverb at the beginning of the second clause,
- use lower case for the first letter,
- place a comma after the conjunctive adverb.

Example:

The Centers for Disease Control estimates that in the United States alone, 23,000 people die each year from infections caused by antibiotic-resistant bacteria; similarly, the World Health Organization estimates that resistant infections causes 700,000 deaths worldwide.

(b) They can introduce a *single* independent clause. The correct punctuation is:
- place the conjunctive adverb at the beginning of the second clause,
- capitalize the conjunctive adverb,
- place a comma after the conjunctive adverb to separate it from the rest of the sentence.

Example:

The Centers for Disease Control estimates that in the United States alone, 23,000 people die each year from infections caused by antibiotic-resistant bacteria. Similarly, the World Health Organization estimates that resistant infections cause 700,000 deaths worldwide.

Practice: Use a discourse connector from the list above to signal a relationship between the two ideas

> Use a discourse connector to (a) join the two clauses and (b) introduce the second clause. Punctuate each correctly.
>
> **Example:**
> Football, also called soccer, is one of the most popular team sports in the world. Almost everyone is familiar with the game.
>
> > *Football, also called soccer, is one of the most popular team sports in the world; consequently, almost everyone is familiar with the game.*
> >
> > *Football, also called soccer, is one of the most popular team sports in the world. Consequently, almost everyone is familiar are familiar with the game.*
>
> 1. Football requires little equipment at the basic level. It is available to young people from most social classes.
> 2. Children from all walks of life play soccer. It is a bond that extends across cultures.

3. Soccer is the highest paying professional team sport. Many children dream of becoming a professional player.
4. The best professional football players are world famous. They are as well-known as film stars.
5. Professional football is viewed by millions. Companies that advertise during games reach a huge audience.

C. Expanding language

Examining discourse connectors for enumeration

The discourse connectors *also*, *in addition*, *furthermore*, and *besides* indicate the presentation of additional information in text. Many writers use these connectors interchangeably. In fact, each conveys a slightly different relationship between new and prior information. Learning to use them properly clarifies the relationship among ideas and sharpens the writer's voice.

Also and *in addition* indicate the presentation of information that <u>parallels previous information.</u> It signals simply that the writer is adding more information. It does <u>not lead</u> the reader to expect the new information to contribute support for a specific idea or argument.

Furthermore indicates the addition of <u>evidence of the same type that was presented previously</u>. It signals that the writer is <u>multiplying evidence to provide support for the topic sentence</u>. It alerts the reader to expect evidence of the same type that deepens understanding of the previous information.

Besides indicates the addition of evidence that <u>reinforces previously presented evidence.</u> It signals that the writer will <u>increase the impact of satisfactory evidence</u> with even more compelling evidence to support the topic sentence. It alerts the reader to expect evidence that goes beyond the norm.

Example 1. Adding parallel information that does not support a point of view.

Read the short paragraph below.

> Ocean garbage patches are expansive accumulations of drifting trash. The patches are made up of tons of floating plastic and other debris. **In addition**, they contain toxic chemical sludge. Most people have heard of the Pacific trash vortex, which is estimated to cover an area the size of France. The less well known Atlantic patch is **also** expanding rapidly.

Note that all of the sentences relate to a single topic, ocean garbage patches. The writer presents interesting facts that increase our knowledge but does not make a point about the garbage. In this paragraph, the connectors "in addition" and "also" simply signal a new piece of parallel information.

Example 2. Presenting multiple examples or sources of evidence to support a point.

> The Great Pacific Garbage Patch endangers the health of our planet. Vast accumulations of floating plastic, debris, and chemical sludge contaminate the water's surface. **Furthermore**, the water below the surface contains concentrations of tiny fragments of debris and chemicals that create a toxic environment. Floating plastic harms or kills marine mammals such as whales, dolphins, and sea turtles by trapping them. **Besides** concerns about the health of the marine environment, human health is at risk as people consume seafood with measurable levels of toxic plastics in their flesh. The contamination of the oceans endangers every aspect of life on earth.

In this paragraph, the author includes a topic sentence with a clear point of view on the subject: ocean garbage patches are dangerous to life. The information provides evidence to support the topic sentence and the discourse connectors signal the nature of the evidence.

<u>Furthermore</u>, indicates more evidence of the same type as the previous sentence. Both sentences present information about the impact of the contamination on water.

<u>Besides</u> indicates evidence to reinforce previous information. It signals that it is even <u>more compelling</u> since it harms human life as well as ocean life.

Practice: Choosing discourse connectors for enumeration

> Below are sets of three sentences that present information on the same topic. Some sets do not present a point of view on the subject and have no topic sentence. Other sets present a point of view and contain a topic sentence.
>
> Read each set and respond to the following:
>
> What is the general topic?
>
> Is there a topic sentence that makes a point about the subject?
>
> Join the first and second or second and third sentences with one of the following transitions: in addition, also, furthermore, or besides. Choose a connector that indicates parallel information or evidence.
>
> Explain why the transition is appropriate for these sentences.
>
> | | |
> |---|---|
> | William Shakespeare wrote 39 full length plays. | Topic: *William Shakespeare* |
> | | Topic sentence? *NO* |
> | Shakespeare wrote 154 sonnets. | Joined: *William Shakespeare wrote 39 full length plays. In addition, Shakespeare wrote 154 sonnets.* |
> | His plays have been translated into all living languages. | Explain: The sentences provide parallel information but do work together as evidence to support a topic sentence. |

Smoking is a destructive habit.	Topic: *Smoking*
Smokers are at increased risk for heart disease.	Topic sentence? *Yes*
The rates for lung cancer are higher among smokers.	Joined: *Smokers are at increased risk for heart disease. Furthermore, the rates for lung cancer are higher among smokers*
	Explain: Furthermore signals that the additional evidence is of the same type as the previous evidence. Both refer to diseases.
Confucius is widely considered one of the most influential individuals in human history.	Topic: Topic sentence?
His influence on Chinese thought began in the fifth century BCE and continues today.	Join:
The Chinese thinker has had an extraordinary impact on modern philosophy.	Explain:
Applications like Facebook and Twitter allow people to stay connected with friends and family around the world.	Topic: Topic sentence?
They provide instant access to information, photos, and personal news.	Join:
The use of social media continues to expand.	Explain:
Water is directly linked to poverty.	Topic: Topic sentence?
Lack of access to potable water causes illness that prevents victims from attending work and school.	Join:
Walking tens of kilometers daily in search of water limits the time available to earn income.	Explain:

Chapter 6

Compare/contrast and cause/effect

Chapter 6 will expand your understanding of organizational patterns used in academic writing. Chapter 5 focused on applying the AWARE cycle to the art and architecture of the enumeration essay. Chapter 6 applies AWARE to compare/contrast and cause/effect essays. It will examine the characteristics of both types of essays and will lead you through the process of developing a thesis statement and body paragraphs for each.

Although all expository essays follow the introduction, body, and conclusion format, the organization of the body paragraphs will vary according to the type of evidence needed to support the thesis statement. Evidence can be defined as a collection of facts and information that has been *organized for a specific purpose*; therefore, the body paragraphs organize evidence according to patterns associated with the point of view in the thesis statement.

In this chapter students will:

- explore the purpose of compare/contrast and cause/effect modes of exposition,
- examine the architecture of compare/contrast and cause/effect essays,
- analyze and write effective thesis statements for compare/contrast and cause/effect essays,
- learn and apply AWARE strategies for planning, writing, assessing, revising, and editing,
- develop body paragraphs with topic sentences and evidence to support compare/contrast and cause/effect thesis statements,
- review and practice causal language and discourse connectors for compare/contrast and cause/effect essays.

A. Compare and contrast

1. Examining compare/contrast

A compare/contrast essay deepens our understanding of at least two subjects by analyzing points of similarity or difference. To establish grounds for the comparison or contrast, both subjects must share points in common. The compare and contrast essay must include:

1. Two or more subjects. They might be people, theories, works of literature, historical events, or policies.
2. The points of comparison or contrast. These are attributes or characteristics that serve as points of comparison for the subjects such as styles, opinions, policies, research findings, or statements.

For example, an essay might look at differences in student outcomes in bilingual and monolingual education. (1) The *subjects* are the students. Subject A is the population of bilingual students and Subject B is the population of monolingual students. (2) The *point of contrast* might include differences in student outcomes such as graduation rates, university completion, social skills, and intercultural awareness.

2. Compare/contrast thesis statements

Expository thesis statements include a topic and a point of view. In addition to indicating the topic, a compare/contrast thesis statement must direct the reader's attention to the explicit relationship between the subjects and the points of comparison or contrast. In a compare/contrast thesis statement, the point of view is the similarities (comparison) or the differences (contrast).

Who or what are the subjects?
What is the point of comparison or contrast?

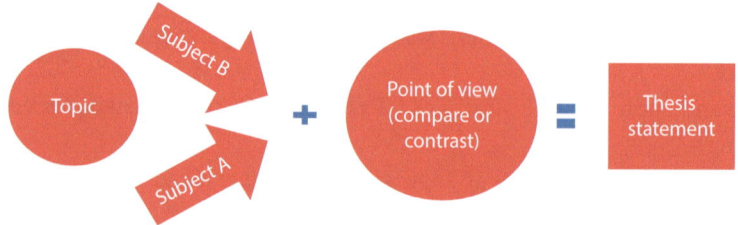

Notice that each thesis statement below explicitly states the topic, the subjects, and the point of contrast or comparison (point of view).

Thesis statement A – Contrast

Although conservationists call for immediate action to regulate overfishing in the oceans, the fishing industry claims it is not necessary.

The thesis statement establishes:
- the topic: overfishing
- the subjects: conservationists and fishing industry
- the point of contrast: need for regulation

Thesis statement B – Comparison

Writing during the Renaissance, William Shakespeare and the novelist Miguel Cervantes revealed deep psychological insights into human nature in their characters.

The thesis statement establishes:
- the topic: Renaissance writers
- subjects: Shakespeare and Cervantes
- point of comparison: insights into human nature

> *Reflection*
>
> *The thesis statement previews the content of an essay or paper for the reader, telling the reader what to expect with regard to the type of content and the mode of exposition.*
>
> *Consider the two thesis statements:*
>
> > *Although conservationists call for immediate action to regulate overfishing in the oceans, the fishing industry claims it is not necessary.*
> >
> > *Writing during the Renaissance, William Shakespeare and the novelist Miguel Cervantes revealed deep psychological insights into human nature in their characters.*
>
> *Do you have a clear idea what the essays will examine? What content might the writer present in the essay?*

3. The architecture of a compare/contrast essay

a. *Body paragraphs*

The organization of body paragraphs in compare/contrast essays must make the relationship between the subjects and the points of comparison or contrast clear for the reader. While the body paragraphs in enumeration are always organized in a linear progression, there are two frequently used organizational patterns for compare/contrast: *subject-by-subject organization or point-by-point organization*. The sample outlines below apply both the point-by-point and the subject-by-subject organizational patterns to an essay that contrasts the standard of living for citizens in Madrid and New York. The essays present evidence related to climate, cost of living, access to the arts, and public transportation for both cities. Notice the difference in the way the evidence is organized.

Point-by-point: Comparison or contrast

In this approach, evidence is organized around the points of contrast. Each paragraph contrasts Subjects A and B with respect to a <u>single point</u>. The topic sentences state the point of contrast and each paragraph develops evidence for Subject A and Subject B.

Point-by-point contrast

Introduction		
Thesis statement: Although New York City and Madrid are two of the grand capital cities of the world, middle class citizens enjoy a higher standard of living in the Spanish city.		

Body Paragraphs		
Point of contrast	Subject A: Madrid	Subject B: New York
Paragraph 1: climate Topic Sentence: While both cities are on the same latitude, the climate of Madrid is milder than New York.	Evidence: – temperatures – precipitation – days of sunlight	Evidence: – temperatures – precipitation – days of sunlight
Paragraph 2: cost of living Topic Sentence: The overall cost of living is lower in Madrid than New York.	Evidence: – price of food – housing – taxes	Evidence: – price of food – housing – taxes
Paragraph 3: access to the arts Topic Sentence: Although opportunities to enjoy the fine and performing arts seem limitless in both cities, the arts are expensive for New Yorkers.	Evidence: – museum fees – visiting artists – theater tickets	Evidence: – museum fees – visiting artists – theater tickets
Paragraph 3: public transportation Topic Sentence: New York and Madrid differ with respect to the accessibility and cost of public transportation.	Evidence: – metro – bus system – train access	Evidence: – subway – bus system – train access

Conclusion (Restatement of the thesis) Clearly, both New York City and Madrid are two of most exciting and vibrant cities in the world; yet, the lifestyle of Madrid is more accommodating to the needs of middle-income residents.

Subject-by-subject: Comparison or contrast
In this approach, the organization pivots around the subjects: each body paragraph presents information about only one subject. All the points of contrast are discussed for Subject A in one paragraph and for Subject B in another. The topic sentences state the subject and point of view that the paragraph will develop.

Longer papers may require several sets of alternating body paragraphs. A potential problem with subject-by-subject organization is that the similarities or differences between the subjects may be vague to the reader because the points of comparison (or contrast) between the subjects do not emerge until the second subject is analyzed. Thus, subject by subject essays may give the impression of two separate descriptions instead of a comparison (or contrast) between the two ideas.

Introduction
Thesis statement: Although New York City and Madrid are two of the grand capital cities of the world, middle class citizens enjoy a higher standard of living in the Spanish city.

Body paragraphs

SUBJECT A: Madrid
Topic sentence: Madrid is one of the most desirable 21st century cities for the middle class.

Point 1: Climate is mild.
– evidence (temperatures, precipitation, days of sunlight)
Point 2. Cost of living is moderate.
– evidence (price of food, housing, taxes)
Point 3: The arts are accessible.
– evidence (museum fees, theater tickets, visiting artists)
Point 4: Public transportation is extensive and inexpensive.
– evidence (metros, bus, train systems and fares)

SUBJECT B: New York
Topic sentence: New York City poses challenges for middle class residents.

Point 1: Climate is extreme.
– evidence (cold winters, hot summers, snow)
Point 2. One of the most expensive cities in the world.
– evidence (real estate, food, taxes)
Point 3: World class art scene but access is expensive.
– evidence (museums, concerts, theater tickets)
Point 4: Public transportation infrastructure is inadequate.
– evidence (subway repairs, bus delays, few trains)

Conclusion (Restatement of the thesis)
Although both New York City and Madrid are considered two of the most exciting and vibrant cities in the world, middle income residents might find the living experiences quite different.

b. *Discourse connectors for compare/contrast*

In the same way that enumeration uses certain words and expressions to signal relationship among ideas, there are discourse connectors that serve as explicit signals of comparison or contrast. The charts below list some frequently used connectors for comparison and contrast. Add any others that you can think of.

Comparison

in the same way	as well as	just as	likewise
similarly	compared with	similar to	in common
not unlike	at the same time as	both	either…or
in addition			

Contrast

although	despite	as opposed to	notwithstanding
but	otherwise	different from	in spite of
even though	however	instead of	still
on the other hand	whereas	yet	while
despite the fact that	in contrast		

The practice exercise below will help you recognize the architecture of the point-by-point comparison essay.

Practice: Reading to write – analyzing comparison

> Read the essay *Nature or Nurture* below. The essay uses a point-by-point organizational pattern to compare similarities between Oskar and Jack, twins who were separated at birth and reunited after more than 45 years.
>
> 1. Underline any discourse connectors or vocabulary that signal comparison.
>
> Science has not provided definitive answers on the nature versus nurture debate with respect to the origins of personality. Nevertheless, the history of identical twins who were raised in different families contributes to understanding genetic and environmental influences. Oskar and Jack were born as the result of a shipboard romance between a German Catholic woman and a Romanian Jewish man en route to the Caribbean. The couple's relationship ended in 1933 shortly after the boys' birth. The mother returned with Oskar to Germany where he was raised as a Catholic and as a Nazi youth. In contrast, the father remained in the Caribbean to raise Jack as a progressive Jew who lived part of his youth on an Israeli kibbutz. Despite having lived their childhoods at opposite ends of the ideological and cultural spectrum, the striking similarities between the two adult men show that genetic heritage plays a significant role in determining personality.
>
> When Oskar and Jack met again in 1979, the physical likenesses and preferences in clothing were apparent immediately. Both men arrived at the airport wearing almost identical wire-rimmed glasses and two-pocket shirts with epaulets. Likewise, the color of the shirts was only a shade apart. The twins also had corresponding short mustaches and receding hairlines. Additional surprising similarities in personality emerged as they got to know each other.
>
> For two people who had never known each other, Oskar and Jack's habits, personalities, and characters were remarkably alike. Both men were absent-minded, read magazines from back to front, and fell asleep in front of the television. Researchers observed that the two men asked similar kinds of questions and exhibited similar mannerisms. Likewise, the emotional temperaments of the twins were comparable as both men experienced explosive anger and suffered from recurrent anxiety.
>
> Similarly, there were uncanny resemblances in the twins' eating preferences and idiosyncratic behaviors. Oskar and Jack enjoyed spicy foods and sweet liqueurs. They both considered sneezing in a crowd amusing. Astonishingly, the men shared two peculiar habits. They

both dipped buttered toast in coffee, and they flushed the toilet before using it. Each twin had the habit of keeping rubber bands on their wrists.

Notwithstanding childhoods that were polar opposites, the inexplicable similarities between Oskar and Jack in adulthood suggest that genetic influences are important factors in personality development. The twins' choice of clothing and their physical appearance were striking in similarity for two people who had not met. Equally remarkable were parallels in the twins' behaviors, idiosyncratic habits, and personalities. Oskar and Jack were a pair of twins who were raised in different worlds but appear to have grown up in the same family.

Adapted from *Psychology: An Introduction*
<http://www.psywww.com/intropsych/ch11_personality/bouchards_twin_research.html>

2. Use the T chart below to guide your analysis of the "point by point" comparison essay. In the right-hand column
   a. answer the questions,
   b. copy the topic sentence,
   c. list the evidence that supports the topic sentence.

	Answers and outline points
Introduction	a. What is the context for the story? b. What were the differences in Oskar and Jack's childhoods? c. What is the thesis statement? d. What point is the author trying to make using the story of Oskar and Jack?
Similarity point 1	Topic sentence/evidence 1. 2. 3 4.
Similarity point 2	Topic sentence/evidence 1. 2. 3. 4.
Similarity point 3	Topic sentence/evidence 1. 2. 3. 4.
Conclusion How does the author restate the thesis?	

> **Reflection**
> *Most students have experience with writing paragraphs or essays that compare or contrast two subjects. Have you written a compare/contrast essay? Has your understanding of compare/contrast changed? How?*

B. AWARE writing: Compare/contrast essay

This section will guide you through writing body paragraphs for a point-by-point comparison/contrast essay on the topic of marriage customs. In the next chapter you will complete your essay with an introduction and a conclusion.

The short article below on marriage during the Roman Empire will serve as a resource. The final essay will contrast Roman marriage customs with modern western marriage customs.

a. **Practice:** *Reading to write – Using a T chart to outline the main ideas*

> 1. Read the article below that discusses marriage during the Roman Empire.
> 2. Create a T chart similar to the one above to take notes on the main idea and evidence for each paragraph.
>
> **Roman Marriage**
>
> Marriage in Roman society was highly structured, and in some ways, similar to contemporary society. According to Roman traditions, brides dressed in white and the wedding was celebrated with a feast and gifts. There were also specific laws that governed marriage and divorce. Despite similarities, many Roman marriage and divorce practices reflect an ancient society that valued men, family, and social class above the notion of romantic love.
>
> Marriage in ancient Rome was often not at all romantic. Rather, it was an agreement between families. Men would usually marry in their mid-twenties, while women married when they were still in their early teens. As they reached these ages, their parents would consult with friends to find suitable partners that could improve the family's wealth or class. Once a suitable match had been made, the process itself was simple. The prospective bride and groom were committed to marry each other at the betrothal, a formal ceremony between the two families. Gifts would be exchanged and the dowry agreed. A written agreement would be signed and the deal sealed with a kiss.
>
> On the wedding day, the groom would lead a procession to his bride's family home, where the bride would be escorted by her bridesmaids to meet her future husband. She would be wearing a tunica recta, a white woven tunic, belted with an elaborate "knot of Hercules." Her hair would be carefully arranged and she would wear an orange wedding veil and orange shoes. After the marriage contract had been signed, there would be an enormous feast. The day ended with a noisy procession to the couple's new home, where the bride was carried over the threshold so she would not trip – an especially bad omen.

> Roman laws governing marriage placed restrictions on who was eligible to marry. A proper Roman marriage could not take place unless bride and groom were Roman citizens, or had been granted special permission, called conubium. Until the lex Julia law was passed by Emperor Augustus in 18 BC, freed slaves were only prohibited from marrying citizens. Citizens were not allowed to marry prostitutes or actresses, and provincial officials were not allowed to marry local women. Soldiers were only allowed to marry in certain circumstances and marriages to close relatives were forbidden.
>
> Roman divorce was as simple as marriage. Just as marriage was only a declaration of intent to live together, divorce was just a declaration of a couple's intent not to live together. Marriage had no legal force of its own but was rather a personal agreement between the bride and groom. As a result, the wedding itself was a mere formality to prove that the couple intended to live together, known as affectio maritalis. All that the law required was that they declare their wish to divorce before seven witnesses.
>
> When she divorced, a wife could expect to receive her dowry back in full and would then return to the protection of her father. If she had been independent before her wedding, she would regain her independence upon divorce. Although the law did not recognize adultery by husbands, under the lex Julia a wife found guilty of adultery might sacrifice the return of half her dowry. Unfaithful wives divorced by their husbands could not remarry.
>
> Roman customs and laws reflected a social order that favored men, and valued class, wealth, citizenship, and property over unions based on romantic love. Families arranged marriages between their children to improve social class and gain wealth. Romans celebrated weddings with traditions that included gifts, feasts, processions, and a white tunic for the bride. Although marriage was considered a personal agreement between the bride and groom, Roman laws maintained strict boundaries between social classes by restricting who was eligible to marry. Divorce was relatively easy and laws favored men, overlooking a husband's adultery but penalizing an unfaithful wife. While modern society still follows many Roman laws and traditions, most people today decide to marry for love.
>
> Adapted from: <http://www.pbs.org/empires/romans/empire/life.html>

1. AWARE: Arranging to write

This writing task is designed to develop confidence and skill in writing. It will not assess the accuracy of your facts or information. Do not conduct research. Use your personal experience, observations, and common knowledge as evidence. Writing from personal knowledge helps the writer develop his or her own voice.

a. *A Venn diagram for generating ideas for a contrast essay on marriage*

There are multiple possible points of contrast between Roman and modern western marriage. A contrast could be made between the ceremonies, the legal processes, the decision making, the motivation of the parties, financial arrangements, and many more.

A Venn diagram helps the writer to create a visual representation of the similarities and differences between topics. Using the reading on Roman marriage and your

T chart notes as starting points, generate ideas on similarities and differences between Roman marriage (Subject A) and modern western marriage (Subject B) customs. You can use the Venn diagram below as a brainstorming tool or choose another brainstorming approach.

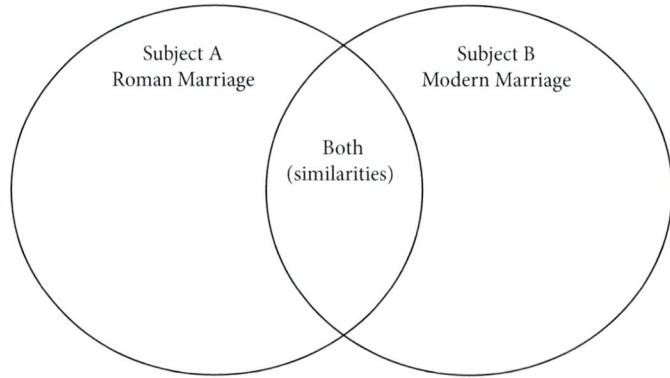

Compare/Contrast: Venn diagram

b. *Practice: Developing a working thesis and a point-by-point outline*

1. Analyze the ideas you generated in your brainstorming on Roman and modern marriage.
2. Write a working thesis sentence for a point-by-point essay that contrasts Roman marriage customs with modern marriage customs.
3. Create an outline for a point-by-point essay with three body paragraphs. List the evidence you will include in the paragraph to support one point of comparison.
4. Create a T chart to use as an outline guide or create your own outlining process.

2. AWARE: Writing

Practice: Using a T chart to draft body paragraphs

Following the T chart outline from "Arranging to write" above, draft your paragraphs. New ideas may emerge during the writing. Make a note of these on your outline but do not develop them at this point. You can develop them during revision.

1. Copy your working thesis.
2. Write a draft for three body paragraphs to support your thesis statement.
3. Include a topic sentence for each paragraph.
4. Present at least one form of evidence for Roman and another for modern western marriage to support each topic sentence.
5. Make a note of any new points of contrast that emerge during the writing. You can revisit these during revision.

Practice: Analyzing a body paragraph for contrast

Read the following sample paragraph.
1. Underline the topic sentence.
2. What is the point of contrast for the paragraph?
3. How many points of evidence are provided for the topic sentence? What are they?

Ancient Roman citizens chose marriage partners based on social contracts that differ radically from modern western unions. In Roman times, marriage was viewed as an agreement between families rather than a union based on love. Roman parents considered the potential for improving social status or wealth when they chose partners for their children. In contrast, modern western marriages are grounded in the notion of romantic love. Each person chooses his or her future spouse based on mutual attraction, emotional compatibility, common interests, and similar lifestyles.

3. AWARE: Assessing

This stage prepares you for the final revisions by assessing the quantity and quality of evidence and the viability of the working thesis. As you review the draft, you will find that some points of contrast are stronger than others. A point of contrast that seemed promising in the outline often does not produce strong direct evidence once it is developed.

a. *Assessing strategy: Evaluating the evidence*

Create a reverse outline for the essay (see Chapter 5) by copying the working thesis and topic sentences. Review your paragraph:

1. Does each topic sentence support the thesis statement directly?
2. Underline any topic sentences that do not directly support the thesis statement. Mark these paragraphs for revision.
3. Is there sufficient evidence to support the topic sentence in each body paragraph? Mark any paragraphs that need additional evidence.

b. *Assessing strategy: Evaluating the thesis statement*

Does the working thesis accurately reflect the supporting points in the reverse outline? If it does, you have a viable thesis statement. If the relationship between the working thesis and topic sentences is not clear and direct, what changes can you make to more accurately reflect the supporting evidence?

For example, the working thesis below is general. In reading through the draft body paragraphs, the writer realized that each paragraph related to social values such as the rationale for marriage, age, and social eligibility. The writer also realized that the modern social values discussed were those of the western countries and modified the thesis to reflect this fact.

> **Working thesis:**
> Roman and modern marriage are different in many ways

> **Analysis of draft:**
> What topics and evidence are presented? What is the relationship of the topics to the working thesis?

> **Final thesis statement:**
> Modern western and ancient Roman marriage customs reflect distinct social values.

c. *From working thesis to thesis statement*

Based on your assessment, rewrite your thesis statement if needed or continue with your original thesis statement. Your thesis statement will guide your revisions.

> Your thesis statement on Roman and modern marriage:

4. AWARE: Revising

a. *Revising strategy: Sharpening the writer's voice with precise vocabulary*

The writer's choice of words affects the clarity of the evidence and the strength of the author's voice. The use of vague and imprecise vocabulary weakens the writer's voice by allowing the reader to interpret a meaning which might be different from the writer's intended meaning.

> **Reflection**
> *What do you think the author is writing about in the sentences below?*
> *Is there enough information for you to say you agree or disagree with the sentences?*
>
> To be safe, everyone should discard old medications.
> Good musicians need to practice regularly.

1. Replace non-specific nouns with specific nouns whenever possible. Non-specific nouns refer to broad categories such as "people," "everyone," "things," "problems," "situations." Non-specific words make the writer's evidence less convincing because readers can misinterpret their meaning. Specific words reflect the author's ideas accurately and clarify the message for the reader.

Non-specific nouns are ambiguous	Specific nouns create clear ideas
To be safe, <u>everyone</u> should discard old medications.	To be safe, <u>parents</u> should discard old medications.
Good <u>musicians</u> need to practice regularly.	Good <u>violinists</u> need to practice regularly.

2. Use precise words for concepts, adjectives, and adverbs. Imprecise language weakens the author's voice by allowing each reader to interpret the meaning differently. For example, what does the concept of "old medications" refer to specifically? Is it a traditional folk remedy, a drug that has expired, or a drug no longer used by family members?

Imprecise concepts, adjectives, and adverbs are open to interpretation.	Precise language creates clear, convincing statements.
<u>To be safe,</u> parents should discard <u>old</u> medications. <u>Good</u> violinists need to practice <u>regularly</u>.	<u>To avoid accidental ingestion by children</u>, parents should discard <u>unused painkillers</u>. <u>Professional</u> violinists need to practice <u>at least five hours daily</u>.

Practice: Precise vocabulary

Rewrite the sentences below.
- Substitute specific nouns for non-specific nouns.
- Use specific concept words, adjectives, and adverbs.

Example: Officials are looking at the problems with the building. *Engineers are calculating the stability of the damaged building.*

1. People promised to help the poor often.
2. Very rich people are healthier.
3. Everyone thinks they can solve the problem.
4. Elderly people suffer for many reasons.
5. The critic said the film was wonderful in every way.
6. I support environmental issues.

b. *Revising checklist*

Read through your paragraphs on Roman marriage. Revise the following as needed.

1. Add additional evidence if needed.
2. Underline non-specific or imprecise words. Substitute precise and specific vocabulary (see also Chapter 4).
3. Review formality of language (see Chapter 1).

4. Check for paragraph unity. Strike out any sentences that do not directly support the topic.
5. Clearly signal comparison or contrast with language and discourse connectors.

5. AWARE: Editing

a. *Commonly confused words in English*

The following words are commonly confused in English. Review the list and refer to it when editing.

Commonly confused words		Meaning
affect	(verb)	to impact or change something
effect	(noun/verb)	a result; to bring about a result
aloud	(adverb)	out loud
allowed	(verb)	permitted
aural	(adjective)	relating to the ears or hearing
oral	(adjective)	relating to the mouth; spoken
complement	(verb/noun)	to add to so as to improve; an addition that improves something
compliment	(verb/noun)	to praise or express approval; an admiring remark
elicit	(verb)	to draw out a reply or reaction
illicit	(adjective)	not allowed by law or rules
ensure	(verb)	to make certain that something will happen
insure	(verb)	to provide compensation if a person dies or property is damaged
foreword	(noun)	an introduction to a book
forward	(adverb)	onwards; ahead
imply	(verb)	to suggest indirectly
infer	(verb)	to draw a conclusion
loose	(verb)	to unfasten; to set free
lose	(verb)	to be deprived of; to be unable to find
passed	(verb)	moved by or went by
past	(noun)	time before
principal	(noun)	most important; the head of a school
principle	(noun)	a fundamental rule or belief
stationary	(adjective)	not moving
stationery	(noun)	writing materials
than	(preposition/conjunction)	introducing the second element in a comparison or contrast
then	(adverb)	at that time; in addition.

b. *Editing checklist*

Using the editing checklist as a guide, read through your paragraphs. Look for errors in grammar, spelling, and punctuation. Sometimes reading the text backwards, sentence by sentence, helps. Pay attention to the points below.

1. Fragments (Chapter 2)
2. Use of commas (Chapter 3)
3. Punctuation for discourse connectors (Chapter 4)
4. Commonly confused word pairs.

C. Expanding language: Comma splices

The comma splice is a common grammatical error in student writing. A comma splice occurs when two sentences are *incorrectly* joined by a comma. Most word processing programs include a grammar checker that highlights comma splices. It is important to understand how to correct them.

Example of a comma splice:

By October 2007, the American stock market reached a pre-recession high of 14,164.43 points, by March 2009, it had fallen to 6,594.44 points.

Examining the statement above shows that it actually consists of the two sentences below. The use of a comma to join them resulted in a comma splice.

By October 2007, the American stock market reached a pre-recession high of 14,164.43 points.
By March 2009, it had fallen to 6,594.44 points.

It is always incorrect to join two sentences with a comma. There are three ways to correct a comma splice:

1. Create two sentences with a period at the end of each.

   By October 2007, the American stock market reached a pre-recession high of 14,164.43 points. By March 2009, it had fallen to 6,594.44 points.

2. Join clauses with a semicolon.

   A semicolon links independent clauses that are closely related in thought and of approximately equal length. The semicolon indicates that the author views both ideas as equal in position or rank.

   By October 2007, the American stock market reached a pre-recession high of 14,164.43 points; by March 2009, it had fallen to 6,594.44 points.

3. Join clauses by creating a subordinate clause. The use of a subordinate clause with a conjunctive adverb (see Chapter 5) indicates that the author considers one idea as more important than the other. In the sentence below, the author is emphasizing the second idea.

   Although the American stock market reached a pre-recession high of 14,164.43 points October 2007, it had fallen to 6,594.44 points by March 2009.

> **Reflection**
> How does the use of semicolons and subordinate clauses reflect the author's voice? Why would you choose to join two sentences with a semicolon or subordinate clause?
> Copy one of the sentences from the exercise below into a word processing program. Use the grammar check. What was the result?

Practice: Comma splices

Rewrite each of the comma splices below using the three correction options above.

Example: The physician completed the scheduled surgery, he began a complicated emergency operation immediately after.

> *The physician completed the scheduled surgery. He began a complicated emergency operation immediately after.*
>
> *The physician completed the scheduled surgery; he began a complicated emergency operation immediately after.*
>
> *After the physician completed the scheduled surgery, he immediately began a complicated emergency operation.*

1. The steam engine produced profound changes in the economic system, it accelerated revolutionary social and cultural changes.
2. Realism is a literary style in which the author attempts to present an accurate imitation of life, in romanticism the author paints an idealized picture of life.
3. An architect designs the aesthetic elements of a building's appearance and functions, an engineer plans for the construction based on math and science calculations.
4. Many doctoral students fail to complete their dissertations, they have worked many years toward their goal.

D. Cause and effect

1. Examining cause and effect

The purpose of a cause and effect essay is to clarify relationships among various phenomena. A cause produces an event or condition; effects are the consequences of an action produced by an event, a person, or phenomenon.

Cause – Who or what produced the action?
Effects – What were the impacts of the action?

Instructors assign cause and effect assignments to assess whether students can analyze complicated relationships among phenomena and explain them clearly.

2. The architecture of cause and effect

Cause and effect relationships are complicated. The writer needs to develop an appropriate thesis statement, use causal language, and follow established organizational patterns to ensure that cause and effect relationships are clear to the reader.

A cause/effect text may focus primarily on causes or primarily on effects. Most cause and effect assignments examine multiple causes or multiple effects. The organization of the essay depends on whether the writer is examining the causes or the effects. The basic organization of cause/effect follows one of two patterns

explain the causes and then show the effects
explain the effects then show the causes

The thesis statement for a cause or effect essay presents the topic + the point of view. It must also signal whether the analysis will focus on causes or effects.

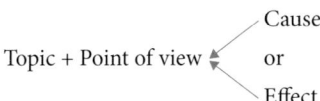

For instance, consider an analysis of the phenomenon of light pollution. Light pollution refers to the artificial illumination of the night sky by electric lights. Some believe that it causes problems for humans, wildlife, and the climate. Scientists, citizens, and politicians must understand both the causes and the effects in order to address the problem. Therefore, an examination of light pollution might focus on the (a) the causes or (b) the effects. Both patterns are examined below.

- What are the causes of light pollution?
- What are the effects of light pollution?

a. *Examining multiple effects: Thesis statements and body paragraphs*

Effects refer to the consequence produced by a person, an event, or a phenomenon.

According to some researchers, the phenomenon of light pollution results in multiple potentially harmful effects on living beings. These include sleep disturbances, interference in animal migration, and disruptions to ecosystems.

The thesis statement below on the effects of light pollution includes the topic (light pollution), and the writer's point of view (harmful to living organisms). It also tells the reader to expect evidence of multiple harmful *effects* on living organisms.

Environmental studies raise concerns over the harmful effects of light pollution on living organisms.

Based on the thesis statement, each body paragraph develops evidence to support one of the main ideas in the outline.

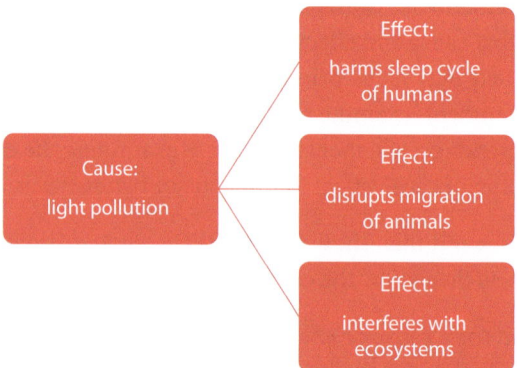

b. *Discourse connectors for effect*

Vocabulary and discourse connectors work together to ensure that each effect is clear and easy for the reader to follow. Synonyms for effects (*result, consequence, outcome*) and action verbs (*confuse, disrupt, interfere, limit*) clarify the nature of the effects. Discourse connectors signal the relationships among ideas, sentences, and paragraphs.

Discourse connectors to signal effects		
accordingly	consequently	since
as a result	for that reason	therefore
and so	hence	thus
because	on account of	

Practice: *Reading to write – Body paragraph for multiple effects*

Read the paragraph below on the effects that light pollution has on bird migration. It develops the main idea for paragraph 2 of the outline above.

1. Underline the topic sentence.
2. Circle the cause and underline the effect in the topic sentence.
3. List the evidence the writer uses to demonstrate the harmful effects of light pollution.

The nighttime glow of lights from large cities confuses migrating birds that use moonlight or starlight to navigate. Many non-native species of birds stop to rest in urban landscapes where suitable food is scarce and so may not consume sufficient calories to fuel their journeys. Consequently, some undernourished birds are not strong enough to complete their migration and die before they reach their destinations. Since ecosystems rely on migratory birds to pollinate plants and control insect populations, a reduced bird population may disrupt the life cycles of plants and animals. Accordingly, municipalities need to consider measures to reduce urban nighttime glow.

Practice 2: *Discourse connectors*

Read the paragraph above again.

1. What discourse connectors indicate effect?
2. What vocabulary is used to show effect?
3. Rewrite the paragraph using different discourse connectors.

c. *Examining multiple causes: Thesis statements and body paragraphs*

Causes refer to the agent, sources, reasons, or events which produce effects. It is possible to analyze multiple causes or a single cause. The example below examines multiple causes for a single phenomenon.

What are the multiple <u>causes</u> of light pollution? According to some researchers, potential causes include light trespass, light glare, and light clutter. The thesis statement below on the causes of light pollution includes the topic (light pollution) and the writer's point of view (disrupts the sleep cycles). It also tells the reader to expect the body paragraphs to present evidence of multiple causes of light pollution.

Thesis statement: The cumulative effects of light pollution disrupt the human sleep cycle

The outline develops three causes for the single effect of sleep disruption.

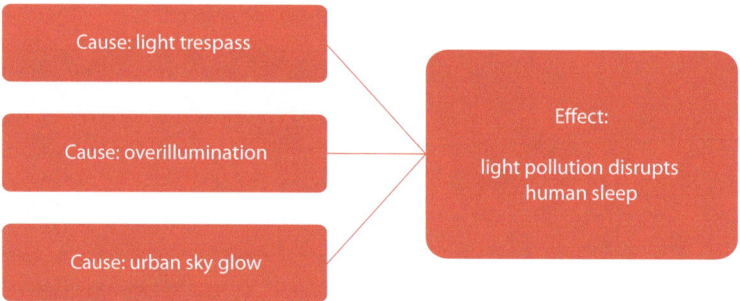

Practice: *Reading to write – body paragraphs for multiple cause*

1. Read the paragraph below. It examines one cause of light pollution (light trespass) which disrupts the human sleep cycle.
2. Underline the topic sentence.
3. Circle the cause and underline the effect in the topic sentence.
4. List the evidence that the writer provides to illustrate the causes.

Light trespass occurs when uncontrolled light reaches places where it is not wanted. Researchers warn that light trespass from multiple sources disturbs the healthy sleep cycle of humans. A common source of light trespass is produced by the illumination of bedroom space from misplaced streetlights. Similarly, the horizontal reflection of light off outside surfaces into windows leads to intrusive nighttime light in bedrooms. Finally, blue light trespass from computers, phones, tablets, and televisions in the bedroom disrupts the body's natural ability to fall asleep.

d. Causal language

Causal relationships in English are frequently signaled with a verb rather than an adverbial connector. The paragraph above uses the verbs *disturb, produce, lead to, disrupt,* and *affect* to signal the type of causal relationship.

Common verbs used to signal cause are listed below. Keep in mind that many verbs can be used to signal cause, depending on the relationship the writer wants to indicate.

cause	produce	lead to	result in
bring about	affect	contribute to	influence

Practice: Causal language

Substitute the verb in the left column for the word <u>cause</u> in the sentence below to indicate the causal relationship.

   Prolonged emotional stress <u>causes</u> physical illness.

What other verbs can you add to the list?

produce	*Prolonged emotional stress produces physical illness.*
affect	
lead to	
result in	
bring about	
inflict	
worsen	
prolong	

Reflection
All of the verbs in the sentence above indicate a causal relationship. How does the meaning of the sentences change with different verbs?

E. AWARE writing: Cause and effect

This section will lead to the production of a working thesis and body paragraphs of an essay that examines multiple causes or multiple effects. The essay is based on your knowledge and experience. It is not a research essay. The focus is on the practical application of AWARE strategies. Choose a topic that you feel you can examine from your personal experiences. Some suggested topics are presented below. You may choose another topic with your instructor's permission.

Examine the causes of:	Examine the effects of:
the popularity of fast food	fast food consumption
a current consumer fad	a current consumer fad
growth in tourism	growth in tourism
poverty	poverty
obesity	obesity
noise, air, ocean pollution	noise, air, ocean pollution
social isolation	computer gaming addiction
	type of technology (automobile, washing machine, cell phone, or another device)

1. Arranging to write: Cause and effect

   a. *Developing a working thesis*

Generate as many ideas as possible on your topic using brainstorming, listing, free writing, clustering, or another approach. Analyze and organize your ideas to narrow the topic into a working thesis. In addition to presenting the topic and point of view, the working thesis statement must signal cause or effect.

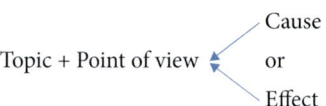

Sample working thesis for multiple effects

1. Topic: *Fast food consumption*
2. Point of view: *contributes to growth in childhood diseases*
3. Cause or effect signal: *contributes*
4. Working thesis: *The increase in fast food consumption has led to a growth in chronic diseases among children.*

Sample working thesis for multiple causes

Topic: *Women's poverty*
Point of view: *worsened by lack of access to clean water*
Cause or effect signal: *worsen*
Working thesis: *The lack of access to clean water in undeveloped communities contributes to women's poverty.*

   b. *Graphic organizers for cause and effect essay*

Using one of the graphic organizers below, or another of your choice, create an outline for your essay. Choose the appropriate organizer for your working thesis.

Graphic outline for single cause with multiple effects

In this case, the graphic outline keeps the writer focused on the topics that show the multiple effects from a single cause. The writer can visualize whether there is evidence for each main idea.

Chapter 6. Compare/contrast and cause/effect   133

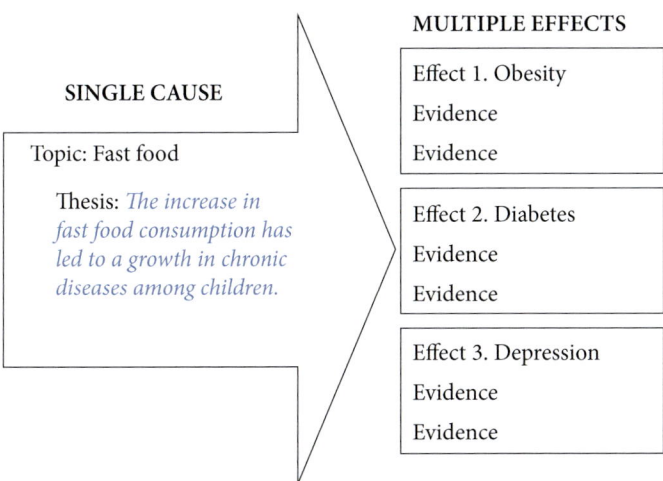

Graphic outline for single effect with multiple causes

In this case, the graphic outline keeps the writer focused on the topics that show the multiple causes of a single effect (women's poverty). The writer can visualize whether it is possible to develop topics with evidence of multiple ways that lack of access to clean water causes poverty among women.

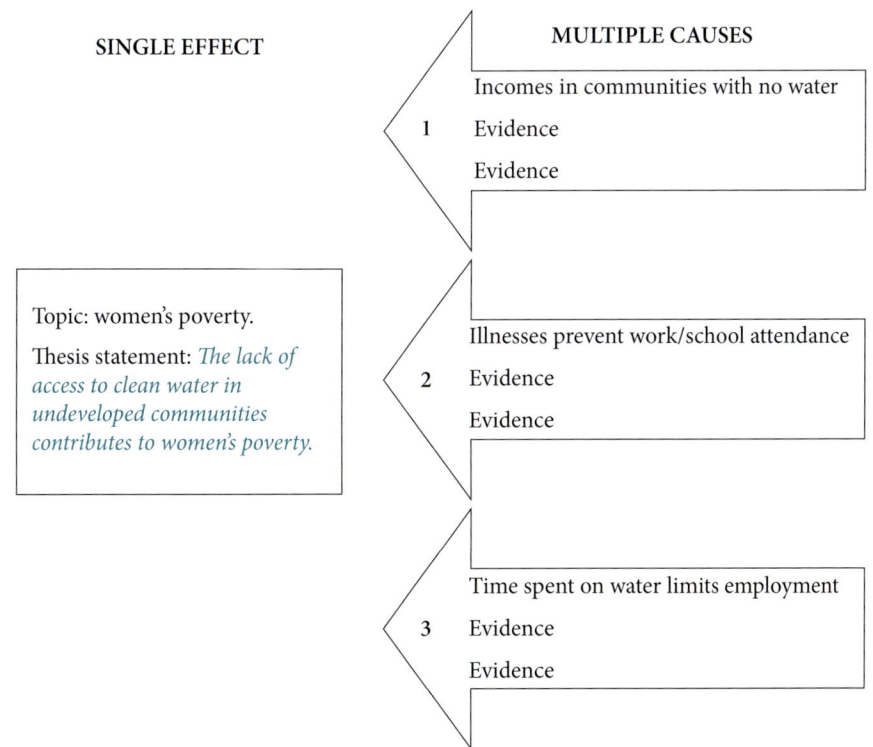

2. **AWARE writing: Cause and effect**

Following the main ideas in your outline, draft three body paragraphs that include:
- a topic sentence,
- at least two sources of evidence (examples, facts, data),
- language or discourse connectors to signal cause and effect.

3. **AWARE: Assessing**

Create a reverse outline for the essay (see Chapter 5) by copying the working thesis and topic sentences.

Answer the following questions about the reverse outline:

1. Does each topic sentence relate directly to the thesis statement? Underline any topic sentences that do not relate directly. These need to be revised.
2. Are there at least two forms of evidence to support the topic sentence in each body paragraph? Mark any paragraphs that need additional evidence.
3. Do you need to revise your thesis statement?
4. Write your final thesis statement:

> Final thesis statement

4. **AWARE: Revising**

Read through the body paragraphs for your cause or effect essay. Pay special attention to the points below and make any changes needed.

Revising checklist

1. Add additional evidence for cause or effect as needed.
2. Underline non-specific or imprecise words. Substitute precise and specific vocabulary (see also Chapter 4).
3. Review formality of language (see Chapter 1).
4. Check for paragraph unity. Strike out any sentences that do not directly support the topic sentences (see Chapter 5).
5. Use appropriate discourse connectors or causal language to signal the relationships among ideas.

5. AWARE: Editing

Affect and *effect* are often confused. *Affect* is usually a verb; it means to impact or change. *Effect* is usually a noun; it means the result of change. Affect is also used as a noun to refer to a display of emotion. It is the root word of "affection."

	Usually	
	Affect as a verb	**Effect as a noun**
Common usage	"Affect" is most commonly used as a verb	"Effect" is most commonly used as a noun
Common meaning	The verb "to affect" means to have an impact or bring about change	The noun "effect" indicates the result of change
Example	The hurricane affected travel.	The effects of the hurricane were devastating.
	Occasionally	
Special usage	Affect can be used as a noun to indicate the display of emotion	Effect can be used as a verb with the meaning "to bring about"
Example	The young woman's face showed no affect at the news of the tragedy.	Mahatma Gandhi effected change by peaceful means.

Editing checklist
Using the editing checklist as a guide, read through your paragraph. Look for errors in grammar, spelling, and punctuation. Try to read the paragraphs backwards, sentence by sentence. Pay attention to the points below.

1. Use of commas (Chapter 3)
2. Punctuation for discourse connectors (Chapter 4)
3. Commonly confused word pairs
4. Correct use of affect or effect for causal relationships
5. Comma splices
6. Fragments.

Chapter 7

Introductions and conclusions

This chapter will examine the role of introductions and conclusions in academic writing. It will provide guided practice in writing effective introductions and conclusions and model concrete strategies for both. You will complete the first full essays in this book by developing an introduction and conclusion for the enumeration, compare/contrast, and cause/effect paragraphs created in previous chapters.

Introductions and conclusions play a powerful role in the communication between readers and writers. They are the writer's first and last opportunity to engage with the reader and they shape the readers' interpretation by previewing and summarizing the writer's ideas.

The success of introductions and conclusions depend on how well they reflect the content of the essay. The AWARE cycle emphasizes the vital role of assessing and revising in creating a strong message and a clear voice. The recursive nature of the AWARE cycle supports the natural evolution of ideas during research and writing; AWARE is designed to give the writer the flexibility to shift focus and adapt the thesis statement. Therefore, writing the introduction and the conclusion *after* the content and organization of a paper is finalized is a sound strategy that many experienced writers use.

In this chapter students will:

- examine the characteristics of effective introductions,
- practice strategies for writing basic introductions,
- write a basic introduction,
- examine characteristics of effective conclusions,
- practice strategies for writing basic conclusions,
- write a basic conclusion,
- develop a full cause/effect essay.

A. Introductions

1. Examining the introduction

Strong introductions engage the reader, provide a context for the thesis statement, and orient the reader to the direction the essay will take. Introductions must always lead the reader to the thesis statement and create a meaningful context for the thesis statement. Although the introduction may be written after most of the paper is drafted, *a working thesis is always developed before the body of the paper.* The working thesis directs thinking and research with the understanding that it may be modified during the process.

The introduction for an essay is usually four to five sentences long; the introduction for a research paper may be several paragraphs long, depending on the topic. The thesis statement is usually placed at the end of the introductory paragraph.

Moves in introductions

Earlier chapters explored the role of shared academic discourse in facilitating scholarly communication. Readers and writers expect academic text to follow norms for language, discourse connectors, and predictable organizational patterns. When these norms are not followed, the writer's message is often lost to the reader. Academic writing relies on another feature of academic discourse, sometimes known as moves, to provide information that helps the reader to contextualize the information and understand the writer's intent.

The term "move" was introduced by the linguist John Swales (1990) to describe the features of language or content that occur regularly in research articles. Moves provide specific information at particular junctures in research articles and other academic texts. Readers expect these moves and rely on them to clarify the writer's intent.

The moves in an introduction show to the reader the purpose and value of examining a topic. For instance, readers <u>expect</u> an introduction to show the relevance of a topic, to create a valid context for examining the topic, and to explain the point of view the writer will examine. If one of these moves is missing, the introduction will be much less effective.

The concept of "moves" in writing is closely tied to the writer's voice. Moves establish the author's position with respect to the information presented. In the case of an introduction, a move states the *writer's choice* of topic, another move clarifies the *writer's understanding* of its relevance, and finally presents the *writer's point of view* in the thesis statement.

Moves do not always occur in the same order and they may vary depending on the purpose of the text, but they are always present in a strong introduction. Effective introductions to student essays include moves that do the following:

a. state the topic and attract the reader's interest,
b. create context for understanding the thesis statement,

c. present a clear thesis statement or research question,
d. orient the reader to the type of evidence to expect.

> **Relevance**
> A clear introduction provides a roadmap that tells the reader what to expect in the essay.

Practice: Reading to write – analyzing moves

Read the introduction to *The Truth about Organic Food* below. Notice how the author prepares the reader by including all of the essential moves in a short introduction.
As you read, look for moves that do the following:

- present the topic and attract the reader's interest
- provide a context for understanding the thesis statement
- present a clear thesis statement or research question/s
- orient the reader to the type of evidence to expect

Answer the following questions:

1. How many sentences are in the introduction?
2. Explain the moves in the right hand column. (Refer to the list above)
3. How does the writer attempt to interest the reader in the first sentence?

The Truth about Organic Food

Many consumers question whether they should care about agricultural techniques if an organically cultivated green pepper looks identical to a conventionally grown pepper. Many people are aware that food grown according to organic principles is free from exposure to harmful herbicides and pesticides, but that is only one small aspect of organic agriculture. A core value of organic farming, preserving the health of the soil, is relevant to everyone because it affects the quality of our food and our ecosystems.

	Move
Many consumers question whether they should care about agricultural techniques if an organically cultivated green pepper looks identical to a conventionally grown pepper.	
Many people are aware that food grown according to organic principles is free from exposure to harmful herbicides and pesticides, but that is only one small aspect of organic agriculture.	
A core value of organic farming, preserving the health of the soil, is relevant to everyone because it affects the quality of our food and our ecosystems.	

2. Strategies for writing the introduction

A four-to-five sentence introduction usually begins with a general statement about the topic and continues with several statements that provide more specific details. An introduction generally ends with the thesis statement. There are a number of strategies that the writer can use to develop strong introductions that include the required moves for an introduction. Three basic strategies are:

- finalize the content of the body paragraphs before writing the introduction,
- determine the background information the reader will need to understand the essay,
- use a general to specific framework to situate the thesis statement within a relevant context.

> **Relevance**
> Good writers employ a number of strategies while writing papers. The difference between effective and less effective writers is how well they use strategies and whether they are appropriate to the task at hand. Adopting strategies requires initial step by step practice. With experience these conscious efforts develop into unconscious strategies that require little thought.

a. *Introduction strategy 1: Finalize the content before writing the introduction*

During the process of writing a formal essay or paper, new evidence may be uncovered, or new relationships among ideas may be identified. The writer may shift the focus of the paper and/or thesis in response to emerging information. Therefore, many writers find it effective to wait until the final stages of the paper before composing the introduction. In this way, the writer has a clearer idea about the information that should be included in the introduction.

During the research and writing process, it is helpful to keep a record of the information that will be needed for the introduction. This can include essential background information, material to contextualize the thesis, and interesting ideas that can engage the reader.

b. *Introduction strategy 2: Background questions for context*

An effective introduction includes key information that allows *any* reader to follow the content of the essay. The background question strategy uses a question framework to determine what background information a reader will need to understand the topic and the thesis. The writer considers "Who", "What", "When", "Where", "Why", and "How" from the point of view of a reader who is not familiar with the topic. Not all of the questions apply to all topics; however, the framework is a sound strategy for analyzing necessary background information for the introduction.

For example, for an essay assignment about the poet Robert Frost, the writer focuses on the poem "Nothing Gold Can Stay". In the introduction, the writer must create a meaningful context for the reader who does not know the poem or the author.

Nothing Gold Can Stay

Nature's first green is gold,
Her hardest hue to hold.
Her early leaf's a flower;
But only so an hour.
Then leaf subsides to leaf.
So Eden sank to grief,
So dawn goes down to day.
Nothing gold can stay.

Frost, R. (1923). New Hampshire, A Poem; with Notes and Grace Notes. Project Gutenberg. Retrieved, November 22, 2020 from https://www.gutenberg.org/ebooks/58611

The essay writer has developed the following thesis statement:

> In his poem "Nothing Gold Can Stay", Frost uses a series of metaphors of nature in spring to lament the inevitable loss of youth and beauty throughout the cycle of life.

What information would a person who is not familiar with the poem need in order to understand the essay?

What	is the topic of the essay?	Poem, "Nothing Gold Can Stay"
Who	does the reader need to know about?	The poet, Robert Frost
When	was the poem written?	Early 20th century
Where	was the poem written?	US, New England
Why	examine this poem?	The beauty of Frost's images and the darker meaning of his poems reflect the opposing forces of nature
How	will I examine the topic?	Show how the various images of nature are metaphors for the inevitable loss of youth and beauty

Once the writer has determined the necessary background information, it needs to be organized into paragraphs. The general-to-specific approach is a sound basic strategy that methodically develops a context for the thesis statement.

c. *Introduction strategy 3: Use a general-to-specific framework to situate the thesis statement*

The general-to-specific approach uses a series of moves that begins by announcing the topic in a broad, general statement. Each succeeding statement creates a context by clarifying or narrowing the focus of the topic. In this way the information moves the reader from a general topic to a specific thesis statement.

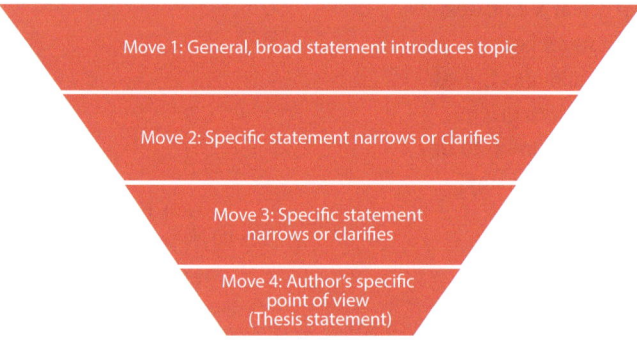

Practice: *Reading to write: General to specific framework*

The following introduction applies the information from the background question strategy above to develop a general-to-specific introduction to the essay on "Nothing Gold Can Stay".

Read the introduction and circle information about "who, what, where, why and how". Notice how the author has included information on all of the questions.

Robert Frost is one of America's most beloved and honored 20th century poets. Frost is best known for poems that use images of nature and rural New England life to explore the human psyche. The deceptive simplicity of his poems and the beauty of the imagery disguise the poet's profound questioning of the basic truths of life. In his poem "Nothing Gold Can Stay", Frost uses a series of metaphors of nature in spring to lament the inevitable loss of youth and beauty throughout the cycle of life.

Notice how the introduction "leads" the reader to the thesis with specific moves. The information becomes increasingly more specific and provides the necessary context for the thesis statement.

Robert Frost is one of America's most beloved and honored 20th century poets.	General statement about the poet and his status.
Frost is best known for poems that use images of nature and rural New England life to explore the human psyche.	Statement explains the topics of Frost's poems.

The deceptive simplicity of his poems and the beauty of the imagery disguise the poet's profound questioning of the basic truths of life.	Statement further narrows the topic to predominant themes in Frost's poetry.
In his poem "Nothing Gold Can Stay", Frost uses a series of metaphors of nature in spring to lament the inevitable loss of youth and beauty throughout the cycle of life.	Thesis presents – the topic (Frost's poem) – <u>writer's point of view</u> (spring theme symbolizes inevitable loss) – <u>specific type of evidence</u> (analysis of metaphors).

Acknowledgement: This exercise is based on an original idea from the Online Writing Lab at Roane State Community College. It has been changed and adapted for this text.

Reflection
1. Review the general-to-specific introduction above. Identify the characteristic moves of an introduction which do the following:
    a. state the topic and attract the reader's interest;
    b. create context for understanding the thesis statement;
    c. present a clear thesis statement or research question;
    d. orient the reader to the type of evidence to expect.
2. How does the writer try to connect the topic to a reader who may not be familiar with US culture or literature?
3. What does the expression "basic truths of life" mean to you?

Practice: Analyzing a general-to-specific framework

The introduction for a compare/contrast essay on Roman and modern western marriage organizes the introduction using a general-to-specific framework. Analyze each statement, and explain how it "leads" the reader to the thesis. Use the framework at the end.

Roman and Modern Western Marriage

Marriage in Roman society was highly structured, and in some ways similar to contemporary society. According to Roman tradition, brides dressed in white and the wedding was celebrated with a feast and gifts. There were also specific laws that governed marriage and divorce. Despite similarities with modern western marriage customs, many Roman marriage and divorce practices reflect an ancient society that valued men, family, and social class above the notion of romantic love.

… (Body of the essay is not included here)

Statement	Move	What does it tell the reader?
Marriage in Roman society was highly structured, and in some ways, similar to contemporary society.	General statement introduces the topic of Roman marriage and modern marriage.	*Reader is introduced to broad topic of Roman marriage but not the specific aspect the author will discuss. The mention of contemporary society generates interest.*

> **Reflection**
> *Examine the introduction. Can you think of additional information or ideas that would make the introduction more interesting to you?*

B. AWARE: Writing the introduction to a compare/contrast essay

The AWARE writing in this chapter will guide you in completing the short essay on *A Contrast between Roman and Modern Western Marriage*. In Chapter 6, you developed a thesis statement and wrote three point-by-point contrast paragraphs. These will be the basis for the AWARE writing practice. Please have these body paragraphs at hand as you begin the next section of the chapter.

1. AWARE: Arranging to write the introduction

a. *Counterpoint in the compare/contrast introduction*

In a compare/contrast essay, the introduction is more complex than a simple enumeration essay. In creating a context for the thesis, a compare/contrast introduction usually establishes a counterpoint as a frame of reference for the thesis statement. In other words, the introduction for a contrast essay begins with a reference to similarities while the introduction for a comparison essay begins with a reference to differences.

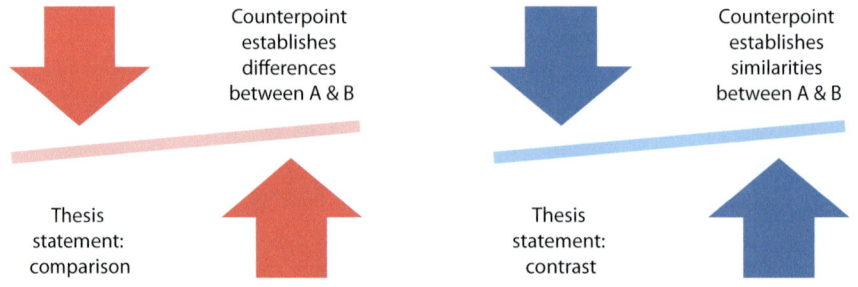

> **Reflection**
> *Read the introduction to the essay on Roman marriage above. Underline the comparisons in the introduction that serve as a <u>counterpoint</u> in a contrast essay.*

b. *Determining the necessary background information*

In Chapter 6, you created a thesis statement and wrote the body paragraphs for a short essay: *A Contrast of Roman and Modern Western Marriage*. The content of these body paragraphs will be unique to you. You will need to write an introduction that reflects the distinct content of your compare/contrast paragraphs.

Practice: Effective introductions

> 1. Review the body paragraphs of your essay.
>   Using the question framework below, determine the information necessary for an effective introduction to your essay *A Contrast of Roman and Modern Western Marriage*.
> 2. Remember that as the writer, it is up to you to determine what information is vital to provide an adequate introduction to your topic.
>
> | Background information for introduction to compare/contrast Roman v. Modern Marriage | |
> |---|---|
> | What | is the topic of the essay? |
> | Who | will the essay discuss? |
> | When | does/did the situation take place? |
> | Where | does/did the situation take place? |
> | Why | examine this topic? |
> | How | will I examine the topic? |

2.   AWARE: Writing the introduction

Write an introduction of four to seven sentences for your compare/contrast essay using a general-to-specific approach. Include all of the necessary background information, a counterpoint to your comparison, and a thesis sentence. What information or facts can you include that would make the topic interesting or relevant to the reader?

3.   AWARE: Assessing the introduction

Practice: Assessing your introduction

> Use the framework below to assess the draft of the introduction for your compare/contrast essay on Roman and contemporary western marriage to see if it has the minimum required elements. Copy the statements that correspond to the elements in the left column. You may include additional information to narrow the topic but at a minimum the introduction should include the points below.
>
> General statement to introduce the topic.
>
> Statement that narrows and contextualizes the topic by establishing a counterpoint.
>
> Additional statement that continues the counterpoint.
>
> Thesis statement with topic and point of view.

4. AWARE: Revising the introduction

Add any of the elements that are missing from the framework above.

Read the introduction from the point of view of someone who is not familiar with the topic. Is there sufficient information to create a context for the thesis statement?

Underline any information or ideas that serve to attract the reader's attention. What can you add to make the topic more interesting or relevant?

5. AWARE: Editing the introduction

Edit the introduction at the same time as the conclusion, in the last section.

C. Conclusions

1. Examining the conclusion

A good conclusion creates a strong finish to a paper or essay. The conclusion may be the last thing an instructor reads before assigning a grade so it is worth the time and effort to construct it well. A conclusion is the writer's last opportunity to ensure clarity by reminding the reader of key evidence and reinforcing the validity of the thesis statement. When a paper has an effective introduction and presents evidence logically, the flow of ideas naturally leads to the conclusion.

Moves in conclusions

The previous section discussed the conventional moves in an introduction. These moves prepare the reader by clarifying the writer's purpose and establishing the context for the thesis statement. Effective conclusions draw the writer's attention to the central ideas in the essay and relate them to the thesis statement. Academic readers look for this information to help them synthesize the evidence and reflect on its relevance. Therefore, the basic moves in a conclusion remind the reader of the original thesis statement, review the key evidence, and underscore the significance of the topic.

At a minimum, academic essays and papers include the three basic moves below. Other genres such as empirical research studies, dissertations, or theses have additional requirements for introductions and conclusions. These will be examined in the chapters on research.

The basic moves in the conclusion to an essay or academic paper include:

- a rephrased thesis statement,
- a synthesis of evidence that supports the thesis statement,
- an affirmation of the significance or relevance of the topic.

2. Strategies for writing conclusions

There are many ways to write a conclusion. This section will examine three basic strategies for composing effective conclusions based on the moves above: reworking the thesis, synthesizing major points, and emphasizing their significance.

The basic structure for a simple conclusion mirrors the introduction. While the introduction moves from general to specific, the conclusion moves from specific to general. The conclusion begins with a reworked thesis statement, synthesizes key evidence, and ends with a general statement that affirms the significance or the relevance of the topic.

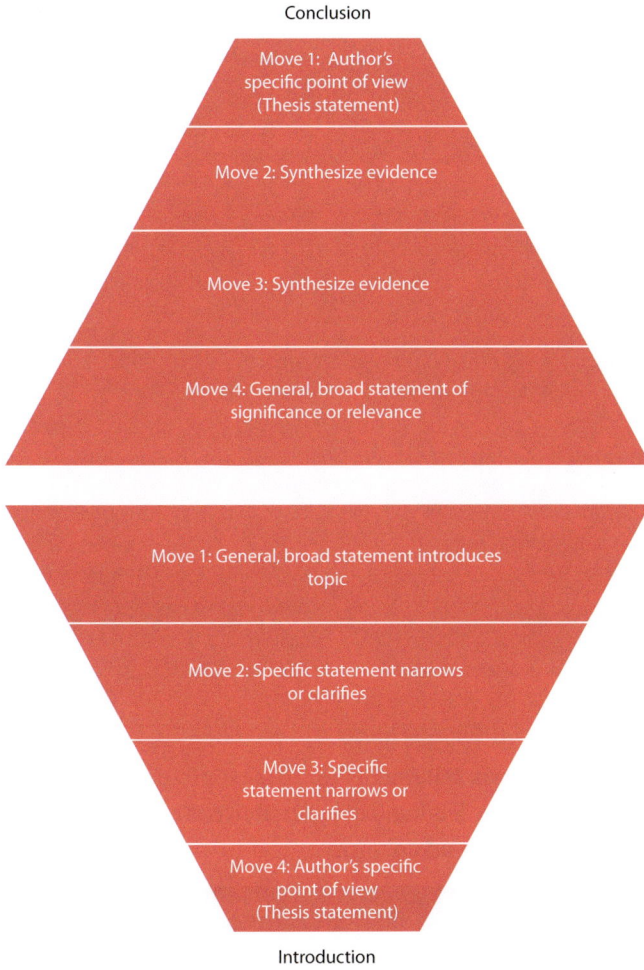

a. Conclusion strategy 1: Rephrase the thesis

Reminding the reader of the thesis statement refocuses attention on the author's purpose and reaffirms the importance of the thesis. It helps the reader evaluate how successful the essay has been in presenting the author's point of view.

Rephrasing the thesis is essentially rewording the original statement so that it does not sound repetitive. In the examples below, the author rephrases the thesis statement while maintaining the original topic and point of view.

Practice: Reading to write – Rephrasing the thesis statement

The original thesis statement in column 1 has been rephrased in column 2.
a. Read the pairs of thesis statements.
b. Underline the topic.
c. Double underline the point of view in each.

Original thesis statement	Rephrased thesis statement
In his poem *"Nothing Gold Can Stay"*, Frost uses a series of metaphors of nature in spring to lament the inevitable loss of youth and beauty throughout the cycle of life.	The metaphors of early spring in the poem *"Nothing Gold Can Stay"* express Frost's sorrow as he contemplates the inescapable fading of youth and beauty.
Despite similarities, many Roman marriage and divorce practices reflect an ancient society that valued men, family, and social class above the notion of romantic love.	Increasing social status, family wealth, and male privilege were more important factors in Roman marriage and divorce than romantic love.
By creating an algorithm that made the photography of a black hole possible, the young female scientist showed the world that women were as capable as men.	The young woman convinced the world that the competence of female scientists equaled that of males when she created an algorithm that made photography of black holes feasible.

Practice: Strategy 1 – Rephrasing the thesis

You have worked with thesis statements for three topics in previous chapters. Copy each thesis statement into the left hand column. Rewrite each thesis statement and put the new version in the right hand column.

Your original thesis statement	Your reworked thesis statement
Enumeration (Downloading music) Compare/Contrast (Roman/modern marriage) Cause/Effect (your topic choice)	

b. *Conclusion strategy 2: Synthesize the major ideas of the essay*

A strong conclusion synthesizes the author's key points. This move reminds the reader of the evidence that the author has presented to support the thesis. To keep the conclusion from sounding repetitive, the original writing is paraphrased, capturing the main points but using different words and phrasing.

Practice: Reading to write – Synthesizing major ideas

> Read the introduction of the essay on Roman marriage above. Notice that in the conclusion below, the author:
> - restates the thesis
> - synthesizes key evidence from the essay
>
> Roman customs and laws reflected a social order that favored men and valued class, wealth, citizenship, and property over unions based on romantic love. Families arranged marriages between their children to improve social class and gain wealth. Romans celebrated weddings with traditions that included gifts, feasts, processions, and a white tunic for the bride. Although marriage was considered a personal agreement between the bride and groom, Roman laws maintained strict boundaries between social classes by restricting who was eligible to marry. Divorce was relatively easy and laws favored men, overlooking a husband's adultery while penalizing an unfaithful wife. While modern western society still follows many Roman laws and traditions, most people today decide to marry for love.

c. *Conclusion strategy 3: Explain the significance of your topic and thesis*

The purpose of the essay is to validate the author's thesis and show its significance. The author does this by presenting convincing evidence to support this point of view. However, an effective paper also persuades the reader that your conclusion is significant and worthy of consideration.

Practice: Reading to write – Explaining the significance of the topic and thesis

> Read the following conclusion from the essay *The Truth about Organic Food*. Notice how the writer:
> - restates the thesis,
> - synthesizes key evidence from the essay, and
> - concludes by affirming why organic farming is important.
>
> When considering the pros and cons of organic produce, the consumer should consider that organic farming does more than eliminate toxic chemicals from our food. Organic farming improves the quality of food and the ecosystem by maintaining healthy soil. While synthetic chemicals harm the micro-biotic activity of the soil, organically farmed soils preserve nutrients that grow healthier and more flavorful produce. In the long run, organically grown food benefits everyone by preserving soil fertility and natural ecosystems.

Practice: Explaining the significance/relevance of the topic

> Reread the conclusion to the essay on *Roman Marriage*. Does the author make a statement that suggests that the topic is significant to the modern person? Underline this statement.

d. *Conclusion strategy 4: Avoid ineffective elements in a conclusion*

Conclusions are the writer's last opportunity to focus the reader's attention on the relevance of the thesis statement and the most important ideas in a paper or essay. Some elements commonly seen in student papers weaken, rather than strengthen, the impact of the conclusion. Keep the following in mind when writing the conclusion:

- Never introduce new ideas, evidence, or facts. All new ideas must be integrated into the body of the text.
- Avoid overused phrases such as "in conclusion," in "summary," or "in closing". The phrases may be heard in formal speech, but they sound trite in written text.
- Do not copy the thesis statement or sentences from the introduction or body paragraphs. Rework and rewrite the statements to help the reader interpret them with a fresh perspective.

D. AWARE: Writing the conclusion

You have already developed an introduction for your essay, *A Contrast of Roman and Modern Western Marriage*. To prepare for the conclusion, please have the introduction and body of the essay on hand.

1. AWARE: Arranging to write the conclusion

Use the framework below to begin writing a concluding paragraph for the essay *A Contrast of Roman and Modern Western Marriage*.

Practice: The elements of the conclusion

> a. Rework your thesis. Paraphrase. Do not simply copy the thesis.
>
> b. Identify one main idea that illustrates/explains the thesis statement.
>
> c. Identify a second main idea that illustrates/explains the thesis statement.
>
> d. Identify a third main idea that illustrates/explains the thesis statement.
>
> e. Write a statement that explains the significance of your topic or shows its relevance to the reader.

2. **AWARE: Writing the conclusion to a compare/contrast essay**

Use the information you developed in the framework above to draft the conclusion to the essay *A Contrast between Roman and Modern Western Marriage*. Write a concluding paragraph of four to six sentences.

3. **AWARE: Assessing the conclusion**

Assess the content of your conclusion to ensure it includes the three basic moves. Does the conclusion:

- rephrase the thesis statement?
- synthesize key ideas that support the thesis statement?
- affirm the significance or relevance of the topic?

4. **AWARE: Revising the conclusion**

The most important move in the conclusion is to bring the discussion back to the thesis statement. Since the purpose of expository writing is to develop convincing evidence for a thesis statement, the reader will evaluate the key ideas in relation to the thesis statement. Both must present the same topic and point of view. At the same time, avoid the impression that the conclusion repeats the introduction through the use of different vocabulary and sentence structure.

a. Align the thesis statement in the introduction with the rephrased thesis statement in the conclusion. Compare the two statements:
   - Are the topics identical?
   - Is the point of view the same?
b. Look for repetitive vocabulary. If vocabulary repeats, substitute a synonym where possible. Sometimes synonyms are not available; however, look for alternatives. The thesaurus in word processing programs is a good resource. If you are not familiar with the word, check its usage in the dictionary.
c. Delete or revise unacceptable elements. Beware of the following:
   - Does the conclusion present new ideas, evidence, or facts?
   - Does the conclusion use expressions such as "in conclusion," in summary," or "in closing?"

> **Reflection**
> *Compare the original thesis statement and the rephrased statement below.*
> *What vocabulary remains the same?*
> *What vocabulary changes?*
> *Does the new vocabulary change the meaning of the thesis?*

> Original thesis:
> In his poem "Nothing Gold Can Stay", Frost uses a series of metaphors of nature in spring to lament the inevitable loss of youth and beauty throughout the cycle of life.
>
> Rephrased thesis:
> The metaphors of early spring in the poem "Nothing Gold Can Stay" express Frost's sorrow as he contemplates the inescapable fading of youth and beauty

5. AWARE: Editing

Edit your conclusion in the next section.

E. Putting it together: Revising and editing a full essay

Merge the introduction, the body paragraphs, and the conclusion of your essay *A Contrast of Roman and Modern Western Marriage* into a single document. This creates a full draft for your essay.

1. AWARE: Revising the full essay

Read through the full draft of your essay, introduction, body paragraphs, and conclusion.

Checklist for revising for content:
1. Review introduction for all necessary background information and a thesis statement.
2. Align the thesis statement in the introduction with the rephrased thesis statement in the conclusion.
3. Underline repetitive words and check for synonyms.
4. Underline non-specific or imprecise words. Substitute precise and specific vocabulary (see also Chapter 4, 6).
5. Change informal language to formal language (see Chapter 1).
6. Check for paragraph unity. Strike out any sentences that do not directly support the topic sentence (see Chapter 5).
7. Use appropriate discourse connectors to signal the relationships among ideas.

2. AWARE: Editing the full essay

a. *Formatting the paper*

Papers should be formatted according to requirements laid out in the description of the assignment. This includes the APA, MLA, Chicago, or other formatting styles. Students should follow the instructor's guidelines for the preferred format. As this book uses the formatting style of the American Psychological Association (APA), the model assignment is formatted in the APA style.

Topic:	Contrast of Roman and Modern Western Marriage
Title page:	Capitalize all names and words with more than 4 letters. Use a double space between items; add an additional double-space blank line after the title.
Title of Paper:	Centered in boldface type.
Length:	5 paragraphs – an introduction, 3 body paragraphs, and a conclusion.
Font:	Times New Roman, 12 points, double spaced.
Paragraphs:	Indent 5–7 spaces, or one tab stop.
Margins:	1 inch (2.54 cm) on all sides.
Page numbers:	Included on each page.

Title of Essay
Your name
Department and University
Course number and title
Instructor's name
Assignment due date

b. *Editing checklist*

Using the editing checklist as a guide, read through your essay. Look for errors in grammar, spelling, formatting, and punctuation. Pay attention to the points below. Look for one feature at a time. Next, read through the entire draft.

1. Use of commas (Chapter 3)
2. Punctuation for discourse connectors (Chapter 4)
3. Commonly confused word pairs (Chapter 6)
4. Comma splices (Chapter 6)
5. Fragments (Chapter 2).

The paper is now ready for submission. Submit the paper according to the instructor's guidelines.

F. AWARE: Independent writing assignments – enumeration essay and cause/effect essay

1. The architecture of the essays

The following assignments are based on the AWARE writing that you completed in Chapter 4 (Enumeration) and Chapter 6 (Cause and Effect). In those chapters, you developed and revised body paragraphs for an enumeration essay and a cause and effect essay. Both assignments follow the architecture for an expository essay represented in the chart below.

Introduction	Present topic and direction of paper General statements move to narrow statements Engage and orient reader Create context for understanding thesis Thesis statement: controls ideas that follow								
Body	Main idea 1 supports thesis			Main idea 2 supports thesis			Main idea 3 supports thesis		
	Evidence supports main idea	Evidence supports main idea	Evidence supports main idea	Evidence supports main idea	Evidence supports main idea	Evidence supports main idea	Evidence supports main idea	Evidence supports main idea	Evidence supports main idea
	supports main idea	supports main idea	supports main idea	supports main idea	supports main idea	supports main idea	supports main idea	supports main idea	supports main idea
Conclusion	Rephrase thesis Synthesize main points Review significance								

2. Essay instructions

To complete the essays, use AWARE strategies to:
1. Write an introduction.
2. Write a conclusion.
3. Complete a final revision and editing.
4. Format the paper.

Assignments

ENUMERATION ESSAY (Chapter 4)

Topic: Downloading music from the internet.

Description of the assignment: Write a short essay that enumerates at least three points to support a thesis statement.

    Write from one perspective or the other

- "Downloading of music from the internet: The consumer perspective" or
- "Downloading of music from the internet: The music industry perspective".

Length: 5 paragraphs (an introduction, 3 body paragraphs, and a conclusion).

Format: APA, Times New Roman, 12 points, double spaced, 1 inch margins on all sides.

Include a title page.

CAUSE AND EFFECT ESSAY (Chapter 6)

Topic: Examine the causes or effects related to an event, phenomenon, or action.

Description of the assignment: Write a short essay that examines least three causes or effects in support your thesis statement.

    Write from one perspective or the other:

- "single cause with multiple effects"
- "single effect with multiple causes"

Length: 5 paragraphs (an introduction, 3 body paragraphs, and a conclusion).

Format: APA, Times New Roman, 12 points, double spaced, 1 inch margins on all sides.

Include a title page.

Part II

Presenting the views of others

Chapter 8

Research to support a thesis

The chapters in the first part of this book focused on the building blocks of texts common to academic writing. Writing tasks and assignments did not require support from the writings of others, allowing students to concentrate on writing practice to develop their own voice.

The chapters in the second part of the book focus on thesis-driven writing based on research for two model assignments: a case study and a research paper. By following the guidelines for the different stages of AWARE writing, students master skills that will benefit them in any discipline and for most assignments they are likely to encounter at university (Nesi & Gardner, 2012).

First, students conduct their own research and present their findings in a case study of a remarkable person they know. The case study then provides a foundation for the second assignment where students place the remarkable person into a socio-historical context. For the second assignment, students identify, evaluate and incorporate the views of others for presentation in their research paper.

Writing research papers entails citing the works of experts. One of the fundamental rules of English academic writing is that the views of others are clearly attributed to the author. Failing to do this is called plagiarism and is a serious breach of academic honesty. Because methods of attributing sources vary between languages, it is important for writers of English as a second language to master the attribution of sources in a manner acceptable to readers of English.

Reporting research is challenging for novice writers. Therefore, this chapter examines the nature of primary and secondary research and provides guidelines and practice in reporting and citing sources.

In this chapter, students will:

- examine the nature of research,
- examine research-based writing,
- examine ways to avoid plagiarism,
- practice quoting, paraphrasing and summarizing the words of others,
- practice reporting sources, and
- practice citing sources.

A. Examining academic research

Academic writing is typically based on evidence from sources researched and reported by others, usually experts. Research is a general term that includes all systematic study designed to find answers to meaningful questions. Research is classified as primary or secondary research depending on the source of the data.

Primary sources are those reported by the writer who also conducted the research; secondary sources are those conducted by others but reported by the writer. Learning to conduct, use, and report research is important preparation for the two final assignments in this book: a case study based on primary sources and a research paper that incorporates both primary and secondary sources.

There are two basic types of research, quantitative and qualitative. These categories of research use different methods of gathering data and different types of discourse to report those data. The two types will be discussed briefly in the next sections.

1. Quantitative research

Quantitative research is, as the name suggests, based on statistical analysis. The goal is often to prove or disprove a hypothesis providing conclusive evidence. The results of experiments or large-scale surveys of opinions use statistics and seek to be objective with minimal interpretation or discussion. Reports of quantitative research tend to use nouns such as *frequency, percentage, correlation, significance, hypothesis, control group, representation, standard deviation, standardized tests, psychometric tests, pre-test, post-test, independent and dependent variables, reliability, and validity* and verbs like *classify, result in, carry out, and compute*. Studies *prove* a hypothesis and present results in *charts* and *graphs*. The natural sciences and social sciences tend to use quantitative research methods.

2. Qualitative research

Qualitative research is used when the goal is to examine the behavior of an individual or a small group. These types of studies are called case studies. A case study is an effort to describe human behavior in the context of the subject's environment in some detail. Qualitative studies are sometimes called ethnographic studies, as some of the research methods have been developed in the field of ethnography. Qualitative research describes phenomena and may interpret and try to explain them. Reports of case studies are likely to contain language which indicates interpretation. Reports of qualitative research tend to use nouns like *perception, assumption, theme, categorization, insight, generalization,* and verbs like *suggest, may,* and *influence*. Reports *support* a view or a hypothesis but cannot *prove* a hypothesis.

> **Relevance**
> Knowing about the different types of research and how it is reported helps the researcher write better. It also helps the reader understand the findings reported in research texts.

> **Relevance**
> Students give many reasons for why they copy information into their own papers. These include lack of time, inability to paraphrase or summarize, and ignorance of English attribution conventions. Regardless, plagiarizing is never acceptable in English writing and can have dire consequences for the student. It is important that students familiarize themselves with their university's plagiarism policy and decide whether plagiarism is worth the risk.

3. Conducting research

Before writing can take place, students are typically required to conduct research that will provide the content for the assigned paper. For most students, this means reviewing secondary sources. Secondary research is usually conducted at the library or through online resources. A student paper based on secondary research presents interpretations, summaries, descriptions, or analyses conducted and written by others, usually experts in the field. Reviewing secondary sources and materials allows the researcher to establish facts, clarify issues, develop a new perspective, or reach a new conclusion. A secondary research assignment requires students to investigate a topic, develop a thesis, select, analyze, and synthesize information from books, journals, or websites written by experts.

In primary research, such as for the case study in the next two chapters, authors report research that they themselves conducted. All disciplines conduct primary research. It is a first-hand account of a study in which the author designs, documents, and presents the findings. Primary research is based on first-hand experience, observation, or experimentation. In primary research, the investigator creates new knowledge through the systematic observation of phenomena or the study of original documents or artifacts. The observations, documents, or artifacts that are used in the study are called primary sources because they provide direct, first-hand knowledge or observation of a person who witnessed an event or participated in an experience. The case study requires the student to become an expert on the topic and then relate his knowledge to others.

Primary and secondary research is an important source of data in academic papers and scholarly studies. Primary and secondary research can support a thesis or an argument, offer insight into key issues, or provide an overview of what is known about a specific topic.

4. Primary and secondary data sources

Primary and secondary research have certain characteristics in common. There should be enough resources to support a thesis or answer a research question. Secondary sources should be reliable, varied, and their publication dates should be appropriate to the project. The reliability of a source depends on the expertise of the author. Ways to identify reliable secondary sources will be revisited in the next chapters. The writer is the expert on the topic of the case study.

Primary resources include: interviews, pictures, audio, video, blogs.

Secondary resources include: books, articles, editorials, reviews, reports, web sites, web journals.

Relevance
Doing primary research is an excellent skill to learn, as it can be useful in a variety of settings including business, personal, and academic.

Reflection
Most adults have conducted primary research in some manner, such as finding out where a person lives or which company has the best price on phones. Think about a time when you had to find information that was not readily available. How did you do it? How did you know that the source was current and reliable?

Practice: *Reading to write*

1. What is your area of study (discipline)?
2. Examine two research articles in your discipline. They could be assigned readings in one of your courses.
3. Read the title, abstract, and subtitles.
4. What type of research do they present?
   a. Is it qualitative or quantitative?
   b. Is quantitative or qualitative research more common in your discipline?
   c. If you cannot find the answer, ask an instructor in one of the courses in your program.
5. Identify 2–3 characteristics of writing that are specific to your discipline.

Reflection
Why is it important for you to know what type of research is most common in your discipline? What implications does this knowledge have for your ability to understand and write about research in your discipline?

In the English-speaking academic community, the writer must present information appropriately, accurately, and concisely and always include a citation that attributes the knowledge to the original author. The remainder of this chapter is devoted to this fundamental requirement in English academic writing.

B. Examining and avoiding plagiarism

This chapter revisits ways to avoid plagiarism that were introduced in the first chapter of this book. Plagiarism is presenting the writing, lyrics, comments, or ideas of another person without crediting the author through proper citation. Plagiarism can originate in web pages, books, songs, films, personal correspondence, interviews, articles, artworks, or any source that presents the words or ideas of others.

Reproducing the original idea of another person by changing the wording of the information through paraphrase or summary without citing the source is also plagiarism. Whether intentional or unintentional, plagiarism is a serious violation of academic honesty and undermines a student's credibility.

The most effective way to avoid plagiarism is to employ strategies that help the writer reproduce others' ideas in his or her own words or attribute authors appropriately when reproducing their words. Strategies for using quoted, paraphrased, and summarized material are presented and practiced throughout this book in the context of the assignments students are working on. The exercises also provide a good opportunity for writing practice.

1. Examining quotations

Although all types of research papers rely on quotation to some extent, incorporating direct quotes is a requirement for the case study based on primary research in the next chapters. However, over-reliance on direct quotations weakens the writer's voice.

Effective academic writing does not involve stringing together quotations from multiple sources. Doing this suggests a lack of understanding of the material or a lack of time to analyze and integrate sources into the final draft. No more than 10% of a paper should be direct quotations.

Writing in the social sciences (psychology, sociology, education, and political science) usually includes a review of relevant research studies. The writer is expected to summarize or paraphrase information from the studies but should only rarely use direct quotations from the original studies.

> *Reflection*
> *Review an academic or professional journal in your field of study and look for the use of direct quotations. How many direct quotations can you find?*

a. Strategies for using direct quotations

Quotations add authenticity and impact only when they are especially important or illustrative of a point.

When to use direct quotations
Use direct quotations cautiously and with a clear purpose in mind. Restrict the use of direct quotations to the following situations:

1. The exact wording of a statement of policy or opinion is <u>essential</u> to the accurate understanding.
2. A passage in a poem, story, novel, or play is used to illustrate a point.
3. Rewording would reduce the impact of the original text.
4. A quote from an interview that gives the interviewee a 'voice' or a larger presence in the text.

> **Reflection**
> *Examine 1–2 articles that use direct quotations. Why do you think the author chose to include a direct quotation? Did it serve a specific purpose? If so, what purpose?*

Presenting quotations
In an academic paper, the writer must integrate quoted material smoothly into the text and provide a citation that clearly attributes ideas to their original author. This type of citation is called an in-text citation. The model presented here is the APA style, but other formats may require other ways to quote. APA style requires an in-text citation for any references made to another source regardless of whether it is paraphrased, summarized, or quoted. A citation must also be included in the list of references at the end of the paper.

The APA discourages the use of direct quotations and prefers paraphrasing sources rather than quoting directly. Use direct quotations only when necessary in conveying exact information. When using direct quotes always include the author's last name, year of publication, and page number of the quote.

Examples of in-text citations are presented in the next section.

Short quotations
Short quotations, fewer than 40 words, are enclosed within double quotations marks. A parenthetical citation is inserted into the text with the information necessary to identify the source. There are three main ways that the citation is typically placed in the text. They are:

1. <u>The author's name is not mentioned in the text.</u> The quote is enclosed in quotation marks and followed immediately by a parenthetical citation that includes the author's last name, the year of publication, and the page number preceded by "p." When the parenthetical citation is directly after the quotation, *the period is placed after the parenthesis of the citation.*

    > He often repeated that "the ancient belief that the dream reveals the future is not entirely devoid of truth" (Freud, 1920, p. 89).

2. <u>The author's name introduces the quotation.</u> The date of publication is placed immediately *after* the author's name in parentheses. The page number is placed at the end of the quotation.

> When Freud (1920) claimed that "the ancient belief that the dream reveals the future is not entirely devoid of truth" (p. 89), many people disagreed with him.

3. <u>The author's name and date introduce the quotation.</u> Only the page number is required in parentheses to identify the source.

> In 1920, Freud claimed that "the ancient belief that the dream reveals the future is not entirely devoid of truth" (p. 89).

To avoid the reader's misinterpretation of the quote, the writer must introduce the quotation (see **a** below) and, if necessary, follow the quotation with an explanation of its significance (see **b** below).

> Example: (a) After reading *The Diary of Anne Frank*, one publisher concluded that "The girl doesn't, it seems to me, have a special perception or feeling which would lift that book above the 'curiosity' level" (Smith, 1950, p. 9). (b) The publisher rejected the perceptions of a young girl whose story touched the hearts of millions.

When reporting a quotation, the writer indicates the person who spoke or wrote the comments. The most common ways to introduce the author of the information are to use the verbs "said" or "told" or the phrase "according to".

To avoid the overuse of "said", "told", and "according to", the writer can substitute another reporting verb to introduce the quotation. Replacing the general "said" and "told" with more specific words also creates a context that makes the meaning of the quotation clearer and more effective. Compare the connotation of the word, *warned* and *claimed* used to introduce the quotations:

> The woman said, "It is too hot to work today."
> The woman warned, "It is too hot to work today."
> Dr. Muller said, "My research has uncovered two new poems written by Shakespeare."
> Dr. Muller claimed, "My research has uncovered two new poems written by Shakespeare."

Practice: *Introducing quotations with reporting verbs*

> Arrange the quotations in an order that reflects **the least (1) to the most (5) certainty** about Dr. Muller's discovery.
> Dr. Muller declared, "My research has uncovered two new poems written by Shakespeare."
> Dr. Muller insisted …
> Dr. Muller argued …
> Dr. Muller suggested …

Below is a list of reporting verbs that can be used as a substitute for "said".

Verbs for making a claim	Verbs for expressing agreement
argue	acknowledge
propose	agree
insist	celebrate the fact that
assert	reaffirm
observe	
believe	
remind us	
claim	
report	
emphasize	
suggest	

Verbs for questioning or disagreeing	Verbs for making recommendations
complain	advocate
contend	plead
deplore the tendency to	warn

Based on They Say, I Say by G. Graff and C. Birkenstein (2012).

Practice: Integrating short quotations into text

Below are genuine comments from publishers who rejected some of the most famous and respected books of all time.

For each quotation:

1. Create two examples
   a. a sentence that introduces the author, and
   b. one sentence that does not.
2. Use a reporting verb or phrase.
3. Add a sentence that explains the significance of each quotation.

Use the Example from *The Diary of Anne Frank* as a guide.

The Diary of Anne Frank.
Date of rejection: 1950,
Publisher: Mr. Smith, Alfred A. Knopf Inc.

Publisher's Comment
"The girl doesn't, it seems to me, have a special perception or feeling which would lift that book above the 'curiosity' level."

Example (a): Author's name is not in the introduction.
After reading *The Diary of Anne Frank*, one publisher concluded that "The girl doesn't, it seems to me, have a special perception or feeling which would lift that book above the 'curiosity' level" (Smith, 1950, p. 12). The publisher rejected the perceptions of a young girl whose story touched the hearts of millions.

Example (b): Author's name introduces the quote.
After reading The Diary of Anne Frank, Smith (1920) concluded, "The girl doesn't, it seems to me, have a special perception or feeling which would lift that book above the 'curiosity' level" (p. 12). The publisher rejected the perceptions of a young girl whose story touched the hearts of millions.

Animal Farm, (George Orwell) Date of rejection: 1944 Publisher: Faber & Faber. *Example (a)* *Example (b)*	*"It is impossible to sell animal stories in the USA."*
The Great Gatsby (F. Scott Fitzgerald) Date of rejection: 1920 Publisher: Montgomery. *Example (a)* *Example (b)*	*"You'd have a decent book if you'd get rid of that Gatsby character."*
Harry Potter (J. K. Rowling) Date of rejection: 1988 Publisher: Orion. *Example (a)* *Example (b)*	*"When the book came in, I thought it was perfectly good – it was certainly well written – but it didn't stand out."*

Long quotations

The APA guidelines state that quoted material of more than 40 words should be presented in a free-standing block style. However, the use of block quotations should be minimal since they tend to obscure the voice of the writer and diminish the cohesiveness of the writing. When using block quotations:

– introduce the quotation with a colon
– do not use quotation marks
– begin on a new line
– indent the text ½ inch from the left margin
– maintain double spacing of text
– place the citation in brackets after the final punctuation in the passage.

Similar to short quotations, there are two common ways to present block quotations.

1. All of the information (author, date, page number) is placed after the block quotation within parentheses. The period is placed outside of the parenthesis.

Example:

From the beginning of modern psychology, dream researchers have maintained that dreams cannot predict the future:

> To be sure the ancient belief that the dream reveals the future is not entirely devoid of truth. By representing to us a wish as fulfilled the dream certainly leads us into the future; but this future, taken by the dreamer as present, has been formed into the likeness of that past by the indestructible wish. (Freud, 1920, p. 89)

2. When the author's name introduces the block quotation, the publication date is placed in parenthesis immediately after the author's name. The page number is indicated in parenthesis at the end of the block quotation.

Example:

Freud (1920) questioned the value of dreams for predicting the future:

> To be sure the ancient belief that the dream reveals the future is not entirely devoid of truth. By representing to us a wish as fulfilled the dream certainly leads us into the future; but this future, taken by the dreamer as present, has been formed into the likeness of that past by the indestructible wish. (p. 89)

b. *Phrases to present quotations*

The phrases below are examples of phrases that explain who is speaking. They can be used to present short quotations and/or long quotations:

As Smith (year) stated, "_____" (p. 9).
Smith (year) proposed, "_____" (p. 9).
According to Smith (year), "_____" (p. 9).
Smith (year) acknowledged, "_____" (p. 9).

For clarifying quotations:

Essentially, Smith (year) confirms, _____.
In other words, Smith (year) believes, _____.
In making this comment, Smith (year) assumes incorrectly that _____.
Smith (year) is proposing that _____.

Practice: Incorporating direct quotations into text using APA format

For each of the quotations below:
1. Write a sentence that introduces the quotation.
2. Format the quotation according to APA style.
3. Include an appropriate APA in-text citation.
4. Write a sentence that explains the quotation.

(The authors, dates, and pages for the quotations below were created for this practice.)

1. From: Natural Resources Defense Council, 2013, page 72
   Climate change is the single biggest environmental and humanitarian crisis of our time. The Earth's atmosphere is overloaded with heat-trapping carbon dioxide, which threatens large-scale disruptions in climate with disastrous consequences.
   <http://www.nrdc.org/globalwarming/>
3. From Tony Margiotta, 2011, page 99.
   One of the greatest minds of all time and the original "Renaissance Man," Leonardo Da Vinci, was centuries ahead of his time with his futuristic inventions and timeless with his epic paintings such as "The Mona Lisa" and "The Last Supper." Leonardo also had a talent for music during his early development years as an apprentice. He sang and played several musical instruments. It is considered that music was only second to painting in his artistic abilities.
   <http://blogcritics.org/one-secret-many-geniuses-have-in/>
4. From: Mary Jones, 2002, page 189.
   Don Quixote, the tale of a Spanish knight driven mad by reading too many chivalric romances, was yesterday voted the best book of all time in a survey of around 100 of the world's best authors. Miguel de Cervantes' tale of misguided heroism gained 50% more votes than any other book, eclipsing works by Shakespeare, Homer and Tolstoy
   <http://www.theguardian.com/world/2002/may/08/humanities.books>

2. Examining paraphrase

To paraphrase is to reword essential information and ideas expressed by another author. It is not a summary of ideas but a rephrasing of short passages, conclusions or opinions. A paraphrase must be attributed to the original source. The length of a paraphrase is approximately the same as the original source. Chapter 1 included paraphrase practice. Below are more opportunities to practice paraphrasing.

A good paraphrase reproduces information from a source by changing both the wording and the sentence structure of the original text. Paraphrases must always be attributed to the original author. The paraphrases are in *italics*.

Example:

> **Original text:** "Most, but not all cacti grow in dry climates. For example, the Christmas cactus comes from the rainforest of South America" (Smith, 2020, p. 8).
>
> **Paraphrase:** *While cacti typically require a dry environment, the Christmas cactus originated in the rainforests of South America* (Smith, 2020).
>
> **Original text:** "Historical records trace the ancient Olympic Games back to 776 BC. They took place on the ancient plains of Olympia in Greece and were dedicated to the Olympian gods. They continued for nearly 12 centuries until 393 A.D. when Emperor Theodosius decreed that all such pagan cults be banned" (Ardley & Ardley, 1989, p. 68).
>
> **Paraphrase:** *For almost twelve centuries, The Olympic Games were held in honor of the Olympian gods. According to historical records, the games began in Olympia, Greece in 776 BC and continued until the emperor Theodosius prohibited "pagan cults" in 393 AD.* (Ardley & Ardley, 1989, p. 68).

> **Relevance**
> Paraphrasing is a valuable skill because it helps students write in their own voice. It is a good alternative to overuse of quotes. Paraphrasing also helps a student understand the main ideas of the original text better.

There are some occasions when it is necessary to reproduce the original wording from the source. Reproducing the original wording is only acceptable when there are no synonyms or because the original wording is essential to the message or meaning of the text:

1. The author's text uses technical or discipline-specific terms that do not have a synonym, such as *cacti or Olympic Games.*
2. The original text uses words in an unusual way or to show irony. The original wording is not changed but it is enclosed in quotation marks.

   She "retired" three years ago but continues to go into the office every day.

Below are some examples of unacceptable (second column) and acceptable paraphrases (third column).

In the first set of examples below, the unacceptable paraphrase 1 maintains the grammatical structure of the text and simply substitutes synonyms for the original words. In the acceptable paraphrase 2, both the wording and the sentence structure have been changed.

	Unacceptable paraphrase 1	Acceptable paraphrase 2
Original sentence	Copies sentence structure and replaces wording with synonyms	Both wording and sentence structure changed
Analysis found dangerous levels of bacteria in multiple samples of water collected from the city reservoir.	Tests documented harmful amounts of bacteria in various samples of water taken from the city reservoir.	When the city conducted tests of water from the reservoir, it found harmful amounts of bacteria in multiple samples.

In the unacceptable paraphrase 3 below, the sentence structure has been changed but the words remain the same. In the acceptable paraphrase 4, both the structure and the wording have been changed.

	Unacceptable paraphrase 3	Acceptable paraphrase 4
Original sentence	Changes sentence structure but repeats original wording	Changed wording and sentence structure
Since his death in 1616, academic scholars have continued to look for symbols in Shakespeare's writings.	The search for symbols in Shakespeare's writings has continued among academic scholars since his death in 1616.	Symbolism in the works of Shakespeare has remained an important topic of scholarly research for four hundred years.

a. *Strategies for writing short paraphrases*

A paraphrase reproduces the meaning of the original source accurately with minimal reproduction of the wording or structure in the original text. Below, strategies for writing short paraphrases are presented along with exercises.

Practice: Writing short paraphrased text

> Below are three short passages taken from different sources. The first example has been paraphrased. Paraphrase the other two using the guidelines below.
>
> 1. Read the text carefully.
> 2. Put the text aside.
> 3. Imagine that you are telling someone what the text said.
> 4. Write your recollection of the text in your own words and structure. Remember to use formal academic language when appropriate.
> 5. Compare it to the original text.
> 6. Does your paraphrase convey the intent and meaning of the text?
> 7. Did you change both the structure and the wording of the text?

Original:	Paraphrase:
1. Africa has the longest river in the world. The Nile is 6,650 km long.	At 6,650 kilometers in length, Africa's Nile River is the longest in the world.
2. A good example of heat radiation is the warming of the earth by the heat rays transmitted by the sun.	
3. Output and new orders shrank as factories came under pressure from the high level of uncertainty over the country's future trading relationship with other countries and from trade wars, which has caused a sharp slowdown in international trade.	

b.   Strategies for paraphrasing direct quotations

With few exceptions it is preferable to paraphrase the speech or writing of others rather than to use quotations. The next assignment in this book is a case study based on students' own data collection using interviews; it is helpful to practice paraphrasing interviewees' responses. When paraphrasing speech (or direct quotations):

- insert "that" after the reporting verb that introduces the sentence
- if the reporting verb is in the past tense, the verbs in the quotation must also be in the past.

Practice: Paraphrasing speech

Paraphrase the following sentences. The first sentence is an example.

1. Paraphrase each sentence using formal language.
2. Use a signal word to introduce the paraphrase.

Example: The store clerk said, "I go an extra mile for my clients".
Paraphrase: *The store clerk remarked that he does more than is required to serve his clients.*

Original 1: Lisa said, "Getting my degree was a piece of cake".	Paraphrase:
Original 2: They said, "The dam will burst if it rains more, so moving the villagers is crucial".	Paraphrase:

c. *Presenting paraphrased passages*

Similar to in-text citations for quotations, paraphrased passages must identify the source of the original text.

> *Smith (2020) observed that while cacti typically require a dry environment, the Christmas cactus originated in the rainforests of South America* (p. 77).
>
> *At 6650 kilometers in length, Africa's Nile River is the longest in the world* (Martin, 2009, p. 179).

Below are guidelines for paraphrasing effectively.

Writing: Paraphrase

Examine an article or book chapter assigned as readings in your program of study. Choose 2–3 passages to paraphrase, employing these strategies:

1. Read the original passage carefully.
2. Without looking at the original text, write down your paraphrase.
3. Mark the note as a paraphrase.
4. Check your paraphrase against the original to make sure it is accurate.
5. Use quotation marks if you decide to use words or phrases word for word.
6. Write down the author, title, year, and page number.
7. Remember to place a period after a citation in short quotes, paraphrases and summaries but before the citation in long quotes.

3. Examining summary

While paraphrasing is appropriate for recounting other author's ideas, writing summaries is an excellent way to understand and present the main points in a primary or secondary source. Summaries are a helpful tool in avoiding plagiarism and are good practice for writing. Summarization involves retelling the main idea(s) of a longer text in your own words. It is important that summaries are relevant to the topic of the paper and that they advance the writer's thesis. Always attribute summarized ideas to the original source/author.

Relevance
Being able to write good summaries helps students separate main ideas from minor details. It is good writing practice and it is a useful skill beyond academic life.

Strategies for writing and reporting summarized material
There are many ways to write a summary. In this section strategies are presented to write effective short and long summaries, along with ways to report the summarized information.

Short summaries
A short summary of a text should only be a few sentences long.

1. Introduce the article in a single sentence:
   - Present the author and date of the article.
   - Use an action verb to indicate how the author presents the information. Does the author study, argue, review, find, consider, assert, investigate, etc.?
   - Identify the central thesis of the article. What does the author claim about the subject?
2. Describe the evidence that the author uses to support the thesis. What type of evidence is presented to support the claim and how is it developed?
3. Explain the purpose of the article. What does the author conclude based on the evidence?
4. Relate the article to a broader context. How does the article relate to other scholarship or a specific audience?

Practice: *Reading to write a summary of an article*

1. Read the article and the four sentences in the summary below.
2. Analyze each sentence in the summary. Locate and underline the content in the article that corresponds to each sentence.
3. Answer the questions that follow each sentence.

Human Personality: Nature or Nurture
Martin Smith
Global University

Science has not provided definitive answers on the nature versus nurture debate with respect to the origins of personality. Nevertheless, the history of identical twins who were raised in different families contributes to understanding genetic and environmental influences. Oskar and Jack were born as the result of a shipboard romance between a German Catholic woman and a Romanian Jewish man en route to the Caribbean. The couple's relationship ended in 1933, shortly after the boys' birth. The mother returned with Oskar to Germany where he was raised as a Catholic and as a Nazi youth. In contrast, the father remained in the Caribbean to raise Jack as a progressive Jew who lived part of his youth on an Israeli kibbutz. Despite having lived their childhoods at opposite ends of the ideological and cultural spectrum, the striking similarities between the two adult men show that genetic heritage plays a significant role in determining personality.

When Oskar and Jack met again in 1979, the physical likenesses and preferences in clothing were apparent immediately. Both men arrived at the airport wearing almost identical wire-rimmed glasses and two-pocket shirts with epaulets. Likewise, the color of the shirts was only a shade apart. The twins also had corresponding short mustaches and receding hairlines. Additional surprising similarities in personality emerged as they got to know each other.

For two people who had never known each other, Oskar and Jack's habits, personalities, and characters were remarkably alike. Both men were absentminded, read magazines from back to front, and fell asleep in front of the television. Researchers observed that the two men asked similar kinds of questions and exhibited similar mannerisms. Likewise, the emotional temperaments of the twins were comparable, as both men experienced explosive anger and suffered from recurrent anxiety.

Similarly, there were uncanny resemblances in the twin's eating preferences and idiosyncratic behaviors. Oskar and Jack enjoyed spicy foods and sweet liqueurs. They both considered sneezing in a crowd amusing. Astonishingly, the men shared two peculiar habits. They both dipped buttered toast in coffee and they flushed the toilet before using it. Each twin had the habit of keeping rubber bands on their wrists.

Notwithstanding childhoods that were polar opposites, the inexplicable similarities between Oskar and Jack in adulthood suggest that genetic influences are important factors in personality development. The twins' choice of clothing and their physical appearance were striking in similarity for two people who had not met. Equally remarkable were parallels in the twin's behaviors, idiosyncratic habits, and personalities. Oskar and Jack were a pair of twins who were raised in different worlds but appear to have grown up in the same family.

Adapted from: http://www.psywww.com/intropsych/ch11_personality/bouchards_twin_research.html

Summary

Smith's essay (2020) examines the lives of identical twins separated at birth to illustrate the role of genetic factors in personality development. The author compares the childhood experiences and adult personalities of Oskar, raised as a Catholic by his mother in Nazi Germany, with those of his twin, Jack, who grew up as a liberal Jew with his Romanian father in the Caribbean. The documented likenesses in the clothing, habits, and behaviors of the adult brothers suggest that genetic predispositions influence personality development. These unexplained similarities in personality traits draw attention to the need for research to better understand the influence of genes on personality development.

1. Smith's essay (2020) examines the lives of identical twins separated at birth to illustrate the role of genetic factors in personality development.

    What is the subject of the essay? Underline the action verb that indicates how the author presents the information. What does the thesis claim?

2. The author compares the childhood experiences and adult personalities of Oskar, raised as a Catholic by his mother in Nazi Germany, with those of his twin, Jack, who grew up as a liberal Jew with his Romanian father in the Caribbean.

    What type of evidence is presented to support the claim and how is it developed?

3. The documented likenesses in the clothing, habits, and behaviors of the adult brothers suggest that genetic predispositions influence personality development.
   What does the author conclude based on the evidence?
4. These unexplained similarities in personality traits draw attention to the need for research to better understand the influence of genes on personality development.
   How does the article relate to other scholarship or a specific audience?

> **Relevance**
> Writing short summaries is especially relevant when reading sources for possible inclusion in a research paper later in the writing process. It reminds the reader/writer of the content of the source without having to reread the source.

Long summaries

The following guidelines may be more appropriate when writing a summary of a longer text. The summary should restate only the main points of a text without giving examples or details.

1. Follow these steps while reading:
   1. Highlight the thesis and topic sentence in each paragraph
   2. Highlight key points/key words/phrases
   3. Highlight the concluding sentence
   4. Outline each paragraph in the margin.
2. Note down the following:
   1. The source (author – first/last name, title, date of publication, volume number, publisher, URL, etc.)
   2. The main idea of the original (paraphrased)
   3. The major supporting points (in outline form)
   4. Major supporting explanations (e.g. reasons/causes or effects).

(Christine Bauer-Ramazani, 2006. Saint Michael's College. Used with permission)

Writing the summary

1. Organize your notes into an outline which includes main ideas and supporting points but no examples or details (e.g. dates, numbers, statistics).
2. Write an introductory paragraph that begins with an in-text citation of the source and the author as well as a reporting verb to introduce the main idea.
3. The main idea or argument needs to be included in the first sentence. Then mention the major aspects that are discussed in the article. For a multi-paragraph summary, discuss each supporting point in a separate paragraph. Introduce it in the first sentence (topic sentence).
4. Support your topic sentence with the necessary reasons or arguments raised by the author but do not include examples or details (e.g. dates, numbers, statistics).

5. In a longer summary, you may need to remind your reader that you are summarizing by using "summary reminder phrases," such as
   - The author goes on to say that …
   - The article/author further states that …
   - (Author's last name) also states/maintains/argues that …
   - (Author's last name) also believes that …
   - (Author's last name) concludes that…
6. Restate the article's conclusion in one sentence.
7. Give a full reference for the citation.

Below is a list of commonly used reporting verbs for writing a summary.

argue	state	refute the claim	suggest	criticize
claim	report	argue against	recommend	
contend	explain			
maintain	discuss			
insist	illustrate			

Practice: Summarizing an article

> Summarize an article you have been assigned to read in your program of study. Create a one to two paragraph summary of 9–15 sentences in all. Use the strategies given above while reading and writing. Remember to include the author, year, title, and publication.

Interviews

Summarizing interviews can be challenging and it is easy to overuse direct quotes. If the interview is in a form that is recoverable (e.g., a recording, transcript, published Questions & Answers), most format styles require the use of the reference format appropriate for the source in which the interview is available. Some examples are given below in the APA format, but other styles may require different formats.

1. In-text citation using a direct quotation from an interview:
   A close friend of the doctor reminded us that: "Doctor Jones always went the extra mile to help the sick" (J. Smith, personal communication, May 7, 2011).
2. In-text citation using a paraphrased material from an interview:
   A close friend of the doctor reminded us that Doctor Jones did much more than was expected to help people in poor health (J. Smith, personal communication, May 7, 2011).

> **Relevance**
> Interviews are important in primary research. Paraphrasing direct quotations from interviews is important when reporting findings in a case study.

Practice: Summarizing an interview

> Interview a friend, fellow student, or classmate about their writing. Ask them:
> > how much they write,
> > how often they write,
> > what kind of writing they do,
> > what kind of words are common to their discipline,
> > what is the main difference between the writing style of their discipline and the kind of writing they do.
>
> Write a four-sentence summary of the answers using the guidelines presented above.

C. AWARE: Writing

1. Writing a summary

Practice: Writing a summary

Below is an exercise to practice summarizing published interviews. Follow the guidelines.

> 1. Choose a famous person and listen to an interview with her/him.
> 2. Write a four-sentence summary of an interview with that person using the guidelines above.
> 3. Include a clear reference for the interview and an introduction to the person and why he/she is famous.
> 4. Incorporate one short quote and one paraphrase of the person's answers.
>
> You can choose any person you admire, but below are examples of websites that can help you locate interviews with distinguished individuals.
>
> The Dalai Lama <www.dalailama.com/messages>
> Nelson Mandela <https://atom.nelsonmandela.org>
> Martin Luther King <https://kinginstitute.stanford.edu/clayborne-carson/interviews>
> TED Ideas worth spreading <www.ted.com>

2. **AWARE: Revising**

Review the interview summary using the checklist below:

> Does your summary contain four sentences?
> Have you avoided copying sentences word for word?
> Does sentence 1 present only the information about the author, title, date, and a central assertion of the interview?
> Does sentence 2 describe how the main message is developed or supported?
> Does sentence 3 lay out the purpose of the interview ('in order to…')?
> Does sentence 4 indicate the audience for the article and its connection to other readings, news, events?

3. **AWARE: Editing**

Read your summary again for the purpose of editing. Answer the questions and edit as needed.

> Have you reported the quote and paraphrase according to the APA format?
> Have you used the appropriate level of formality?
> Have you used appropriate reporting verbs and avoided generic words such as "said"? Underline the verbs you have used.
> Have you used sentence fragments, comma splices or run-on sentences? If so, correct them according to the guidelines from Chapters 2, 3, and 6.

Chapter 9

Conducting research for a case study

Part I of the book taught you to develop effective expository essays by putting your own ideas into writing. It helped you master the building blocks of expository writing and a repertoire of strategies that apply to most academic writing tasks. The following chapters apply these concepts and strategies to conducting research and writing papers based on primary and secondary sources.

Chapter 9 begins the process of research writing by examining the case study genre. The case study method produces a close, in-depth, and detailed examination of a subject situated in a real world context. The chapter presents and demonstrates strategies for collecting, analyzing, organizing, and evaluating data based on primary sources. The chapter also presents strategies for developing a case study research question. By the end of the chapter you will have completed research for your case study and will be ready to write the final paper in Chapter 10.

Case studies have traditionally been used in disciplines such as law, business and medicine. They are used with increasing frequency in the social sciences, natural sciences, and health sciences. Conducting a case study adds depth, accuracy, and context to students' understanding of the topic. Equally important, a case study demonstrates students' ability to apply theoretical concepts to real world situations. Since case studies are gaining prominence as teaching and assessment tools in almost all academic fields, it is important to understand the principles and strategies for conducting this type of research.

This chapter will prepare students for writing a case study. Students will:

- examine the theory and methodology of conducting a case study,
- develop a research question to guide research,
- explore a variety of primary sources and research methods,
- conduct primary research and evaluate sources,
- organize data into an outline for the case study, and
- practice a variety of strategies that support the research process.

A. Examining the case study

The case study is based on qualitative research methods. As seen in Chapter 8, qualitative research explores the underlying reasons, factors, and motivations of a small sample of subjects. The case study method investigates the qualities that make a subject unique, remarkable, or interesting. It develops a more detailed picture of the subject and tells a more complete story than other research methods. The subject of a case study may be a person, an organization, a group, or a problem. By investigating a subject in its real world context and considering political, social, historical, or personal circumstances, case studies create a deep understanding of the subject. On the other hand, the narrow scope of a case study limits the generalizability of the findings to a larger population.

Case study research is used in many disciplines. Case study assignments at university tend to fall into two categories: analytic or problem-oriented. An analytic case study concentrates on collecting detailed information in order to produce a rich understanding of a subject. A problem-oriented case study focuses on uncovering and understanding the origins of a real world problem in order to propose viable solutions.

The case study you will conduct in these chapters is an analytic case study. An analytic case study may be descriptive or explanatory. The purpose of both is to uncover distinctive characteristics of the subject in a specific context. A descriptive case study investigates what is taking or took place while an explanatory case study investigates how or why something is taking or took place.

This chapter examines the process of writing a case study and guides you through the "Arranging-to-write" stage of a case study. In Chapter 10 you will write a draft of the case study using the preparation and research conducted in this chapter.

> **Relevance**
> Good writers employ a number of strategies at different stages of writing an essay. Using a strategy begins as a conscious effort and develops into an unconscious strategy that requires little thought.

1. Defining the case study assignment

The case study you will conduct in the next two chapters is an analytic case study of a single subject. Your investigation will use multiple sources of data to describe or explain the unique characteristics and qualities of your subject.

Description of the case study assignment

> Topic: **A Remarkable Person I Know**
> For example:
> - a family legend,
> - an overlooked hero,
> - an unrecognized community activist,
> - a personal mentor,
> - a quietly courageous friend.
>
> Length: 800 words (3–4 pages).
> Format: APA, Times New Roman,12 points, double spacing.
> Evidence should reference at least three primary sources.
> Evidence should include at least one short quotation and one paraphrase in the text.

2. The building blocks of the case study

There are many types of case studies and each has specific requirements. Depending on the topic and the scope of research, a case study can vary in length from a few paragraphs to 50 or more pages. Case studies cover a range of options with respect to subjects, sources, methods, and approaches to data analyses. Therefore, it is almost impossible to define a universal method or design for a case study. However, at a minimum, all case studies are based on the following basic building blocks:

- a subject,
- a research question,
- sources of data,
- data collection (methods and planning),
- data analysis (review, organization, evaluatation), and
- a written document that presents the case study.

The next sections will explain the process of choosing a subject, formulating a research question, and conducting research. The AWARE section of the chapter will lead you through the process of arranging to write your case study. The research that you conduct in this chapter will provide the data for writing your case study in Chapter 10.

3. Conducting research for a case study

Conducting research is not a linear process. This is especially true when working with the first three building blocks (subject, research question, and sources) for a case study. Formulating a research question is shaped by the accessibility of subjects and availability of data sources. All three elements need to align before research can begin.

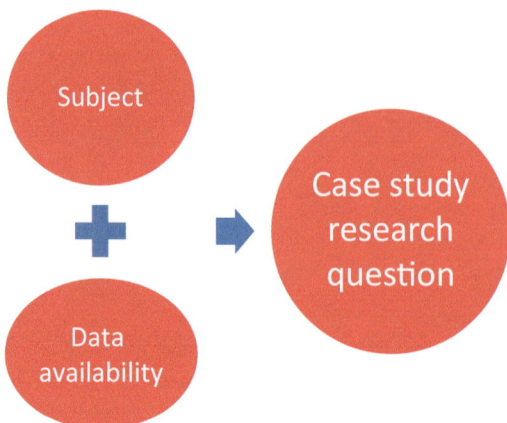

a. Select the subject/participants

Case studies can focus on a single participant or a small group of participants. The subject may be a person, an organization, a group, or a problem. Before selecting a subject, it is important to consider factors such as time and access to data. How much data are available, where the sources are located, and whether data can be accessed within the timeframe of a study influence a student's choice of subject.

John's research subject

Our example student, John, would like to investigate the qualities that led his deceased grandmother, Sarah Woodward, to become a successful business entrepreneur in the 1940s. She transformed a shoe factory that was ready to declare bankruptcy into a profitable company that was sold for millions of US dollars in 2012.

John must first consider what data are available. Can data sources such as family documents or business records, relatives who knew the grandmother, or public records be found? On the other hand, will people who knew his grandmother personally or professionally agree to participate in the study by providing an interview and supporting documents? Are there other sources of public data available that document the qualities of this person?

Informed consent

Informed consent is a formal written statement that explains the study, its purpose, the participants' role, and any procedures for obtaining data. It also explains whether the researcher will maintain the confidentiality of the participants. Both the researcher and the participants sign the form.

When investigating a living person or an operational program or institution, some sources of data require permission from the subject. You must always get permission from the person you want to use as a subject of your study. You should also ask the people you interview for permission to use the information they have provided. It is essential not to harm or compromise participants by revealing inappropriate information or information that can be traced back to them.

> *Reflection*
> *What are your institution's policies for gaining permission from subjects in a study? Where might you find these?*

b. *Define the research question*

Expository writing presents a thesis statement near the beginning of the essay and repeats it in the conclusion. In an essay assignment, the writer generally begins with sufficient knowledge of the topic to generate a working thesis. Because qualitative research is an open-ended process of discovery, the writer begins with little knowledge of what the investigation will find. Thus, the writer uses a research question, rather than a thesis statement, to guide the data collection.

Understanding research questions

A "research question" is the explicit statement of what the study will investigate. It is a question posed by the writer to define the direction and goal of his or her research. The research question provides a focus and sets boundaries for the topics that the researcher will explore in relation to the subject of the study. After sufficient research has been conducted, the research question can be reformulated into a working thesis.

John's research question

John's research question might ask:

> *What factors contributed to the success of my grandmother, Sarah Woodward, as a female business entrepreneur in England during the 1940s?*

John's thesis statement might say:

> *My grandmother's leadership, keen insight, and wartime economics propelled her to create a shoe empire during World War 2.*

A research question that is too narrow requires minimal research and is usually answered with simple facts. Thus, it does not create a rich understanding of the subject. On the other hand, a broad research question is generally beyond the scope of a university case study assignment since it requires collection and analysis of large amounts of data.

The characteristics of a viable research question include:

<u>Clarity</u>: the purpose of the research is easily understood without additional information.

<u>Focus</u>: the question is narrow enough to be answered within the scope of the study.

<u>Complexity</u>: the answer requires analysis and synthesis of multiple data sources. It cannot be answered with "yes" or "no" or factual information.

Strategies for writing effective research questions for a case study

The strategies below help in formulating effective case study research questions. They narrow and define the research topic and still leave room to explore different directions.

- Begin the question with *What or How*. These words reflect an open-minded stance to uncovering new ideas.
- Define the participants and the setting associated with the study.
- Focus on a single concept as a starting point. While research often uncovers unexpected information that warrants further investigation later, always begin with a defined focus.
- Use verbs such as "describe," "report," "assess," "determine," "identify," "affect," "relate," or verb phases such as "associated with" in the question. The verbs reflect the exploratory nature of case study research.

The examples below show how research questions can be narrowed and defined.

Case study research questions

Broad case question	Revised case study questions
John's original question:	John's revised question:
What made my grandmother a remarkable business woman?	What factors contributed to the success of my grandmother, Sarah Woodward, as a female business entrepreneur in England during the 1940s?
Why do students abuse alcohol at this University?	What factors contribute to alcohol abuse among honor students at this University?
How does pay affect employee productivity at a small company?	How did a pay increase affect the productivity of the billing department supervisor at Megaphone company?
How do patients rate care in the cardiac unit of a large hospital?	What aspects of post-surgery care do patients report as most beneficial at Miracle Hospital?
How do trade tariffs affect orange growers in Israel?	What is the impact of trade tariffs on family-owned orange farms in Israel?

Reflection
What are the advantages and disadvantages of using a thesis statement during the research stages of a case study? What do you see as the advantages/disadvantages of using a research question at the beginning of a study?

Practice: Identifying the elements of an effective case study research question

Analyze the research questions in the chart below. Identify the elements of an effective case study question.

Case study research question	How/What	Single concept	Verbs	Subject/participant	Setting
Example What factors contributed to the success of my grandmother, Sarah Woodward, as a female business entrepreneur in England during the 1940s?	What	Success as a business woman	Contribute	Grand-mother	England 1940s
What factors contribute to alcohol abuse among honors students at Superior University?					
How did a pay raise affect the productivity of the billing department supervisor at Megaphone company?					
What aspects of post-surgery care do patients report as most beneficial at Miracle Hospital?					
What is the impact of trade tariffs on family owned orange farms in Israel?					

c. Identify primary data sources

Qualitative researchers collect data using an array of methods including interviews, observation, focus groups, surveys, and document review. A case study relies on multiple primary sources and a variety of methods to create a holistic description of the subject in its original context.

Data sources and collection methods must be carefully planned in advance. The writer must identify the availability of potential sources and the feasibility of gathering the data within a given time frame in order to determine if the subject and research questions are viable. New sources will likely surface during the research process which may be incorporated later.

As discussed in Chapter 8, primary sources are original records created at the time an event occurred. Primary sources include letters, manuscripts, diaries, journals, speeches, interviews, memoirs, photographs, observations, artifacts, audio recordings, and movies or video recordings as well as archival records produced by government agencies, businesses, and organizations. Many scholars consider newspapers produced at the time of an event as primary sources; however, other scholars view newspapers as secondary sources since reporters usually write about events that happened to someone else. The examples below distinguish primary from secondary sources.

Primary source	Secondary source
Mahatma Gandhi's autobiography, *The Story of My Experiments with Truth,* is a primary source. The information comes directly from first-hand recollections of the events. It was written in the time frame of Mahatma Gandhi's life.	Louis Fischer's book, *The Life of Mahatma Gandhi,* is a secondary source. It provides a second hand account of events and was written decades after Gandhi's death.
Data from research polls are considered primary data, because the information is collected directly from sources.	An expert's comments on the significance of the data are a secondary source. The comments provide one person's analysis of the data.
A section of text or a quotation from an original work of literature is a primary source in a literary analysis. It reproduces the author's original words.	An interpretation of the quote or literary criticism is a secondary source. It gives the commentator's opinion about the original words.

Practice: *Identifying primary sources in context*

Choose a famous non-living person whom you admire. Find examples of first-hand information about that person from primary sources of the types below.
- A quotation from a newspaper article reporting an event involving the person.
- An original written paragraph or a transcription of part of an interview given by the person.
- Two to three sentences reporting archival data or other statistics.

d. *Collect the data*

Researchers need to collect the data that are most relevant to their research questions and carefully record and document the information for later analysis. Rushing into data collection without a formalized plan can lead to wasted time and gaps in the data. After accessible and credible data sources have been identified, the researcher needs a formal plan for gathering the data. While plans need to be flexible, they are essential in keeping the research on track. A plan helps the researcher prioritize, create a timeline, and ensure that all necessary resources are available.

Strategies for planning data collection

There is no single way to create a data collection plan. Each researcher develops a document that reflects the needs of his or her study. Creating a data collection guide is a strategy for planning and prioritizing the data collection process. The data collection guide lists the potential sources, accessibility, and additional required resources. The format aids the researcher in confirming whether there is sufficient diversity of data sources and methods. John created a data collection guide to track an array of primary sources for information about his grandmother and to identify necessary resources prior to collection.

John's data collection guide

Research Question: What factors contributed to the success of my grandmother, Sarah Woodward, as a female business entrepreneur in England during the 1940s?				
Data source	Method of collection	Accessibility	Resources needed	Time range
Aunt Catherine	Interview	Phone	Prepare questions; video recorder	Present
Researcher's mother	Interview	In person	Prepare questions; video recorder	Present
Sarah Woodward's (SW) journals	Document review	Aunt Catherine	Photocopies of original journal	1940–1952
Newspapers	Document review	Central library	Microfiche reader; online	1942–1946
Grandmother's correspondence	Document review	Company archives Permission from Board of Directors	Photocopies of documents	1940–1948
Labor and economic statistics	Records analysis	Online, registration required	Register for access to site	1940–1948

Methods of data collection
Below are strategies for collecting data from three of the most commonly used primary sources in student case study papers.

Documents and archival records
Document review can serve as the main source of data or can support and strengthen other sources. It can also help to situate the subject in the socio-historical context. Documents can fill in details that a participant may not remember.

It is important to determine whether there is time and opportunity to locate and access documents. Specifying criteria or patterns prior to examining the sources will make the search more efficient. The steps below will guide the process of reviewing documents.

1. Create a list of documents to explore.
2. Decide what types of content to look for.
3. Gather relevant documents.
4. Make copies of originals for annotation.
5. Develop a plan to organize and document relevant data.
6. Consider ethical issues such as confidentiality.
7. Ask questions about document credibility and bias (e.g., Who produced the document? Why? When? What type of data?).

Interviews
Interviews play a prominent role in case study research because they are a window into the thought, motivations, and interpretations of the subjects and participants. Before conducting an interview, plan to obtain the required permissions or informed consent and plan the documentation process.

Audio or video recordings are the most accurate way to document an interview but written notes may be the only option. Regardless, there must be a formal record of the interview if it is to be used as evidence. Transcribe relevant portions of audio or video recording into a written document for analysis.

Good interviewers recognize that certain types of questions are more likely to elicit meaningful responses and deepen understanding of the subject. Closed or structured questions following an interview guide fall at one end of the continuum. In this type of interview, the researcher asks a set of questions that are prepared prior to the interview. Structured interviews focus on gathering specific types of information.

Unstructured or open-ended interviews fall at the opposite end of the continuum. In this type of interview, the researcher has a focus and goal that guides the discussion, but questions tend to be open-ended. One of the purposes of unstructured interviews is to get the interviewees to express themselves freely.

Below are some strategies for conducting interviews that will yield good data.

- Prepare clear and concise questions focused on your research question.
- Avoid *Yes/No* questions. Prepare questions that encourage the interviewee to elaborate.
- Avoid bias in questioning. Do not preface questions with statements such as *"Don't you agree… or "Isn't it the case that…"*. Such statements suggest that the researcher is looking for a response which conforms to an established idea.
- Be ready to conduct a second, or third, follow up interview if needed to clarify points.

Observations

Observations are valid data when they are systematically recorded in a permanent record. Always record the subject, date, time, and duration of each observation in an observation log. The log provides a useful index for accessing observation data.

The traditional way to document observation data is to record what you observe though your five senses in written field notes. Field notes can be recorded via traditional pen-and paper notes or through electronic media. Electronic recording methods such as video and audio are valuable and accurate records; however, any data that you use as evidence in your paper must be transcribed into a written record for analysis.

Beware of the *Observer's Paradox*. The *Observer's Paradox* refers to the effect that observations have on the people being observed. Being observed may influence the subject's behavior in some way.

Documenting sources during data collection

It is very important to document all resources during collection. Going back to find sources later while finalizing the reference list is very time consuming, especially when weeks or months have passed since they were collected and analyzed. It also leads to inaccuracies.

Below is a list of some of the ways to document the sources for inclusion in the paper and the reference page:

- Index cards – while reading, write the bibliographical entry on one side of the card and notes, comments, quotes, paraphrases on the other side.
- Do the same using electronic index cards.
- Use an electronic management program that automatically formats the citation according to the formatting style assigned such as APA, Chicago, MLA or another format style as directed by the instructor.

e. *Analyze the data*

Information which has not been analyzed or interpreted is raw data. The researcher needs to go through a process of analysis to convert raw data into usable evidence. Depending on the type of study and the quantity of data, the process may require multiple stages of review and analysis.

Analyzing data for a basic case study typically uses a three stage process:

1. Review sources and identify data related to the research question by finding recurring themes in the data.
2. Organize and code the data thematically.
3. Evaluate the relevance as well as the quantity/quality of data for each theme.

The sections below examine and practice basic strategies for analyzing raw data.

Strategies for reviewing data

The initial review of the data focuses on identifying any information that is of potential use in answering the research question. The initial review provides a broad holistic view of the available data. As you read through each data source, look for any facts, examples, statistics, or comments that relate to the research question. Mark the data by underlining, circling, highlighting, adding a sticky note, or creating written notes to signal any data that may provide insight into the research question.

Some suggestions for reviewing common data sources are discussed below. Consult online sources or research textbooks for guidelines for other sources of data.

There is no one way to analyze documents, but the analysis should be guided by the research question. Below are some strategies for reviewing documents:

- Highlight or annotate any information related to the research question in the document.
- Examine the document's form, letterhead, paper, handwriting or typing. What do they reflect about the life and times of the subject?
- What evidence in the document helps you understand why it was written?
- Note what the document tells you about your subject and life at the time it was created.
- Is there a quote that illuminates the research question?
- Note any questions that arise from the examination of the document.
- Record the type of document, where it was found, and the author.

Observations

Read through observation notes or a transcript of the video observation. Highlight and note any concepts or ideas that relate to the research question.

Photographs
Study the image for several minutes. If the photo is large, cover sections with a piece of paper and examine each part in detail. If you are working with a photocopy, highlight relevant information. Create a record of:

1. The identity of people, objects, place, time, or activities.
2. Anything that needs to be identified.
3. Anything that appears relevant.

Audio visual materials
The initial analysis will determine if there are any data related to the research question. If it contains useful data, those sections of the audio or video will need to be transcribed into a document for analysis. As you review the transcript of the recording, take notes on the following:

1. Where the recording was found and what led you to this data source.
2. Who speaks in the recording.
3. The date, time, place, and audience.
4. Facts or quotes that reveal anything about the life and times of your subject.
5. Facts or quotes that relate to the research question.

Strategies for organizing the data
The first review of sources will produce a pool of potential data that needs to be sorted and classified as a basis for analysis. There are many ways to organize qualitative data. Each researcher chooses an approach based on the scope of the study and the type of data.

The next sections examine two basic strategies for organizing qualitative data. These strategies will serve as the methods of analysis for your case study data:

- Coding data thematically and creating an index.
- Presenting data in a thematic order.

Coding the data
Coding is a basic strategy for sorting disparate sources into categories. A code is a shorthand notation (word, letter, or symbol) used as a label for any data related to a specific concept or topic. Data labeled with the same code are grouped together for analysis. Data gathered from all sources, including all transcripts, documents, observations, notes, memos, and visual evidence need to be reviewed and coded.

Coding helps the researcher to identify repeating patterns and interpret what the data say about the research question. There are many approaches to coding and researchers often use multiple cycles of coding to refine the data and understand them more deeply. The case study in this book uses thematic coding as the principal method of data analysis.

Thematic coding, also known as topic coding, categorizes data according to themes. A theme, and its corresponding code, is created when the researcher notices that multiple data sources say something similar. Some patterns that suggest a theme are:

- points that are mentioned repeatedly across the data;
- information that suggests unique circumstances, standards, or procedures;
- points that contradict or support one another;
- explicit connections (among persons, sites, documents, procedures, objects, etc.);
- implied connections (among persons, sites, documents, procedures, objects, etc.).

Follow the guidelines below to code data thematically:

1. After the <u>first review of the data</u>, find any data that you marked. Does it relate to any other data? Are there any patterns or relationships that suggest a theme?
2. Create a code for any themes that you notice. Use a word, symbol, or letters that remind you of the theme. Keep a list of the codes.
3. Read through all of the data <u>a second time.</u> Whenever you notice data that relates to a theme, color-code it with a highlighter or sticky note. Use one color to highlight all data related to the same code.
4. Create additional codes for any new themes that you identify during the review.
5. Transfer themes and codes into a code index (see next section).

Creating a code index

A code index is a table where the researcher records the themes and codes used in data analysis. Before constructing a code index, read through the data a third time. Make any necessary changes, additions, or deletions in the codes. Copy the themes and codes into a simple table.

John's code index

John reviewed data from interviews, family documents, newspapers, company records. As he reviewed his data, he looked for patterns and connections in the data. Several potential themes emerged. For example, John noted repeated references to the lack of professional opportunities for women before WW2. Each time data related to this theme appeared, John highlighted it in a designated color. As John continued his review, he identified six themes. He created codes for each and color-coded his data. John recorded his themes and code in an index where he could reference them easily.

Theme	Code
Limited opportunities for women before WW2	Limited opportunities.
New leadership opportunities for women during WW2	New opportunities.
Support of friends and colleagues	Support
Family Life	Family
New manufacturing opportunities arose during WW2	Manufacturing opportunities
Created profitable business through innovation	Innovation

A thematic data table

Coded data need to be organized into a format where they can be referenced and evaluated. A thematic data table arranges the sources in a visual framework that creates an overview of all of the themes and supporting data. The table allows the researcher to track and evaluate the data.

Constructing a thematic data table

Before constructing the data table, read through the data a third time. Make any necessary changes, additions, or deletions in the codes.

1. Create a table with two columns and multiple rows.
2. In the left-hand column, record a theme and code in each row.
3. In the right-hand column, record data concepts and sources that correspond to each theme/code.
4. Create additional themes/codes if they emerge during the review.

Evaluating the potential of themes and data sources

1. Analyze each theme. Does it illuminate the research question in some way?
2. Eliminate themes/categories that do not address the research question directly.

John's thematic data table

John reviewed data from interviews, family documents, newspapers, company records, and Sarah Woodward's (SW) journal. After multiple data reviews and amendments to his coding, John was ready to organize. He followed the steps outlined below:

1. He created a table with themes and codes in the left hand column.
2. He read through his data a fourth time. When he found data marked with the code, he recorded each concept and its source in the corresponding right hand.
3. John analyzed each theme to determine whether it provided insight into the research question.
4. As John evaluated his themes, he determined that the family theme did not provide any insights into the research question. He eliminated it as a data source for the case study.
5. Based on his analysis, John decided to continue to develop the remaining five themes to explain his grandmother's success.

Research Question: What factors contributed to the success of my grandmother, Sarah Woodward, as a female business entrepreneur in England during the 1940s?	
Theme	**Data concepts and sources**
New manufacturing opportunities during WW2 *Manufact op*	New markets (*The Daily Times*, 1940–1942) Synthetic materials available (letter, advertising brochure) Women enter workforce Shortage of military boots (*Weekly Standard*, *Daily Times*, 1940–1942, SW journal)
Family life *Family*	Happy marriage (letters) 4 children Husband "Charlie" at war (military records) Husband killed in action
Limited opportunities for women before the war *Limited op*	Low education for women (*Office for National Statistics*) Few job ads for women before the war (*Weekly Standard*, 1940) Employment Statistics (Census, 1939)
New leadership opportunities for women during WW2 *New op*	Labor shortages, ads for women (*Weekly Standard*, 1938–1943) "She worked hard and became a leader on a production line" (interview with aunt, personal letters) Factory supervisor went to navy; SW replaced him (company records, SW journal) Shortage leather limited shoe production; SW looked for alternative sources (interview with mother, company letters) Company in debt (company records, interview with aunt)
Support of friends and colleagues *Support*	Magda helped at the factory (interview with mother) Comments on friends' help (SW journal)
Innovation created profitable business *Innovation*	New manufacturing techniques (memos, training manual) Hired and trained women (personnel records) Changed to manufacturing military boots (production inventory, 1943–46) Shift to synthetic leather (purchase orders, 1943–1946)

Strategies for evaluating the data

In addition to determining whether the themes relate directly to the research question, the writer needs to evaluate whether there is sufficient quality and quantity of evidence for each theme. Themes with weak or insufficient data and those that do not address the research question directly must be eliminated, no matter how interesting they are.

Triangulation

As the term implies, triangulation refers to the use of at least three sources of data to establish the credibility of a research finding. Presenting data from a single source, such as an interview with one person, limits credibility. A combination of data from multiple participants or sources such as observations, interviews, historical records, newspaper articles, or other primary sources strengthens the researcher's interpretation. By using multiple data collection methods in the case study, the writer is able to triangulate data in order to strengthen the research findings and conclusions.

Evidence evaluation matrix

An evidence evaluation matrix is a strategy used to evaluate the number of and types of data sources supporting each theme. When the matrix is completed, the number and variety of sources for each is apparent. Themes with fewer than three sources are eliminated. Alternately, the writer can conduct more research to see if additional sources are available for a theme.

To use an evidence evaluation matrix to triangulate data for a case study:

1. Create a table with a column for each theme and at least five rows.
2. Enter the sources from the data table in the corresponding column.
3. Evaluate the number and variety of sources.
4. Eliminate themes that contain fewer than three sources, or conduct additional research.

John's evidence evaluation matrix

John created a matrix with a column for each of the five themes in his data table. Referring to his data table, he will list the corresponding concepts and data sources below each theme. When the table is completed, John will evaluate the data. If a theme has fewer than three sources of data, he will eliminate it from his final paper or conduct additional research.

Research Question: What factors contributed to the unusual success of my grandmother, Sarah Woodward, as a female business entrepreneur during the 1940s?				
Limited opportunities for women before WW2	New manufacturing opportunities during WW2	Support of friends and colleagues	New leadership opportunities for women during WW2	Innovation created profitable business
Low education for women (Office for National Statistics).				
Few job ads for women before the war (Weekly Standard, 1940)				
Employment Statistics (Census, 1939)				

Practice: Data triangulation

1. Complete the evidence evaluation matrix above by listing the data concepts and sources from John's thematic data table above.
2. Evaluate the number and variety of sources.
3. Eliminate any themes that contain fewer than three data sources.

Reflection
Review the themes in the matrix above. Do they provide any insights into the research question? Does John have enough information to create a thesis statement?

f. Create an outline for the case study

With the labor intensive and time consuming process of data collection and analysis complete, the writer is ready to create an outline to guide writing the first draft. One option is to use the two-column format from previous chapters. Another is to use a spider map.

Two-column format
To use the two column format, first determine the order of presentation of the themes from the final data table. There are many ways to organize the data in a case study. Three basic methods are:

A. Narrative account. Data themes are arranged in the order in which they took place. This allows the writer to tell a story.
B. Dramatic presentation. Data is arranged so that the themes with greatest impact are presented last. This allows the writer to emphasize the most powerful point.
C. Most important to least important. The most important themes are presented first and the minor themes follow in order of importance. This helps engage the reader from the start.

Spider map
Information can also be organized using a spider map. The spider map is useful if the writer is unsure of the order of presentation. Visualizing the information in this way can help the writer decide what order to use.

John's outline
As John began to prepare his outline, he was unsure of how to order the data presentation. He decided to begin his draft with a spider map.

Chapter 9. Conducting research for a case study   199

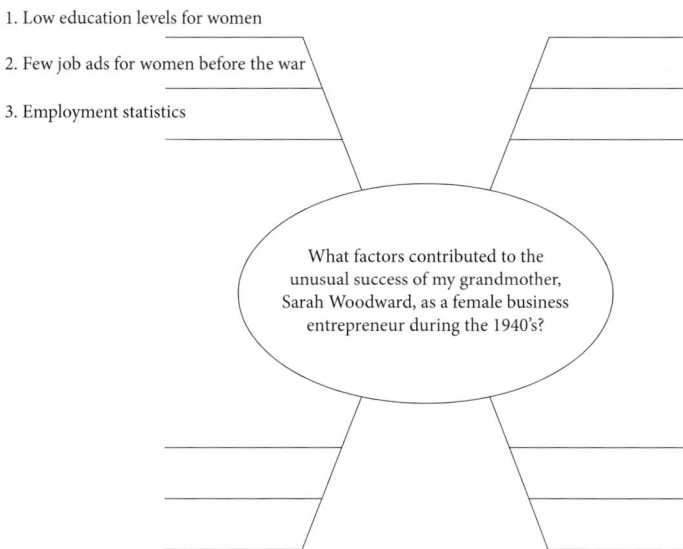

Practice: *Organizing data for the outline*

1. Complete the spider map for John Woodward's case study.
2. When the map is complete, reflect on the themes.
3. Recommend an order of presentation for John's themes.
4. Explain why you make this recommendation.

B. AWARE: Writing a case study

The case study assignment is described above. Review the assignment before continuing.

1. Arranging to write a case study

In arranging to write your case study, you will apply the principles and strategies from the previous sections. Before you begin each of the tasks below, review the corresponding information in the pages above.

a. *Choosing the subject for the case study*

The subject for the case study assignment is a person who is remarkable or heroic in some way. The individual you choose must be known to you personally. It may be someone in your present life, someone from your family history, or someone who is a local legend. Do not choose a famous person for your subject. Instead focus on an ordinary person whose heroic qualities or remarkable accomplishments deserve recognition. Your story will show what makes this person unique.

The research paper you will develop in the final chapters of this book will use secondary sources to create a socio-historical context for the subject of this case study. Therefore, the subject of your case study should have some relevance to the events, trends, or moods of the times.

When choosing a subject, consider whether data is available and accessible. As we saw in the previous section, data collection can include interviewing the subject and/or his or her family and friends, observing the subject in a relevant setting, and/or consulting artifacts such as documents, public records, photographs, films, letters, and business records that reflect the life of the person. Places and objects important to the person may also be sources of information. These could be favorite vacation places, private letters, family stories, photo albums, social media (Facebook, Twitter, etc.), blogs, audio or video recordings, or other artifacts.

Below are some guidelines for choosing the remarkable person who will become the subject of your study.

> **Relevance**
> The topic of this research was chosen because familiar content enables the writer to focus on writing strategies and clarifying his or her message.

Practice: Generating ideas for a subject of the study

> Write down some thoughts on the questions below.
> 1. Most families have stories about family members that are passed down from generation to generation. Start with those stories. Could any of these personal stories suggest a subject for the study?
> 2. Are there any stories about people from the area/town/neighborhood where you, or people you know, live or lived at one time?
> 3. Is there a period of time that was remarkable for some reason and during which people you know lived?
> 4. What occupations have family members or people known to you had? Is there one that stands out for some reason?
> 5. Did someone you know do something extraordinary like save a life, make life changes that took courage, or improve their community?
> 6. Has someone you know done something unconventional and forward-thinking for their time?
>
> Once you have done this, list any of the interesting persons you can think of and what makes them possible subjects for the assignment. Hopefully, this will result in finding more than one possible candidate.
> Keep in mind that there should be enough material for an 800-word case study (3–4 pages).

Practice: Focused free writing

> If you have chosen your subject, or are considering more than one, use the following questions to guide your final decision.
>
> 1. What do I know about this person? What is the source of my information? Is it a person, a letter, a family story? Is the source reliable? Is the information accurate?
> 2. What further information is needed?
> 3. How, where, and when can this particular information be found?
> 4. Who can be interviewed or observed?
> 5. What do I hope to learn from the research?

Reflection
Based on your answers to the questions above, think about whether the candidate and his or her experiences fit the assignment. How does the candidate's personal story reflect the social, political, economic, and historic contexts in which it took place?

Practice: Identifying the subject of the case study

> The subject of my study is:
> What makes the person remarkable?

b. Formulating a research question

Now that you have chosen a subject for the case study, you need a research question to guide your data collection. During the writing phase, the research question will be reformulated into a thesis statement.

Practice: Generating ideas for a research question

> Use your preferred strategy to generate ideas (mapping, listing, clustering, etc.) about a research question.
>
> 1. List some of the specific aspects of the person's life that are worthy of exploration. Can the topic be broken down into parts that are suitable for research?
> 2. What kind of data is needed? Are the sources accessible? Where?
> 3. Is there enough material for 3–4 pages?
> 4. What questions do you have about the person's life or accomplishments?

Practice: Writing the research question

1. Begin the question with *What* or *How*. These words reflect an open-minded stance to uncovering new ideas.
2. Define the participants and the setting associated with the study.
3. Focus on a single concept as a starting point. While research often uncovers unexpected information that warrants further investigation later, always begin with a defined focus.
4. Use non-directional verbs such as "describe," "report," "assess," "determine," "identify," "affect," "relate," or verb phases such as "associated with" in the question.

Write your research question here:

Reflection
What is the purpose of a research question? Think about a time when you started to write a paper without really knowing what you were going to write about. How did that go? How will your research question guide your research and make it more focused and deliberate?

c. Planning to collect primary data

Remember that the qualitative research process is unpredictable, especially in the early stages when you choose your subject, consider your resources, and collect data. In planning for data collection, think about the availability and accessibility of two types of primary sources: existing data sources and primary data sources that you will collect yourself.

Existing sources

In planning your data collection, consider whether any of the following existing sources can provide information on your subject:

- Recorded or transcribed interviews with people who have first-hand knowledge of the subject of the research.
- Recorded or transcribed interviews with people who lived during a particular time period.
- Videos, films, documentaries.
- Personal correspondence such as journals, diaries, and letters.
- Newspaper and magazine articles with factual accounts written at the time of the event.
- Photographs, maps, postcards, posters produced during the period of the event.
- Speeches which have been recorded or transcribed.
- Government records and data (census, taxes, birth, death, marriage, military).

Data you will collect
There are other sources which you will need to collect yourself. These include:
- interviews with the subject,
- interviews with people who know the subject,
- observations of the subject engaged in a certain activity.

Practice: *Creating your data collection guide*

> Based on your assessment of the existing and new data sources you want to include in your study, fill in the following matrix with as much information as you can.
>
> Your case study data collection guide
>
> Your research question:
>
> | Data source | Method of collection | Accessibility | Resources needed | Time range |
> |---|---|---|---|---|
> | | | | | |

d. Analyzing the data

Your data analysis will go through three stages:

- reviewing sources and identifying data related to the research question,
- coding and organizing the data thematically,
- evaluating the relevance as well as the quantity/quality of data for each theme.

Transfer themes and codes to a code index. Before constructing the data table, read through the data again. Make any changes, additions, or deletions in the codes.

e. Organizing the data

Practice: *Record your themes and codes in a code index*

Case Study Data Collection Guide	
Theme	Code

Organize your coded data in a thematic table
1. Create a table with two columns and multiple rows.
2. In the left-hand column, record a theme and code in each row.
3. In the right-hand column, record data concepts and sources that correspond to each theme/code.
4. Create additional themes/codes if they emerge during the review.
5. Analyze each theme. Does it contribute to understanding the research question in some way?
6. Eliminate themes/categories that do not address the research question or those with weak data.

Practice: Construct a data table

Case Study Thematic Data Table
Your research question:

Theme	Data concepts and sources

Evaluate the data
Now that you have coded and organized your data, you need to ensure that you have adequate credible data to support each theme. You may decide that you have too much data and eliminate the weakest theme. You may decide that that there is insufficient data for one of the themes and decide to conduct more research. All researchers uncover far more data than they can use, and all find it hard to discard data that has taken so much time and effort to find, code, and organize. However, your paper will be less credible if you include themes with weak or insufficient data, no matter how interesting the information may be.

(a) Triangulation
Because you have gathered data from multiple sources using a variety of methods, you have a strong pool of data. Triangulation will ensure that each of your themes has sufficient number and variety of sources for each theme.

Chapter 9. Conducting research for a case study

(b) Evidence evaluation matrix
Create an evidence evaluation matrix to triangulate the data for a case study. Use the chart below. Enter the sources from the data table in the corresponding column. Evaluate the number and variety of sources. Eliminate themes that contain fewer than three sources, or conduct additional research.

Practice: Create an evidence evaluation matrix

Case study evidence matrix				
Research question:				
Theme 1	Theme 2	Theme 3	Theme 4	Theme 5

Prepare to outline the case study
Consider the order in which you will present your themes. Choose the order that best reflects the story you want to tell about your remarkable person. Use either <u>narrative account</u>, <u>dramatic presentation</u>, or order from <u>most to least important</u>.

Create an outline for the case study
Using any of the outline formats from previous chapters and sections, create an outline for your essay. The spider map presented earlier is included below.

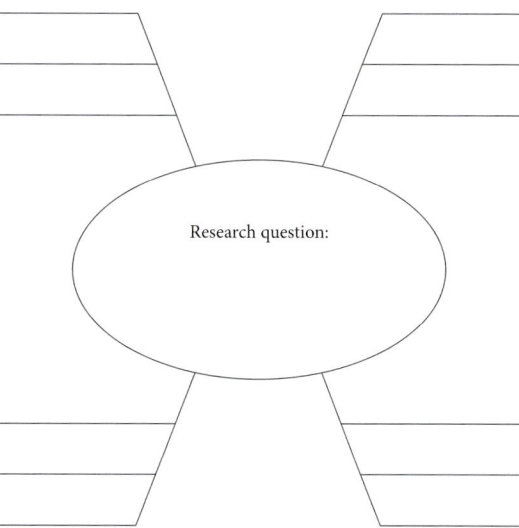

Chapter 10

Writing the case study

Chapter 9 led you through the Arranging-to-write phase of the case study. It examined principles and strategies for formulating a research question, conducting research, analyzing data, and creating an outline for the case study. In this chapter, students will write the final case study document. Students will complete the Writing, Assessing, Revising, and Editing stages of AWARE to produce a case study research paper.

In this chapter students will:

- reformulate the research question into a working thesis statement,
- examine the principles and practice strategies for presenting evidence,
- examine the use of in-text citations,
- write the body of the case study,
- write the introduction and conclusion.

A. Writing the case study

The same principles and strategies used in writing the body of an expository essay apply to the case study paper. The data, organized thematically, will be developed into body paragraphs and will provide evidence to support a thesis statement. While the process of planning the expository essays began with a thesis statement, the case study used a research question to guide data collection and analysis. Writing the case study will begin with reformulating the research question into a thesis statement based on the themes in the case study outline. The strategy of writing the introduction and conclusion after the body paragraphs have been drafted also applies to research papers.

The type of evidence used in the case study differs from the essays in Part I of the book. Whereas the essays presented evidence from your own experience and knowledge base, the case study answers a question using primary data from other people, institutions, or documents. These sources need to be documented and the ideas attributed to their original sources. This chapter will examine how to provide proper citation for primary sources in the body paragraphs. The use and citation of secondary sources will be presented in Chapter 11.

1. From research question to thesis statement

Both thesis statements and research questions are used to define the purpose and direction of an academic writing task. A thesis statement presents the topic and the point of view the writer will develop, whereas a research question defines the direction and parameters the research will take.

Thesis statements are generally used in student papers, while research questions are used in major research papers. Your case study began with a research question because not enough information was available about the subject to create a thesis statement. Now, the themes developed through research and data analysis provide the information necessary to reformulate the research question into a working thesis statement. Research is a process of discovery. The working thesis statement may change as new relationships come to light through analysis or if additional research provides new or expanded information. Writers update their working thesis statement frequently during the writing process as they learn more about their topic.

A thesis statement expresses in one sentence the point and purpose of your case study. It will present the subject (a remarkable person) and point of view (the qualities that make this person remarkable). The point of view signals to the reader what type of information you will present about your subject. The thesis statement defines and limits the scope of evidence you will present to show the reader why your subject is/was remarkable. The thesis:

- determines content and structure of the case study,
- serves as guide that helps the reader focus on key ideas,
- states the subject + a clear point of view about the subject, and
- is usually in the introductory paragraph.

The thesis statement for the case study is actually an answer to the research question that guided the study. John's research looked for answers to explain what made his grandmother a successful business entrepreneur. His thesis statement will give John's point of view about his grandmother's success based on his research. The case study will present primary data as evidence to validate John's point of view about his grandmother.

Reformulating John's research question into a thesis statement

> Broad Topic: A Remarkable Person I Know
>
> **John's research question:** What factors contributed to the success of my grandmother, Sarah Woodward, as a female business entrepreneur during the 1940s?
>
> John's thesis statement will answer his research question. To create a thesis statement that reflects his knowledge of the subject, John answered these questions:

> 1. Who is the subject of the case study? Sarah Woodward, my grandmother.
> 2. What themes have I developed in my outline that demonstrates unique qualities?
>
> John identified four themes that answer the questions through his data collection and analysis:
>
> a. Limited opportunities for women prior to WW2
> b. New manufacturing opportunities during WW2
> c. New opportunities for women in leadership during WW2
> d. Innovation in the factory.
>
> 3. How do these themes relate? John found that these data connected his grandmother's success to *two special qualities*: (a) ability to innovate and respond to emerging opportunities, and (2) insightful leadership that brought out the best in people. John will present evidence to support his point of view in his paper. John wrote the following working thesis for his case study.
>
> **John's working thesis statement:** By turning a failing factory into a thriving business with innovative ideas and insightful leadership, Sarah Woodward's remarkable entrepreneurship demonstrated that women were as capable as men.

John's thesis statement presents:

a.	The subject:	Sarah Woodward
b.	The point of view:	Turning a failing factory into a thriving business with innovative ideas and insightful leadership demonstrated remarkable entrepreneurship and showed that women were as capable as men.

2. Presenting case study research

The content of the case study must validate the thesis statement by presenting convincing evidence in the body paragraphs. Evidence, as we saw in previous chapters, is data that has been analyzed and organized to answer a question. In the Arranging-to-write phase of AWARE, you analyzed and organized data into several themes. These themes will serve as the evidence for your thesis statement.

In presenting evidence, novice academic writers sometimes mistakenly believe that reworded, paraphrased, or summarized material does not require citation. In fact, original ideas or expressions of any kind require full attribution regardless of how they have been modified. Plagiarism includes the failure to provide citations when reproducing ideas by changing wording, rewriting, paraphrasing, or summarizing the original work. Always provide citations for information from any source, including web pages, books, songs, films, personal correspondence, interviews, articles, and artworks, to the creator. Incorporating the ideas from a primary or secondary source in a paper without crediting the original author is plagiarism. Whether intentional or unintentional, plagiarism is a serious breach of academic honesty and may result in serious consequences.

The outline developed in the Arranging-to-write phase serves as your guide for drafting the body of the case study. Most writers find that first drafts reveal the need to make changes in content, focus, or organization as they write or revise during the revising stage. As you write, you may need to refocus your themes, find additional data, or make other changes.

John's final case study outline was developed by analyzing and organizing data into four themes supported by multiple sources of data. The variety and number of sources create convincing evidence for each theme. In turn, individual themes work together to create convincing evidence for his thesis statement.

John's final outline

John's working thesis statement:

By turning a failing factory into a thriving business with innovative ideas and insightful leadership, Sarah Woodward's remarkable entrepreneurship demonstrated that women were as capable as men.

Theme	Data concepts and sources
Limited opportunities for women before the war Limited op	Low education for women (Office for National Statistics) Few job ads for women before the war (Weekly Standard, 1940) Employment Statistics (Census, 1939)
New leadership opportunities for women during WW2 New op	Labor shortages, ads for women (Weekly Standard, 1938–1943) "She worked hard and became leader on production line" (interview aunt, personal letters) Factory supervisor went to navy; SW replaced him (company records, SW journal) Shortage leather limited shoe production; SW looked for alternative sources (interview with mother, company letters) Company in debt (company records, interview with aunt)
New manufacturing opportunities during WW2 Manufact op	New markets (The Daily Times, 1940–1942) Synthetic materials available (letter, advertising brochure) Women enter workforce Shortage of military boots (Weekly Standard, Daily Times, 1940–1942; SW journal)
Innovation created profitable business Innovation	New manufacturing techniques (memos, training manual) Hired and trained women (personnel records) Changed to manufacturing military boots (production inventory, 1943–46) Shift to synthetic leather (purchase orders, 1943–1946)

Four principles guide the drafting of the body paragraphs of the case study. These are:
1. Present evidence thematically.
2. Report primary research in the past tense.
3. Build cohesion.
4. Include in-text citations for all primary and secondary data sources.

a. *Present evidence thematically*

The research for this case study produced a large quantity of data which was analyzed and organized thematically. Because of the amount of data involved and the need to provide sufficient evidence to create a deep and close understanding of the subject, most themes are likely to require several paragraphs to develop fully. Therefore, within each theme, the data needs to be organized and presented in a series of paragraphs.

One way to organize the material into paragraphs is to group the data into sub-themes or subtopics. For example, one of the themes in John's final outline is "New leadership opportunities for women during WW2". It includes the subthemes of opportunities for women to access jobs that were previously unavailable, Sarah Woodward's work on the production line, and the effects of material shortages. John will need to present evidence for each of these subthemes and connect them to leadership. Each subtheme is developed in one or more paragraphs.

b. *Report primary research in the past tense*

The past tense is generally used to report findings from primary research. The general terms "results" or "findings" refer to the principal insights gained from research. The themes developed in the previous chapter are the results or the findings of your research.

Whereas the use of the past tense to report research suggests that the findings are limited to one particular study, the use of the present tense implies that the findings are generalizable to a larger population. Consistency of verb tense is important in creating a clear voice. Use the past tense for reporting verbs and for evidence verbs. In the example below the reporting verbs (claim, explain) as well as the verbs used to describe the data (feel, rely) are all in the past tense.

> *Female students <u>claimed</u> that they <u>felt</u> frightened when walking on campus at night.*
>
> *Most students in the study <u>explained</u> that they <u>relied</u> on Wikipedia as their main source of information.*

c. *Build cohesion*

As academic writing assignments become longer, the principle of cohesion assumes additional importance. As we have seen in previous chapters, cohesion maintains the flow of information from one sentence or paragraph to another. Cohesion is the glue that binds disparate parts of an essay or research paper into a single message that supports the thesis. Cohesion helps the reader understand relationships among complex ideas and see connections among multiple sources of data. Cohesion contributes to a clear authorial voice by keeping the reader focused on the author's message.

> **Reflection**
> *What role has cohesion played in your writing? How has your understanding of cohesion changed? Which of the cohesive devices (organizational patterns, paragraph unity, discourse connectors, concluding sentences) do you think will help your writing the most and why?*

Effective writers incorporate a variety of cohesive devices in their texts. They:
- present information that conforms to rhetorical organizational patterns,
- use discourse connectors to link new information to prior information,
- maintain paragraph unity by including only information related to the topic sentence,
- use a concluding sentence to sum up the paragraph.

Part 1 of the book examined the first three factors. The following section will examine the role of concluding sentences in creating cohesive text.

d. *Concluding sentences*

Whereas topic sentences tell the reader the topic and focus the paragraph will develop, a concluding sentence sums up the central ideas in the paragraph. The concluding sentence may restate the topic sentence in different words or it may sum up important evidence. Although not all paragraphs require a concluding sentence, the writer needs to consider whether one is needed to help make a clear connection between two paragraphs.

Concluding sentences create cohesion in two ways. They can refocus the reader's attention on the main idea of the paragraph and they can make a connection between the current paragraph and the next paragraph.

To refocus the reader's attention on the main idea, concluding sentences may:
- summarize the main focus of paragraph,
- repeat key words or phrases (or their synonyms) used in the topic sentence,
- use discourse connectors that signal a conclusion such as *therefore,* thus, *consequently, to sum up.*

To make a connection to the content of the next paragraph, concluding sentences may use one of these devices:
- include vocabulary or concepts from the topic sentence of the next paragraph,
- use language or discourse connectors that preview (*future, the following, another, other factors,* etc.),
- suggest comparisons or contrasts.

Practice: *Reading to write: John presents evidence for a theme*

> Examining the paragraphs from a section of John's draft case study will help illustrate the principles examined above. In the draft paragraphs below, John develops evidence to support one of the themes from his outline (above). The parenthetical citations indicate the sources for the primary data presented.
>
> 1. Read through the draft of the body paragraph that John wrote to develop evidence for one of the themes in his outline.
> 2. After the first reading, answer the questions below.
>
> The opportunity for Sarah Woodward to rise to a leadership role was made possible by the labor shortages that arose during the war. As men left the work force to serve in the war, The Weekly Chronicle ("Doors Open", 1940) reported that jobs which were previously closed to women began to open for women in London. In fact, city employment records (Office for National Statistics [ONS], 1941, 1945) showed that prior to 1941, fewer than 3% of factory workers were women; however, the number of women workers increased to 48% by 1945. In an interview (E. Woodward, personal communication, 2019), Sarah's sister explained that because her husband was fighting at the front, Sarah needed additional income to care for her family. She began work as a factory floor sweeper and within a month was given a job cutting leather for shoes. Sarah wrote daily in a personal journal (S. Woodward, personal communication, 1941–1946). Sarah's journal entries chronicled her promotions and rise to a supervisory position. Within two years of the director's departure for the war, she was appointed director of the factory. Although the war opened new doors for many women at the factory, Sarah was the only woman who moved from the factory floor to the executive office at the shoe factory.
>
> Sarah's hands-on executive leadership style created a culture of trust and collaboration that encouraged innovation. According to her sister, Sarah built trust and won respect through her caring management style and her deep appreciation of her workers (E. Woodward, personal communication, 2019). Internal memoranda from Sarah to her employees (S. Woodward, personal communication, 1941–46) provided many examples of hands-on engagement with workers and factory systems. For example, after she was promoted to director, Sarah requested a post on the production line. She wanted to learn to perform various essential jobs and fully understand what each worker's job entailed before making changes. Not surprisingly, workers respected her hands-on leadership style. Her employees valued her openness to new ideas and her faith in their judgment. The local newspaper ("Factory Miracles", 1945) published interviews with factory employees who said that the shared responsibility between workers and management had improved productivity and morale. The resulting partnership between Sarah and her workers set the stage for future innovations that would save the company.
>
> Sarah believed that collaborative leadership would empower workers to find ways to overcome shortages of materials and make the company profitable again. Sarah wanted to create a company culture that rewarded employees risk taking. In a letter to her

husband (S. Woodward, personal communication, 1942), Sarah expressed her intention to create "a collaborative partnership between workers and management" which would give workers "the courage to innovate and change without fear of failure." As a result, the solution that allowed the company to surmount the shortage of shoe leather originated with her factory workers. Internal memos (R. Grimes, personal communication, 1943) show that an employee, Ruth Grimes, prompted Sarah to investigate the possibility of using synthetic leather for the production of boots. This innovation led to a dramatic increase in profits (ONS, 1946) at a time when many industries closed due to critical shortages (Zahang, 1999). Thus, Company Annual Reports (Companies House, 1940–45) show that a woman led her company from debt to profitability by empowering employees.

Practice: Examining John's paragraphs

Analyze the series of three paragraphs above. Answer the following questions:

1. Which theme (from the outline) has John developed?
2. Identify the topic sentence for each paragraph.
3. What is the subtheme developed in each paragraph?
4. How many types of evidence does John synthesize to support the topic sentence?
5. Do all of the topic sentences support the thesis statement?

Topic sentence/Subtheme	Evidence
1	
2	
3	

Practice: Examining concluding sentences

1. Copy the topic and concluding sentences from each of the three paragraphs.
2. Answer the questions that follow. Refer to the section on concluding sentences above to help with your analysis.

Topic sentence	Concluding sentence
Paragraph 1	
Sarah Woodward's rise to company leadership was made possible by the labor shortages that arose during the war.	Although the war opened new doors for many women at the factory, Sarah was the only woman who moved from the factory floor to the executive offices at the shoe factory.

1. What ideas are repeated in <u>both</u> the topic sentence and concluding sentence?
2. What words or phrases (or their synonyms) from the topic sentence are repeated in the concluding sentence?
   leadership in the company = executive offices
   leadership was made possible by labor shortages that arose during the war = war opened new doors for women

3. What discourse connectors were used?
   None
4. Does the concluding sentence preview the next paragraph? If so what devices does it use?
   The concluding sentence uses the word executive which is repeated in the topic sentence of the next paragraph.
   Comparing Sarah to the other women and the discourse connector "although" suggests Sarah was unique.

Paragraph 2

1. What key ideas are repeated in both the topic sentence and concluding sentence?

2. What words or phrases (or synonyms) were repeated from the topic to the concluding sentence?

3. What discourse connectors were used?

4. Does the concluding sentence preview the next paragraph? If so, what devices does it use?

Paragraph 3

1. What key ideas are repeated in both the topic sentence and concluding sentence?

2. What words or phrases (or synonyms) were repeated from the topic to the concluding sentence?

3. What discourse connectors were used?

4. Does the concluding sentence preview the next paragraph? If so what devices does it use?

Practice: Cohesion

1. Based on the topic sentence below, what might be the topic of the previous paragraph?

   Sarah Woodward's rise to company leadership was made possible by the labor shortages that arose during the war.

2. Based on the concluding sentence below, what do you think the topic of the next paragraphs might be?

   Thus, Company Annual Reports (Companies House, 1940–45) show that a woman led her company from debt to profitability by empowering employees to find new opportunities.

Reflection
One of the ways that introductory and concluding sentences create cohesion is by creating a link between the information in two paragraphs. Scan an article in an academic journal or a chapter in a scholarly book. Can you find two examples of concluding sentences that clearly connect a paragraph to the next one?

e. *Include in-text citations for all primary and secondary data sources*

An academic paper requires the writer to synthesize ideas, facts, and information from many sources. Synthesis in writing refers to the process of drawing together different sources of information that collectively create a new insight or single perspective. Thematic analysis is a form of synthesis. A theme is a new way of looking at the data and, it is an original creation of the writer. On the other hand, all primary or secondary sources used in a theme are creations of *other* authors; therefore, they must be credited to the original source, even if the material is paraphrased or summarized. Each piece of data must be attributed to the original author within the paragraph. The APA format uses the author-date method to reference sources in the text. Citing quotations and paraphrases was presented in Chapter 8. In the next section, citation conventions are revisited, this time in the context of the case study assignment.

3. Citing sources in the case study: APA

Because academic writing relies extensively on the synthesis of research, learning to cite sources accurately is a critical skill for all students. Before writing any assignment or paper, verify the formatting style required for the assignment and consult the corresponding guidelines.

APA style uses two methods of citation: the in-text citation and the reference list. In-text citations are placed within the body of the paragraph while the reference list is located at the end. The in-text citations and the references work together. All recoverable sources cited in the paper must be included in the reference list. This is so the reader can find them if needed.

- The in-text citation places identifying information in parentheses within the body of a paragraph to signal the source of the material. It provides the author's surname and a date. The in-text citation allows the reader to locate the full reference in the list at the end of the document.
- The reference list is located at the end of the document. Each entry in the list includes all of the information a reader needs to locate and retrieve a source.

The following first section provides an overview of in-text citations for common types of primary sources. The formatting of reference lists will be presented in a later section of the chapter.

a. *Basic in-text citation style*

The case study assignment includes both published and unpublished primary sources. Citations are necessary for information from both published and unpublished sources. <u>To avoid any missing citations in the final paper and the reference list, it is important to include a citation for all sources during the writing</u>. Keep a list of all the sources used for the reference list at the end of the paper.

The basic format for APA in-text citations is the author-date method. While some sources may require special modifications, mastering the basic format for APA in-text citations helps the writer stay focused on the message while integrating sources into the paragraphs. This applies to any format the writer is using. Below is a basic recap of APA rules for three situations.

1. **Basic author-date citations** place the surname of the author(s) and the date of the publication in parentheses:

   Shortages of electricity and oil affected manufacturing during both wars (Zhāng, 2018). Recent studies show that "shortages of materials affected clothing manufacturing during both wars" (Zhāng, 2018, p. 89).

2. **An author's surname used in a reporting phrase** is not repeated in the parenthetical citation. When the author's surname appears in the text, only the date is placed in parenthesis:

   Zhāng (2018) found the greatest effect of shortages of materials fell on clothing manufacturing during both wars.

   Quotations require a page number in separate parenthesis after the quotation.

   Zhāng (2018) reported that "shortages of materials affected clothing manufacturing during both wars" (pp. 89–90).

3. **For multiple authors,** substitute the ampersand symbol (&) for the word "and" in the parenthetical citation:

   Shortages of materials affected clothing manufacturing during both wars (Zhāng & Smith, 2018).

   In the signal phrase, use the word "and" between the authors' names.

   Zhāng and Smith (2018) found the greatest effect of materials shortages fell on clothing manufacturing during both wars.

Author-date format	Examples	With page numbers for quotations
(Last name + year)	Shortages of materials affected manufacturing during both wars (Zhāng, 2018).	Recent studies show that "shortages of materials affected clothing manufacturing during both wars" (Zhāng, 2018, p. 89).
Last name in narrative (year)	Zhāng (2018) found the greatest effect of materials shortages fell on clothing manufacturing during both wars.	Zhāng (2018) found that "clothing manufacturers endured crippling shortages of materials during both wars" (p. 89).
(Multiple last names + year)	Shortages of materials affected manufacturing during both wars (Zhāng & Smith, 2018).	Recent studies (Zhāng & Smith, 2018) show that "shortages of materials affected manufacturing during both wars" (p. 89).
Two last names in signal phrase (year)	Zhāng and Smith (2018) found the greatest effect of materials shortages fell on clothing manufacturing during both wars.	Zhāng and Smith (2018) found that "clothing manufacturers endured crippling shortages of electricity and oil during both wars (p. 89).

Determining the author

Organization as author. The author of a source will not always be a person. It may be a group, such as a corporation, an agency, a ministry, or an institution. In this case use the name of the group as the author. If the source will be used more than once in the paper, include an abbreviation in parenthesis. Substitute the abbreviation for the full name in subsequent citations.

Basic Format: (Name of the organization, year)

The name of the organization is used in the reporting phrase or in the parenthetical citation.

> According to the rules of the American Psychological Association (2020), the references list includes only sources that were cited in the paper.

In subsequent citations, the abbreviation may be used instead of the full name.

First citation: (American Psychological Association [APA], 2020)

Subsequent citation: (APA, 2020)

Missing information

Writers must make every effort to find missing information. However, it is not always possible, especially when using primary sources. The in-text citation must still provide information to identify the source.

- If the author of the sources is identified as "Anonymous", cite Anonymous in the in-text citation.
- If the date cannot be determined, use the abbreviation n.d. for "no date".
- If the author cannot be determined, put the title of the source in place of the author. If the source title is long, use only the first two or three words from the title.
    - Capitalize important words in titles.
    - Italicize titles of books or reports.
    - Place titles of articles and documents in double quotation marks.

b. *In-text citations for personal communication*

APA treats unpublished or non-archival information as personal communication. This includes personal interviews, emails, non-archived discussion groups, letters, memos, telephone conversations, lectures, and other similar sources. These sources are considered unrecoverable information because a reader is unlikely to be able to access them. Since private communication is not recoverable, it is not included in the reference list.

However, all personal communication requires an in-text citation when it is used in a research paper. The in-text citation for all personal communication consists of the first initial and surname of the person, the phrase "personal communication," and the date, all enclosed in parentheses.

Example: (S. Woodward, personal communication, May 4, 2019).

Communication between the researcher and participants
APA classifies letters, memos, telephone conversations, lectures, and interviews between the researcher and another person as *personal communication*.

The in-text citation is the same for quoted or paraphrased data collected by the researcher. For example, in conducting interviews with Susan Stanford, a friend of Princess Diana, the researcher recorded the following comment: "Princess Diana always went the extra mile to help the poor."

Example using a direct quotation from an interview:

> A close friend of the princess reminded us that "Princess Diana always went the extra mile to help the poor" (S. Stanford, personal communication, May 7, 2011).

Example using paraphrased interview material:

> A close friend of the princess reminded us that Princess Diana did much more than was expected to help the impoverished (S. Stanford, personal communication, May 7, 2011).

Unpublished primary documents
The case study assignment includes both published and unpublished primary sources. APA also treats correspondence and other documents held in the private collection of an individual or organization as personal communication because there is no direct, reliable path for readers to access the sources.

The term "private communication" includes many types of sources and the source will not be available in the reference list to provide more detailed information. To ensure that the reader has all the information necessary to understand the source, the writer should use as much identifying information as possible in the narrative of the paragraph. For example, in the sentence below the writer includes information about the type of correspondence and the recipient in the narrative. The reader has a clear idea of the nature of the communication based on the information in the narrative and the parenthetical information about the author and date.

Example: Internal memoranda from Sarah to her employees (S. Woodward, personal communication, 1941–46) provided many examples of hands-on engagement with workers and factory systems.

Practice: Examining John's in-text citations

> As noted above, the purpose of the in-text citation is to direct the reader to the full information in the reference list. Since personal communication is not recoverable and not included in the reference list, the writer should include enough information in the narrative to help the reader understand the origin of the source.

> The in-text citations below are from the draft by John that you read above.
>
> 1. Find each citation in the text.
> 2. Based on what you know about the rules for in-text citations, explain your understanding of the source.
>
> | | |
> |---|---|
> | ("Doors Open", 1940) | *The narrative explains this is from a newspaper The Weekly Chronicle. The citation uses the first two words from the title of the article in place of the author's name. The source will be listed by the title of the article in the references list.* |
> | (Office for National Statistics [ONS], 1941; 1945) | |
> | (E. Woodward, personal communication, 2019) | *The paragraph states that this is from an interview conducted by John Woodward. It is not a recoverable document and, therefore, not included in the reference list.* |
> | (S. Woodward, personal communication, 1941–1946) | |
> | ("Factory Miracles", 1945) | |
> | (S. Woodward, personal communication, 1942) | |
> | (R. Grimes, personal communication, 1943) | |
> | (ONS, 1946) | |
> | (Companies House, 1940–45). | |

4.   Writing the introduction to a case study

With the body of the case study drafted, the writer can determine what information should be included in the introduction. The introduction and the thesis statement provide the background information for understanding the subject and the research. The introduction creates a context for the case study that:

- engages the reader's interest in the subject,
- provides a context for understanding the subject,
- focuses the reader's attention on the nature of the case study, and
- presents a clear and concise thesis.

Although there are many ways to write introductions for case studies, to be effective an introduction must always lead the reader to the thesis statement and provide the background necessary to understand the thesis. An introduction to a short case study is usually four to seven sentences long; the introduction for an extensive research paper may be several paragraphs long, depending on the topic.

> **Reflection**
> *Do you consider writing the introduction to a paper easy or difficult? Explain your response. Has your understanding of the purpose and content of an effective introduction changed during this course and if so, how has it changed? If it hasn't changed, why is that?*

Strategies for writing the introduction

The underlying principles and strategies for writing an introduction apply to most academic papers, including a short case study. Chapter 7 presented two strategies for writing the introduction: the question framework and the general-to specific-approach. Review the full discussion of these strategies in Chapter 7. Both strategies methodically develop a context that will prepare the reader for the case study.

Practice: *Reading to write – analyzing John's introduction*

> Below are two drafts of introductions written by John for his case study. Read each and underline the thesis statement. Which paragraph gives you a better understanding of the context in which the events unfolded? Why?
>
> **Introduction 1**
> My grandmother, Sarah Woodward, was a heroic woman who opened doors for women to have careers. In the past, middle class women took care of the house and children while men took financial responsibility for the family. When women entered the workforce and professions, they confronted many obstacles but were often as successful as men. Although today's young girls take for granted the opportunity to develop a fulfilling career and raise a family, the idea of combining the two roles is actually a relatively new phenomenon in this country. While her husband was stationed in France, Sarah took over a shoe business and cared for her children under very difficult circumstances. By turning a failing shoe factory into a thriving business with innovative ideas and insightful leadership, Sarah Woodward demonstrated that women were as capable as men.
>
> **Introduction 2**
> Although today's young girls take for granted the opportunity to develop a fulfilling career and raise a family, the idea of combining the two roles is actually a relatively new phenomenon in this country. Until WW2, it was rare for a woman to have a profession, depending instead on financial support from her husband for herself and her children. As increasing numbers of men went off to fight in the war, women took on many of the traditional male jobs and, despite the skepticism of many, were every bit as successful as men. My grandmother, Sarah Woodward, was one of those heroic women who opened doors for women to have careers. While my grandfather was stationed in France, Sarah took over a failing London shoe business and managed to care for her children during the most difficult war years. By turning a failing factory into a thriving business with innovative ideas and insightful leadership, Sarah Woodward's remarkable entrepreneurship demonstrated that women were as capable as men.

> **Reflection**
> *Which of the two introductions do you feel is more effective?*
> *Explain why.*

Practice: Determining background information for John's introduction

A writer becomes so familiar with his topic, that it is easy to overlook details that the reader will need. To ensure that the reader has all the information necessary to comprehend the essay the writer should introduce the topic as if the reader does not have any knowledge of the topic. The question framework reminds the writer to include the details the reader needs to know.

Reread the two introductory paragraphs above.

Use the framework below to compare the paragraphs.

What additional information does the second paragraph present? How does it change your understanding of "difficult circumstances"? How does it change your understanding of "stationed in France"?

Do these details change your understanding of the thesis statement?

Question framework		Introduction 1	Introduction 2
Who	is the subject of the case study?		
What	is the case about?		
When	did it take place?		
Where	did the most important events take place?		
Why	is it important?		
How	what point of view will the essay support?		

Practice: General to specific strategy for John's introduction

The general-to-specific approach begins with a broad general statement. It gradually develops a context by clarifying and narrowing the topic, leading the reader to the thesis statement.

Read each statement below. Comment on how each sentence clarifies or narrows the topic.

Although today's young girls take for granted the opportunity to develop a fulfilling career and raise a family, the idea of combining the two roles is actually a relatively new phenomenon in this country.	*Introduces broad topic of women in the workplace by linking the phenomenon to the past.*
Until WW2 it was rare for a woman to have a profession, depending instead on financial support from her husband for herself and her children.	*Clarifies when the change began (WW2) and the situation until that time.*

> As increasing numbers of men went off to fight the war, women took on many of the traditional male roles, and despite the skepticism of many, were every bit as successful as men.
>
> My grandmother, Sarah Woodward, was one of those heroic women who opened doors for women to have careers.
>
> While my grandfather was stationed in France, Sarah took over a failing London shoe business and managed to care for her children during the most difficult war years.
>
> By turning a failing factory into a thriving business with innovative ideas and insightful leadership, Sarah Woodward's remarkable entrepreneurship demonstrated that women were as capable as men.

5. Writing the conclusion for the case study

The conclusion guides the reader to revisit the thesis statement and recall the most important evidence. It is more than a simple restatement and summary. The conclusion is the last opportunity for the writer to make a case for the validity of the evidence presented to support the thesis statement. It is also an opportunity for the writer to share a reflection on the value of the research. Many, but not all, disciplines and instructors expect a statement with the writer's reflection on the significance or implications of the findings as they relate to the context presented in the introduction. Check with the instructor about the use of reflective comments.

Strategies for writing the conclusion

An effective introduction and well organized evidence leads naturally to the conclusion. An effective conclusion should review the major themes in the case study and relate them to the thesis statement. It should also help the reader consider the significance of the research and connect it to a broader context. The three strategies presented below have been adapted from writing introductions and conclusions in chapter 7. They also apply to the case study.

Strategy 1: Rephrase the thesis statement

Rephrasing the thesis statement from the introduction refocuses the reader's attention on the purpose of the study and reaffirms the point of view the writer presented. It helps the reader evaluate how successful the case study research was in validating the thesis statement. When rephrasing the thesis statement for a case study, identify the subject and explain the point of view using synonyms and changing the syntax so that it does not sound repetitive.

Original thesis statement from the introduction	Rephrased thesis statement from the conclusion
In his short poem "Nothing Gold Can Stay" Frost uses beautiful images of the golden buds of trees in early spring as a metaphor for the inevitable loss of youth and beauty that is part of the natural cycle of life.	In Frost's poem, the ephemeral gold of budding leaves symbolizes the march of time and the inevitable loss of youth.
Despite similarities, many Roman marriage and divorce practices reflect an ancient society that valued men, family, and social class above the notion of romantic love.	While modern society still follows many Roman laws and traditions, most people decide to marry for love.

Practice: Examining the introduction and conclusion for John's case study

Below are drafts of John's introduction and conclusion to his case study. Underline the thesis statement in the introduction and the paraphrased thesis in the conclusion.

Introduction
Although today's young girls take for granted the opportunity to develop a fulfilling career and raise a family, the idea of combining the two roles is actually a relatively new phenomenon in this country. Until WW2, it was rare for a woman to have a profession, depending instead on financial support from her husband for herself and her children. As increasing numbers of men went off to fight the war, women took on many of the traditional male jobs and, despite the skepticism of many, were every bit as successful as men. My grandmother, Sarah Woodward, was one of those heroic women who opened doors for women to have careers. While my grandfather was stationed in France, Sarah took over a failing London shoe business and managed to care for her children during the most difficult war years. By turning a failing factory into a thriving business with innovative ideas and insightful leadership, Sarah Woodward's remarkable entrepreneurship demonstrated that women were as capable as men.

Conclusion
Like most women in the pre-WW2 era, Sarah had minimal education and no employment experience; nevertheless, she took full advantage of the opportunities that opened for women during the war. As Sarah ascended from factory worker to manager, she earned the trust and respect of her employees through collaborative leadership, creating a strong partnership that would sustain future change. Sarah surmounted the challenge of worker shortages and materials with the keen insight that allowed her to recognize the potential of new materials, new markets, and the female labor force. In the last years of the war, Sarah

took the company from financial crisis to profitability by shifting to the production of durable army boots made of synthetic materials and by training women to operate and maintain heavy equipment. Undoubtedly, studying Sarah Woodward's life revealed a remarkable person who recognized opportunity and tapped into her hidden talents to achieve remarkable success. Sarah's life illustrates how untapped human potential will flourish when opportunities are available; it is a reminder that society benefits when girls and women can access the same educational and career opportunities as boys and men.

Strategy 2: Synthesize the major themes in the case study
The conclusion should synthesize the main themes from the research. Remember that synthesizing is the process of pulling together different sources that collectively create a new insight or single perspective. Synthesizing the themes reminds the reader of the evidence presented to support the thesis statement. To keep the conclusion sounding fresh, do not copy sentences from the body paragraphs. Instead, paraphrase as much as possible by capturing the main points of each theme, using different language and structure.

Practice: Reading to write – analyzing synthesis in John's conclusion

1. Reread the conclusion to John's case study.
2. Copy the sentence that synthesizes each theme in the column below.

Theme	Synthesis of theme from John's conclusion.
Limited opportunities for women before the war	Although Sarah had minimal education and no work experience, she took full advantage of the opportunities that opened for women during WW2.
New leadership opportunities for women during WW2	
New manufacturing opportunities during WW2	
Innovation created profitable business.	

Strategy 3: Comment on the significance of the case study findings
The purpose of a case study is to create a deep and full picture of a subject. The findings from a case study apply only to the subject of the study and are not generalizable to a wider population. Nevertheless, by relating the results to a broader context, the writer makes a statement to the reader about why the research was worthwhile and what insights it can provide.

Practice: *Explaining the significance of John's case study*

> Reread the conclusion of John's case study.
>
> 1. John includes a statement that suggests that the topic is significant today.
>   Write the statement here:
>
> 2. The conclusion of the case study of Sarah Woodward makes a statement that affirms the significance of her accomplishments for the reader or wider audience.
>   Write the statement here:

> *Reflection*
> *Do you consider writing the conclusion to a paper easy or difficult? Explain your answer. Has your understanding of the purpose and content of an effective conclusion changed during this course and if so, how has it changed? If it hasn't changed, why is that?*

B. AWARE: Writing the case study document

1. AWARE: Arranging to write

a. *From working thesis to thesis statement*

In writing your thesis statement avoid vague words like "interesting," "negative," "exciting," "unusual," and "difficult", because they are hard to support. Abstract, catch-all words like "society," "values," or "culture" need limiting and clarification. For example, "pre-war society", "Christian values", and "Korean culture" clarify the concept for the reader.

b. *Reformulating your research question into a working thesis statement*

> Write your research question:
> Your thesis statement will answer this research question. To create a thesis statement that reflects your research and analysis, consider the following questions.
>
> 1. Who is the subject of the case study?
> 2. What themes have you developed in your outline that demonstrate unique qualities?
>   a.
>   b.
>   c.
>   d.

> How do these themes relate? What characteristics of the subject do the themes demonstrate?
> 3. If two ideas emerge, can you join related topics into a unified idea using compound or complex sentences? Two topics can be connected using coordinating conjunctions (like *and, but, for, nor, or, so, yet*), subordinating conjunctions (such as *through, although, because, since*), or another type of subordination to join two statements.
>
> Write your working thesis statement:

2. AWARE: Writing the draft of the case study

a. *Writing the body paragraphs*

Following the instructions and the outline developed in Chapter 9, write the first draft of the body paragraphs. The final paper should be about three to five pages long. Most experienced writers find that the first draft is the longest version. As you revise and reorganize, the paper will become more concise.

Here is a checklist for developing the body of the case study:

1. Present evidence thematically, according to your outline. Some themes may contain subthemes and require multiple paragraphs. Develop only one theme, or subtheme, per paragraph.
2. Begin each paragraph with a topic sentence.
3. Present at least three sources of data to support each theme (triangulation).
4. Use the past tense for primary data and reporting words.
5. Cite each source in the text using the author-date method (author, date).
6. End the paragraphs with a concluding sentence, whenever possible.
   Include at least one quote and one paraphrase in your paper (see instructions in ch. 9).

The first draft of the body of the essay is now complete. The next step is to combine the body paragraphs with an introduction and concluding paragraphs. This will be done in the next section.

b. *Writing the introduction*

Use the question framework and general to specific strategies to generate the information you need for your introduction

Question framework considers all of the key information the reader needs.	
Who	is the subject of the case study?
What	is the case about?
When	did it take place?
Where	did the most important events take place?
Why	is it important?
How	what point of view will the essay support?

> **General to specific approach for the introduction**
> Use the general-to-specific approach to generate ideas for the introduction. Be sure to include all of the essential information from the question framework above.
>
> General statement
> Clarifies the topic
> Narrows topic
> Thesis
>
> Using the information you generated above, write a draft of your introduction. Remember that the introduction should be four to seven sentences long and end with the thesis statement.

c. Writing the conclusion

A good conclusion reviews your major points and relates them to the thesis. Three strategies will help you generate the information you need for your conclusion and organize it into a paragraph that reminds the reader of your thesis statement and the themes that you used to support it. In this section you will rephrase your thesis statement, synthesize the key evidence from your case study, and write a statement that affirms the significance of your study.

> **Rephrase your thesis statement**
>
> | Original thesis statement your introduction | Rephrased thesis statement |
> |---|---|
> | | |

> Synthesize the themes from your outline. Focus on the idea that you think is most convincing in each theme.
>
> | Theme | Synthesis of theme from your outline |
> |---|---|
> | 1. | |
> | 2. | |
> | 3. | |
> | 4. | |

> The following questions can help you reflect on the broader significance or implications of your research.
> - What, if any, is the significance of your findings (your themes) to you?
> - What, if any, is the significance of your findings (your themes) to an academic discipline?
> - What are the implications of the case study finding to a broader context?
> - Did any factors emerge that are not relevant to the case study but worthy of note?

Congratulations, you have completed a full draft of your case study. The final phases of AWARE, Assessing, Revision, and Editing will help you prepare it for submission.

3. AWARE: Assessing

From previous chapters, you know that before revising, you need to assess your evidence and reevaluate your working thesis statement. Sometimes what appears to be strong data in an outline is not effective when put into a paragraph. As you develop the idea, it may not relate as directly to the thesis as you expected. Alternatively, when you read a draft of the findings, you may find that they create a different understanding of the subject than you expected.

a. Assessing strategy: Evaluating the evidence for the case study

It has already been established that the evidence for a thesis statement will be grouped according to themes/findings with multiple sources of data. To assess the quality and quantity of the evidence, create a reverse outline for the body of your case study (see Chapter 5) by copying the topic sentences.

As you read each topic sentence, ask yourself:

1. Which of the themes from my outline does the topic sentence belong to? Mark any paragraphs that do not belong to a theme for revision or deletion.
2. Does the topic sentence add support to the thesis statement? Mark any paragraphs where the topic sentence does not relate directly to the thesis statement for revision.
3. Does each paragraph present strong evidence to support the topic sentence? Look for three sources of data for each theme. Mark for revision any themes or paragraphs that need additional evidence.

b. Assessing strategy: Evaluating the working thesis statement

Once you have assessed the evidence for the case study and determined the final content, you need to assess whether your working thesis still accurately reflects the point of view from your thesis statement. Remember that the thesis statement defines the content of the case study and the themes presented in the case study must relate directly to the thesis statement.

> **Realigning the working thesis statement**
> Write your current working thesis statement below. Underline your point of view on your subject.
> _____
> _____
>
> 1. What are the findings/themes you have decided to include in your final draft?
> _____
> _____
> _____
> _____
> _____
> _____
>
> 2. Does your working thesis accurately reflect the themes in your reverse outline?
> 3. Has the point of view in your thesis statement changed based on new information or a new perspective on the data?
> 4. Do you need to revise your thesis to reflect these changes?
>
> Write your revised thesis statement here:
> _____
> _____

4.   AWARE: Revising

As you revise, pay special attention to the following elements that were introduced in this chapter:

- presenting evidence thematically
- reporting primary research in the past tense
- including in-text citations for all primary and secondary data sources
- building cohesion.

Read through the draft and check for the following:

1. Are the paragraphs organized thematically? All paragraphs related to the same theme should be grouped together to maintain a logical organization. Reorganize if needed.
2. Check that the past tense is used consistently for reporting primary data and in the signal verbs that introduce data.
3. Identify every data source and confirm that an in-text citation is provided for each.
4. Do you use concluding sentences to sum up the paragraph? Add concluding sentences to strengthen the cohesiveness of the message.

Read through the draft a second time following the checklist below:

Revising checklist

1. Add additional evidence where needed.
2. Underline non-specific or imprecise words. Substitute precise and specific vocabulary (see also Chapter 4).
3. Substitute formal language for informal language (see Chapter 1).
4. Check for paragraph unity. Strike out any sentences that do not directly support the topic sentences (see Chapter 5).
5. Use appropriate discourse connectors or causal language to signal the relationships among ideas.

5. AWARE: Editing

Editing the case study paper will focus on formatting and compiling the reference list according to the APA style. Please confer with the instructor as to which format is required for your assignment.

a. *Formatting the paper*

> Review this checklist for formatting:
> 1. Are your name and title on the paper and in the correct format?
> 2. Are the font, font size, line spacing, and margins according to the guidelines?
> 3. Does the case study conform to the requirements for length?
> 4. Are all the in-text citations appropriately cited?
> 5. Are the recoverable sources also included in the reference list?
> 6. Are you following the appropriate format for citations and the reference list?

b. *The APA reference list*

The final step of writing a case study is to compile the reference list. The model uses the APA format. If you have been keeping a list of references as you write, this task will be much easier. You will need to focus primarily on formatting and finding any missing information for your references.

APA style uses a reference list rather than a bibliography. Unlike a bibliography which includes all of the sources consulted during research, a reference list credits *only* the sources cited in the paper. Each entry in the reference list contains all of the information the reader needs to locate and retrieve the source.

All sources cited in the body of the paper must appear in the reference list; likewise, only sources cited in the text will be included in the reference. However, in-text citations credited as "personal communication" are not included in the reference list since these are not recoverable. See information in Section A, "Citing Sources in the Case Study" above for more information on personal communication.

Below are the basic building blocks of the APA reference list.

Layout of the APA reference list
- New page
- <u>Center</u> the word "References" in bold at the top of the page
- <u>Double space</u> all references.
- Use a <u>hanging indent</u> by beginning the first line of each entry at the margin and indenting all of the others one half inch. Most word processing programs have a setting for hanging indents.
- <u>Alphabetize</u> works by the last name of the first author for each reference.

c. *The building blocks of an APA reference citation*

According to the seventh edition of the Publication Manual of the APA (2020), each entry in a reference list should include four elements: author, date, title, and source. An APA reference should provide answers to four questions a reader needs to locate a source.

1. Who created it? (author)
2. When was it published? (date)
3. What is it called? (title)
4. Where can I retrieve the work? (source)

While APA citations include the four building blocks (author, date, title, and source) there are as many variations as there are sources. As we saw in examining in-text citations, the author or date may not be available; there are many types of books and numerous types of periodicals. Many sources will require a modification of the basic format. For this reason, all writers need to consult a style guide or style manual regularly.

Nevertheless, by mastering the basic building blocks, writers will be able to format most references without consulting a style manual. The rules below apply to APA reference lists. If you are using another formatting style, consult that style manual. Some basic rules apply to formatting the majority of sources.

d. *Formatting sources in the reference list*

Below is an overview of the basic rules for formatting references. The most generic reference citation (the book) as well as frequently used primary sources such as newspapers and government documents will be examined. Formatting references for secondary sources such as edited books and journal articles will be examined in Chapter 12.

Separate the four building blocks of the reference citation
Use a period *between* each of the elements and at the end of the reference:

Author. Date. Title. Source.

Exception:

Online source citations that include web addresses do *not* end in a period.

Authors' names
1. Reverse the name of the author, putting the surname first, followed by the initials.
2. Use a comma after the author's surname.
3. Use a period after the initials of the author's given names.
4. In references with multiple authors, separate authors with a comma between them.
5. Substitute an ampersand symbol (&) for the word "and" when listing multiple authors.

Example:

Author, A. A., Author, B. B., & Author, C. C.

When no name is available for the person or organization that created the source, the title of the document is placed in the author's position in the reference.

Example:

All 33 Chile miners freed in flawless rescue. (2010, October 13).

Capitalization
APA style uses two methods of capitalization for titles in the reference list.

<u>Sentence case</u> (mostly lower case words) is used for titles of *books and articles*. These are generally independent sources rather the parts of a larger work.

1. Capitalize the first word of the title.
2. Capitalize proper nouns.
3. Subtitles: Capitalize the first word.

Example:

Student plagiarism in the internet era: A wake-up call.

<u>Title case</u> (all major words capitalized) is used for titles of *periodicals* such as a journal or newspaper.

1. Capitalize the first word in a title/heading or subtitle/subheading.
2. Capitalize all important words (nouns, verbs, adjectives, adverbs, and pronouns) in the title/heading and the second part of hyphenated words.
3. Capitalize all words of four letters or more.

Italics

APA places some titles in normal typeface and others in italics.

Use italics for titles of independent sources such as:

- Books
- E-Books
- Periodicals
- Dissertations/theses
- Reports/technical papers
- Works of art

Use normal typeface for titles of article or book chapters that are part of a larger work.

Example:

Yang, A., Stockwell, S., & McDonnell, L. (2019). Writing in your own voice: An intervention that reduces plagiarism and common writing problems in students' scientific writing. *Biochemistry & Molecular Biology Education*, *47*(5), 589–598. https://doi-org/10.1002/bmb.21282

e. *Summary of formatting rules for references*

Books

Include:
1. Author
2. Year of Publication
3. Title
4. Source

	APA FORMAT	EXAMPLE
One author	Author, A. A. (Year of publication). *Title of work*. Source.	Kendi, I. X. (2018). *How to be an antiracist*. Random House.
Two to seven authors	Author, A. A., & Author B. B. B. & Author, C. C. (Year). *Title of work*. Source.	Fromkin, V., & Rodman, R. (2018). *An introduction to language*. Cengage Learning.

Newspapers

Include:
1. Author
2. Date of publication
3. Title of article
4. Title of newspaper
5. Page numbers
6. URL for online newspapers

For online newspapers, provide the URL of the home page to avoid nonworking URLs.
Not all elements may be found on certain newspapers, so use the information available.

	APA FORMAT	EXAMPLE
Newspaper (print)	Author, A. (Year, month, day). Article title. *Newspaper Title*, pp. x–x.	Jacobs, A. (2019, September 17). A shadowy industry group shapes food policy around the world. *The New York Times*, p. D1.
Newspaper (Electronic)	Author, A. (Year, month, day). Article title. *Newspaper Title*. Retrieved from URL.	Jacobs, A. (2019, September 16). A shadowy industry group shapes food policy around the world. *The New York Times*. https://www.nytimes.com/

Reports
1. Name of the author
2. Date of publication
3. Title of article
4. Report number, if available
5. Page numbers
6. URL for online report

If there could be any confusion about the country of origin for a government report, include the country name.

	APA FORMAT	EXAMPLE
Government report (print)	Government author. (Year). *Title of report: Subtitle of report if applicable* (Report No. 123). Source.	US Copyright Office. (1981) *Circular R1: Copyright basics* (Publication 341–279/106). Government Printing Office.
Government report (online)	Government author. (Year). *Title of report: Subtitle of report if applicable* (Report No. 123). http://xxxxx	Great Britain Department for Business, Innovation and Skills. (2011). *Bigger, better business: Helping small firms start, grow and prosper*. https://www.gov.uk/government/uploads/system/uploads/attachment_data/file/32225/11-515-bigger-better-business-helping-small-firms.pdf
Web Document, Web Page, or Report		
	Author. (Date). Title of article. *Title of the resource*. http://www.someaddress.com/full/url/ or http://doi.org/10.0000/0000	British Broadcasting Corporation. (2019). *BBC Group annual report and accounts 2018/19*. https://downloads.bbc.co.uk/aboutthebbc/reports/annual-report/2018-19.pdf Angeli, E., Wagner, J., Lawrick, E., Moore, K., Anderson, M., Soderland, L., & Brizee, A. (2010, May 5). *General format*. http://owl.english.purdue.edu/owl/resource/560/01/

f. Sample reference list

The reference list below is made up of the sample references used above.

References

Angeli, E., Wagner, J., Lawrick, E., Moore, K., Anderson, M., Soderland, L., & Brizee, A. (2010, May 5). *General format*. http://owl.english.purdue.edu/owl/resource/560/01/

British Broadcasting Corporation. (2019). *BBC Group annual report and accounts 2018/19*. https://downloads.bbc.co.uk/aboutthebbc/reports/annualreport/2018-19.pdf

Fromkin, V., & Rodman, R. (2018). *An introduction to language*. Cengage Learning.

Great Britain Department for Business, Innovation and Skills. (2011). *Bigger, better business: Helping small firms start, grow and prosper*. https://www.gov.uk/government/uploads/system/uploads/attachment_data/file/32225/11-515-bigger-better-business-helping-small-firms.pdf

Jacobs, A. (2019, September 16). A shadowy industry group shapes food policy around the world. *The New York Times*. https://www.nytimes.com/

Jacobs, A. (2019, September 17). A shadowy industry group shapes food policy around the world. *The New York Times*, p. D1.

Kendi, I. X. (2018). *How to be an antiracist*. Random House.

US Copyright Office. (1981). *Circular R1: Copyright basics* (Publication 341279/106) Government Printing Office.

Yang, A., Stockwell, S., & McDonnell, L. (2019). Writing in your own voice: An intervention that reduces plagiarism and common writing problems in students' scientific writing. *Biochemistry & Molecular Biology Education*, 47(5), 589–598. *https://doi.org/10.1002/bmb.21282*

Chapter 11

Conducting research for an academic paper

In this chapter, students will begin working with published sources in preparation for the final research paper. The general topic of the research paper is still the same: A remarkable person, but secondary sources are used to situate the primary research of the case study in its social and historical context. A research paper differs from a case study in purpose, discourse, and length. The research paper assigned in this chapter may be characterized as an expository paper based on a literature review within a multidisciplinary field that includes the humanities and social sciences. The paper thus follows the academic writing conventions of those discourse communities.

Writing a research paper requires students to review what experts have said about their chosen topic. These sources are called secondary sources because the support for the thesis comes from someone other than the writer. This chapter will guide students through the Arranging-to-write phase by presenting strategies to help them identify, organize, and evaluate the scholarly writings of others that are relevant to their research topic.

In this chapter, students will:

- rework the thesis from the previous case study to reflect the new context,
- find secondary sources to support the thesis,
- evaluate the reliability of sources,
- organize relevant sources according to themes,
- report on secondary sources,
- cite secondary sources in text and in a list of references,
- write a detailed outline of the paper based on the data collected.

> **Relevance**
> The research paper is one of the most common university assignments. Most research papers include a review of the literature. Strategies for finding, evaluating, reporting, and citing secondary sources for a literature review are important for study in all academic disciplines.

A. Examining the research paper

The assignment in this chapter is to find and organize sources for a research paper that places the remarkable person into a larger socio-historical context. The primary research from the previous case study will serve as a starting point for some of the content of this new paper and may be used to support its thesis. This chapter will present guidelines for students to find and review published sources that will provide the social and historical context for the subject of the case study. Students will analyze the impact of social events on their subject by examining historical evidence of changes in family structures, religion, war, migrations, technology, the economy, education, or other factors that influence the lives of individuals. In the next chapter, students will synthesize their findings into a literature review paper.

The research paper will include an introduction, a literature review, research from the case study, and a conclusion. As with other assignments in this book, the introduction and conclusion will be written after the body of the research paper and the literature review have been developed.

1. The literature review

Most research papers include a literature review in some form. A literature review is a synthesized overview of knowledge about a topic. The review develops a clear, logical argument and synthesizes relationships among findings that have been identified. A literature review leads the reader to the importance of the research question. The length of a literature review varies depending on the type of paper. For this relatively short paper, the literature review should be four to five pages long.

There are several ways to organize a literature review. Most literature reviews have a short introduction defining the topic, a body of paragraphs that can be organized in different ways, and a short summary at the end. The literature review can be organized chronologically according to when the studies were conducted, methodologically according to the type of studies reviewed, or thematically according to the themes a group of studies addresses. The literature review for this paper will be organized thematically.

Organizing the literature review thematically is based on grouping of secondary sources by their topic. Often, they are discussed in the order of their importance from the most important to the least important, or from the most general to the most specific. The studies that support each identified theme are synthesized. It is important to synthesize the findings by topic (theme) rather than summarize the findings from each source and present them author by author. Below are two examples of paragraphs from literature reviews that are organized by themes.

Practice: Reading to write 1: A review of the literature

> The example below is taken from the body of a literature review on the relationship between national identity and nature conservation. This example paragraph combines the thematic and chronological approaches.
>
> The theme of the paragraph is the notion of wilderness as natural landscape. This appears in the topic sentence which is underlined.
>
> Within the paragraph, the sources present how humanities scholars have approached the concept of wilderness chronologically beginning in the 1980's until 2001.
>
> The concluding sentence summarizes the discussion (underlined) before introducing the theme of the next paragraph in the last sentence.
>
> The last sentence suggests that the theme of the next paragraph is a review of more recent studies that argue for more varied approaches to understanding the socio-political relations between nation and nature (underlined).
>
> <u>Early work in environmental humanities tended to take a sharply critical approach to wilderness, focusing on the cultural construction of supposedly "natural" landscapes.</u> The rise of climate change awareness in the 1980s had been framed by narratives about "the end of nature" (McKibben, 1989, p. 9) in which a once-pristine wilderness is degraded by humans to the point of disappearance. In response to this popular discourse, environmental historian William Cronon critiqued the concept of a pure, pristine nature to be preserved from human influence, arguing that ideas like "wilderness" are themselves products of particular human cultures and histories. In his influential essay "The Trouble with Wilderness" (1995), Cronon traces how the ideal of untouched wilderness, anxiety over its loss, and the political will to preserve it has been central to American national identity, entwined with religious motifs and colonial frontier mythologies. Following Cronon, the racial and class politics of wilderness preservation was a theme taken up by several scholars in the late 1990s and early 2000s, who researched the material effects of conservation politics on indigenous and rural Americans (Catton, 1997; Spence, 1999; Jacoby, 2001). The US National Park system became the dominant paradigm for analyzing relations between conservation, nationhood and nationalism. <u>However, this approach has sometimes led to a narrowly US-centric perspective that fails to engage closely with the meanings and materialities of "wilderness" in different contexts. Recent work has begun to challenge this paradigm and argue for more varied approaches to understanding the socio-political relations between nation and nature.</u>

Practice: Reading to write 2: A review of the literature

> The theme of the sample review paragraph below is introduced in the topic sentence (underlined). The theme is the low student retention rates in Massive Online Open Courses (MOOCS).
>
> The author begins by introducing studies that have measured retention and then lists some of the reasons that may explain why many students do not complete MOOC courses.

> The author then lists possible reasons for the low retention rates such as inappropriate measurements, unsuitability of this type of learning environment, and student intent. Each reason is supported by two or more expert sources.
>
> The author concludes the paragraph by summarizing the content of the paragraph (underlined).
>
> The average number of beginning students who complete MOOC courses is very low or around 7% (Gaebel, 2013, 2014; Jordan, 2014). Critics suggest that there are many reasons for this high drop-out rate. Koller et al. (2013) and Reich (2014) question whether success in MOOCs should be measured by completion rates, arguing that retention should be considered within the context of student intent. Koller et al. (2013) compare this to measuring a book's success solely on the proportion of individuals who read it cover-to-cover and remind us that retention is also a problem in traditional college courses. Adamopoulus (2013) claims that MOOCs are simply unsuitable learning environments for most students. Other issues have also been mentioned that may affect retention, including the fact that changes in students' personal circumstances may reduce their motivation to complete a course (Beaven et al. 2015). A dominant discussion is the influence of student intent (Koller et al., 2013). Participants in LMOOC may sign up out of curiosity, never intending to pursue the course. On a similar note, Sokolik (2015) points out that participation in a MOOC is voluntary, entailing no obligation to complete the course. All these factors demonstrate that there is reason to question the concept of 'drop-out' in a MOOC. Finally, the 7% retention rate may be misleading due to the inaccuracy of applying traditional metrics of higher education to MOOCs.
>
> Adapted from a student paper and used with permission.

Before preparation for writing can begin, it is important to understand the requirements for the assignment.

2. Understanding the assignment

It is important to understand the purpose and general structure of a research paper assignment, but requirements of each discipline may vary slightly. Students should always examine carefully the guidelines for an academic assignment. The guidelines for the research paper on a remarkable person are below.

Description of the research paper assignment

> Write a thesis-driven research paper that places the individual in the case study and their personal circumstances in a socio-historical context. The paper should include an introduction, a literature review, and conclusions.
>
> General topic: The socio-historical context of the life of a remarkable person.
>
> Length: 1200 words (six to seven pages)
>
> Format: APA, Times New Roman, 12 points, double spaced.
>
> All sources must be cited with correct in-text citations. Each citation must also be included in the list of references at the end of the paper.

> The paper must be based on a minimum of five sources (in addition to the primary sources from the previous essay). The sources must include:
> one scholarly book,
> two peer-reviewed scholarly articles,
> two scholarly websites.

3. Examining the new working thesis

The new research paper will require a new working thesis. In some disciplines the working thesis may be called a research question. The new working thesis will guide the review of the literature and help the researcher choose the appropriate sources for review. The working thesis is formulated in the beginning, with the understanding that it may be modified or changed as data are collected and analyzed. This modification will lead to a thesis expressing the writer's point of view.

Students have already begun the research process by collecting primary data about a remarkable person. The case study was driven by a thesis that will provide the basis for the development of the new working thesis. Themes including family structures, religion, war/crisis, migrations, technology, the economy, or education can guide the initial search for sources for the research paper.

The working thesis is the map that both directs the writer's thinking and choice of sources to review and keeps the writer focused. A writer who is guided by a working thesis can make more effective choices of sources to support the thesis. Remember that the thesis must make a claim about the significance of an aspect of social history for a defined time period during the lifetime of the remarkable person from the case study. The secondary sources chosen must provide evidence to support this claim.

Sometimes the writer uncovers sources that reveal evidence for new ideas or may not find sources to support what seemed to be a strong idea. When this happens, the writer may evaluate and change the working thesis or research question to reflect the new sources. This is the nature of research. The final thesis statement must always reflect the new evidence.

The sample thesis from the previous chapters might be (working thesis):

My grandmother's leadership, keen insight, and wartime economics propelled her to create a business empire during World War 2.

This working thesis will provide the initial idea for a working thesis for the sample research paper. Students can use a mind map/cluster diagram to begin the process of placing the remarkable person into a socio-historical context. Below is the example of the student, John, writing about his grandmother, has begun jotting down the ideas that might be worth pursuing further based on the themes of war, technology, migration, family structure, economics, and education:

Examining ideas to develop a new working thesis: John's example

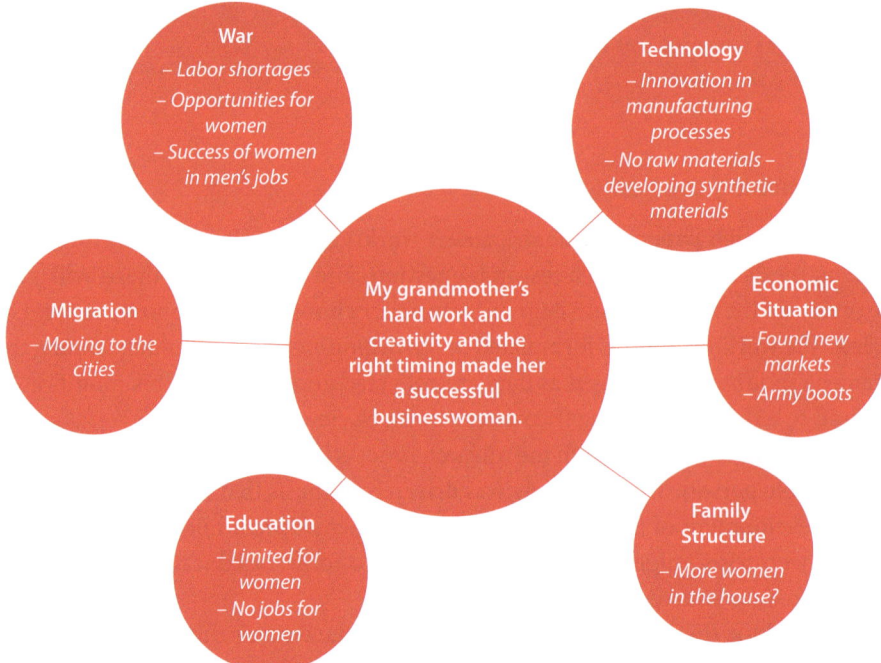

Based on these ideas, this is a possible new working thesis:

World War 2 brought about social changes that changed the lives of women like my grandmother.

In this thesis, the topic is "*World War 2 brought about social changes*" and the point of view is "*changed the lives of women like my grandmother*".

This will become the working thesis that guides the review of the literature.

4. Developing a new working thesis

Below is a diagram to develop a new working thesis.

Brainstorming to develop a new working thesis

> Use brainstorming to create a mind map/cluster diagram like the example below for your working thesis.
> 1. Rework your thesis from the case study to reflect the new focus of the research paper. The goal is to put the remarkable person into a larger social and historical context.
> 2. Use themes that are relevant to your topic.

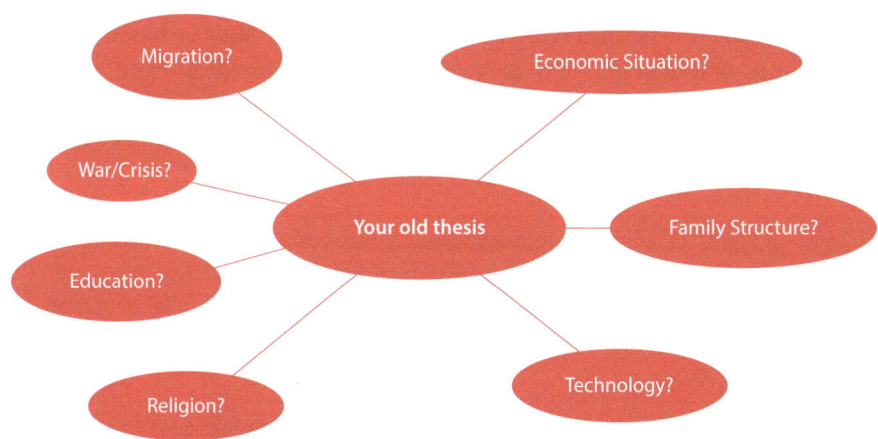

Use the following guidelines to write a working thesis based on the diagram you created above.

A working thesis

> Develop a working thesis for the new paper based on the mind map created in the previous task.
> 1. Read the working thesis out loud.
> 2. Circle the topic and underline the point of view.
> 3. Does the thesis inform the reader about the content of the research paper?
> 4. Keep this working thesis/research question for incorporation into your research paper later.

> **Relevance**
> A working thesis guides and limits the search for secondary/published sources and minimizes collecting sources that are irrelevant to the topic.

You will use the new working thesis to guide your search for supporting secondary sources for the research paper. However, before examining sources, the paper should be formatted.

5. Formatting the research paper

Formatting the paper at the outset saves work later in the writing process. Documenting all sources using the correct citation format is important while reviewing the literature for appropriate sources for the new research paper. Revisit Chapter 10 for formatting using APA.

Keep in mind during the review process that the paper must be based on a minimum of five sources in addition to the primary sources from the previous case study. The sources must include at least: one scholarly book, two peer-reviewed scholarly articles, and two reliable websites in addition to sources from the case study. Documenting sources appropriately is the topic of a later section in this chapter.

> Format your paper. The guidelines for the assignment state that students should use the APA format for the research paper. The font is Times New Roman and the font size is 12 points. All sources must be cited with correct APA in the text and in the list of references.

B. Examining published sources: A review of the literature

Research papers in all disciplines are based on a review of existing literature with very few exceptions. However, not all disciplines require a literature review to be presented in a separate section in the paper. It is important for students to examine research articles and chapters in their field of study to determine how the state of knowledge is presented.

> *Reflection*
> *Examine one or two articles in your field of study and review their subsections. Describe each article's structure and the order in which the subsections are presented. Is it a research article? How do you know? If it is not a research article, what type of article is it?*

Most university students are required to use scholarly sources for writing their academic papers. Below are some examples of secondary sources:

- biographies
- histories
- literary criticism
- book, art, and theater reviews
- newspaper articles that interpret events
- editorials, reviews, reports, websites, web journals
- scholarly books and articles
- publications about the significance of research or experiments
- analysis of a clinical trial
- review of several experiments or trials
- literature reviews

Depending on the topic and theme, a research paper may require supportive evidence from different types of research, both quantitative and qualitative (see Chapter 8 for a review).

Quantitative studies use statistics to demonstrate general trends, demographics, or opinions of large populations or groups, and so on. This type of evidence may be required to give background information in a research paper about a remarkable individual.

Qualitative studies based on interviews and other ethnographic data may provide an historical perspective and context for an individual's life.

1. Disciplinary literacy – academic genres

Each research discipline has a specific methodology of hypothesizing, collecting, and analyzing data and different ways of discussing and presenting results. This variation is reflected in the way academics discuss their studies, both in the vocabulary they use and in the way the text is written. It is quite possible that the same word is used with different meanings or different nuances of meaning in sources from different disciplines, as in the following example:

> Standards of *discipline* have increased as a result of the new program.
> Computer Assisted Language Learning is a new *discipline*.
>
> Learning about all depression *treatment* options will help decide which one is the most appropriate.
> The experimental study included a *treatment* involving explicit teaching of grammar.

Conducting secondary research is made easier when the researcher/student pays attention to the discourse and text structure of the different sources. This will help the student understand the textbooks, articles and other materials in their courses as well as express themselves in spoken language.

> **Relevance**
> Many students are familiar with literary genres from reading and writing about fiction in their EFL classes. Disciplinary literacy refers to genres of a discipline. One way to become familiar with the genre of a discipline is to develop a personal glossary of terms used in lectures, texts, and other materials in one's program of study.

2. Strategies for finding sources

Secondary research requires visiting a library or doing a web search to find appropriate resources.

The sample working thesis in this section is:

World War 2 brought about social changes that changed the lives of women like my grandmother.

This sample working thesis will guide John's search for relevant sources.

There are many sources available on the same topic and millions of documents on the web, so even a guided search might yield thousands of results. It is therefore important to search according to the guidelines presented by the library search system or online search engine to narrow down results to the appropriate documents for the purpose at hand.

While searching, it is often difficult to distinguish scholarly and popular literature. Journals, magazines, and newspapers are important sources for current information in all disciplines. News articles can be reliable sources of information on events and issues of public concern. Popular articles reflect the tastes of the general public and are often meant as entertainment. Scholarly or peer-reviewed journal articles are written by scholars or professionals who are experts in their fields.

Writing research papers usually requires working with scholarly articles. Journals that contain scholarly articles are also called academic, peer-reviewed, or refereed journals. Journals usually indicate whether they are peer-reviewed. Articles in peer-reviewed journals have been evaluated by other experts in the field prior to being published and are therefore considered reliable. Most scholarly articles:

- have an abstract,
- contain an introduction, a literature review, sections describing the study and results, a discussion and conclusions,
- have full citations of their sources in the form of a reference list at the end,
- are written by scholars in the field,
- list affiliations of the authors,
- use discourse specific to their discipline.

One general strategy to find sources is to examine the list of references in the scholarly publications. Often the same references will start reappearing on many reference lists. Most likely, this is because these frequently cited references are landmark studies or important contributions to the discussion on that topic and are therefore worth examining for possible inclusion in the research paper.

The student in our example writing about his grandmother begins the search by looking for sources that relate to the status of women during World War 2. The following example demonstrates how John narrowed down his search:

Using the working thesis to identify sources

> The sample working thesis is: *World War 2 brought about social changes that changed the lives of women like my grandmother.*
>
> The topic is: WW2 brought about social change at home.
>
> The point of view is: WW2 changed the lives of women like my grandmother.
>
> The larger socio-historical context is: WW2
>
> The specific context is: WW2 affected the lives of women who took on different non-traditional roles.
>
> The changes included: Women working outside the home, many taking on management positions not open to them before the war.
>
> Specifically, for the remarkable person (grandmother): she found an outlet for her creativity and hard work.
>
> The search should focus on: The status of women during World War 2.
>
> The key words might be: WW2, women and WW2, the home front, women and the workforce, women in management during WW2.

3. Identifying sources

Use the following guidelines to narrow your search for relevant sources.

Use your working thesis to identify sources

> Your sample working thesis is:
>
> The topic and point of view are:
>
> The larger socio-historical context is:
>
> The specific context is:
>
> The changes included (if relevant):
>
> Specifically, for the remarkable person:
>
> The search should focus on:
>
> The key words might be:

The literature review presents ONLY sources that are relevant to the working thesis. Regardless of the topic, the paper should be based on enough reliable resources to give a full picture of the chosen topic.

The next sections present strategies for reading, evaluating and choosing published sources guided by the narrowed search criteria.

> **Relevance**
> Papers assigned at university are often based on reviewing secondary sources. Practicing effective strategies to find, evaluate, and choose the relevant sources will benefit students in all academic work.

4. Strategies for choosing reliable and relevant secondary sources

Depending on a writer's preferences and the type of research review, there are many strategies an author may use to evaluate and choose reliable sources to address the research question. Below are basic guidelines that will help the inexperienced writer choose the most helpful and relevant sources. The strategies for choosing and evaluating scholarly sources in the library are generally the same as for evaluating sources online. A basic rule is to use multiple sources that are diverse and written by reliable experts.

> **Reflection**
> *Conducting a web search can be a time consuming, often frustrating experience. What strategies do you employ to find the information you need? How might you benefit from an online tutorial on ways to evaluate online material?*

a. Quantity and diversity of scholarly sources

There should be enough resources to support the thesis. This assignment calls for the use of one scholarly book, two scholarly articles, and two scholarly websites. Sources can come from books, articles, editorials, reviews, reports, websites, or web journals. Novice writers sometimes rely heavily on one source with the result that the research paper becomes a summary of that source. An effective literature review includes multiple different sources that address the identified themes and strengthen the thesis.

b. Date of publication

The date of publication should be appropriate to the project. If the topic is a current event, resources that are recent and reflect current attitudes are most appropriate. If conducting historical research, choosing a variety of resources from different time periods might be in order.

c. Quality and reliability

The quality and reliability of the material depend on the expertise and purpose of the author. First and foremost, it is important to determine whether the author is an authority on the topic. Look for articles in scientific journals or book chapters published by a reputable publisher. The article/book chapter has most likely been reviewed by experts and is, therefore, reliable. Choose authors affiliated with reputable universities and institutions and choose official and public websites rather than personal websites.

Below are checklists for evaluating printed and online sources.

> **Relevance**
> Recognizing the reliability of a source saves time and helps students choose the best sources for their papers. This is a critical skill that applies to any search for information a student may undertake.

5. Evaluating sources

> Use the criteria presented below to evaluate a scholarly article or book chapter you are considering using as a source for your paper.
>
> If the answer is yes, examine the source further.
> If the answer is no, this is not an acceptable source.
>
> – Is the article in a scientific journal published by a reputable publisher or by a reputable organization?
>   Yes _____ No_____.
> – Is the author affiliated with a reputable institution?
>   Yes _____ No_____.
> – Is the tone or the text objective and balanced?
>   Yes _____ No_____.
> – Is the publication a newspaper or journal that expresses the views of a political organization with a certain agenda? If so, it is not likely to be objective.
>   Yes _____ No_____.
> – Are the conclusions supported by data or is it an opinion piece?
>   Yes _____ No_____.
> – Are the conclusions supported by other scholarly works?
>   Yes _____ No_____.
> – How does the content relate to your topic?
>
> The article is most likely worth examining further if the answer was yes to all of the above.

Evaluating the reliability of a web source

> Because of the vast number of resources on the web, each website needs to be critically evaluated for the reliability of the information it presents.
>
> Choose a website you believe contains information relevant to your research question. Below are some guidelines to determine the reliability of the website:

> - Is the website commercial or public? Public websites often have the domain .org, .edu, .gov. These may give indications as to the authority and objectivity of the authors. URLs which end in .com are commercial.
> - The URL of this website is:
>   http://_____
> - What credentials make this site scholarly or valuable to your research? Is the institution or organization that sponsors the site reputable?
>   Consult subpages that often appear under headings such as: *About us, About the organization, Background, Philosophy*. Is there evidence suggesting that the information is accurate and reliable and authoritative?
> - Is the author affiliated with a reputable institution?
> - Is the tone or the text objective and balanced? If the audience is other scholars, the writing has most likely been reviewed by experts and therefore reputable.
> - Is the website updated?
> - Is the content relevant to your topic, if so, how?
>
> If the answer is yes to these questions, the website is most likely reliable and relevant. If the answer is No to any of these questions, or if you cannot find a clear answer, the website may not be reliable and relevant.

C. Reading and documenting selected sources

Potential sources have now been identified and documented based on the narrowed search criteria guided by the new working thesis. A preliminary examination suggests that the sources are both relevant and reliable. At this point it is time to review the sources to determine which of them could be included in the research paper.

Reading published sources is a skill that requires practice. It is important to keep in mind whether the text will be useful to support the thesis of the paper, in this case, on a remarkable person.

1. Strategies for reading secondary sources

Below are some guidelines of what to look for while reviewing that will help you in your choice of sources for more detailed evaluation.

a. *Strategies for reading a scholarly book*

1. Read the title of the book. Look up the meaning of any unknown words. What does the title tell about the book's content?
2. Examine the table of contents.
3. Read the introduction and conclusion or the first and last pages.

b. *Strategies for reading an article*

1. Read the abstract of the article.
2. Read the introduction and conclusion of the article. Find the thesis statement/ research question in the introduction and the research findings in the conclusions.

This process will likely lead to a selection of a sub-group of sources that seem relevant and need further review. Below are strategies to read selected sources more closely to determine whether they are likely to be relevant to the topic.

c. *Strategies for reading selected sources*

1. Read through the chapters/articles actively.
   - The topic sentences should indicate the content of the paragraph.
   - Read the first and last paragraph of selected chapters in a book.
2. Highlight passages that seem to be especially relevant.
3. Write down impressions while reading.
4. Write down the author's central thesis and evidence that supports the thesis.
5. What makes this author a credible expert?
6. How does the text relate to the topic?
7. Cite the source fully.

> **Reflection**
> *Think of the successful strategies you have used to skim and scan texts. Are these appropriate for this task and if so, why or why not?*

The next step is to evaluate the relevance of sources you identified previously.

2. Evaluating the relevance of selected sources

Now it is your turn to read and evaluate sources you have chosen to use to support your thesis. Please follow the guidelines that are repeated from above.

Evaluating the relevance of selected sources

> Read two of your selected sources, an article and a book chapter. Use the strategies below to determine the relevance of the sources to your thesis.
>
> 1. Use the strategies presented below to read a book chapter.
>   a. Read the title of the book. Look up the meaning of any unknown words. What does the title tell about the book's content?
>   b. Examine the table of contents.
>   c. Read the introduction and conclusion.

> 2. Use these strategies to read the article
>   a. Read the abstract of an article.
>   b. Read the introduction and conclusion of an article. Find the thesis statement/research question in the introduction and the research findings in the conclusions.
> 3. Determine whether they are appropriate to include in your list of sources to support the working thesis.
>
> Do the same for any other sources you are considering for inclusion in your research paper.

3. Documenting selected sources

It is important to document all sources while reading them. Going back to find cited sources while composing the reference list is very time consuming.

a. *Documenting sources during the literature review*

As you review the literature, document the following information using the APA format:

1. Name of author(s)
2. Date of publication
3. Title of publication
4. Article and/or book title
5. Title of journal (if applicable)
6. Page numbers if the source is an article
7. Page number where quote or source is found
8. Indicate whether the notes are quotes, paraphrases or summaries.

Citation software is useful for keeping a record of chosen sources. There are several good tutorials online for learning how to use citation software.

b. *Using APA for in-text citations and the list of references*

Starting a list of references at the beginning of the literature review will save time at later stages of writing. Writers edit the list of references at the end. According to the APA format style, a list of references starts on a separate page at the end of the research paper under the heading *References*. The list of references is in alphabetical order according to the last name of the first author and includes only those sources that are cited in the paper. The list of references is double spaced and uses a hanging indent. All sources cited in the text must be included in the list of references at the end of the paper.

Using the APA format style to cite primary sources is covered in Chapter 9. Below are basic rules for citing secondary sources such as articles, books, and websites. There are also examples of how to cite in text and how to list the same sources in the *References* at the end of the paper.

In-text citations of secondary sources (articles and books) follow the author-date method.

One author:

Smith (2017) claims ...
He claimed that children are good language learners (Smith, 2018).
"Children are good language learners" (Smith, 2019, p. 39).

Two or more authors:

Jones and Smith (1996) or Jones, Smith and Brown (1996) suggest...
In the '90s the prevailing view was ... (Jones & Smith, 1996).
"after a direct quote" (Jones & Smith, 1996, p. 11).
Moore & Jones (2019) contend...

Three or more authors:

Include only the name of the first author followed by et al. if mentioned previously.
Jones et al. (1996) proposed ...
The authors (Jones et al., 1996).

An online article:

If the article has an author:
(Smith, 2017).

If the web page has no author use the title in the author's place:

(The wonders of listening, 2006).

If the web page has no date:

(The wonders of writing, n.d.).

Example: In-text citation

Smith (2019) argues that there is an optimal age for learning languages and that this view is supported by many different studies (Smith, 2017, 2018; Jones, Smith & Brown, 1996). Smith goes on to claim that "the youngest children are the best language learners" (Smith, 2019, p. 39). However, Moore & Jones (2019) contend that this issue is more complex. They point to studies by Jones & Smith (1996) and Jones et al. (1996) whose findings suggest that the youngest children may not be the best language learners. In the 1990s, the prevailing view was that the optimal age for language learning might be from 9–11 years of age (Jones & Smith, 1996; Jones et al., 1996). Studies by Jones et al. of over 60 students from 9–11 and 15–18 years demonstrate that "the younger age group outperformed the older group" (p. 11). The research team then replicated the study 10 years later with the same results. More recently, studies have shown that children aged 9–11 are also better listeners (The wonders of listening, 2006), but that older students are better at learning how to write in a second language (The wonders of writing, n.d.).

The in-text citations appear in this form in the reference list.

References

Jones, B., & Smith, J. (1996). Young children learning language. *Fine Journal, 5*(2), 45–63.
Jones, B., Smith, J., & Brown, A. (1996). The wonders of reading. *The New Journal, 12*(3), 4–22.
Moore, C., & Jones, B. B. (2019). *Writing English for research*. Grand Publishers.
Smith, H. (2019). *The wonders of language acquisition*. Very Good Books Publishers.
Smith, J. (2018). The wonders of writing. *The New Journal, 11*(3), 5–19.
Smith, J. (2017). Student writers. *Journal of Writing 1*(3). http://journalofwriting.org/writing/academicwriting/
"The wonders of listening". (2006). http://www.uuu.edu/hh/about/listeningwonders.html
"The wonders of writing". (n.d.). http://www.uuu.edu/hh/about/listeningwonders.html

Practice: Documenting selected sources using the APA format

Document one article and one book you are reviewing.
Include:

1. Name of author(s)
2. Date of publication
3. Title of publication
4. Page numbers of article
5. Page number where quote or source is found

Begin the reference list by listing these entries according to the APA format.

Relevance

It is important to write down all the relevant information about the sources you are reading. This is more efficient than going back and trying to find the sources in the last stages of the writing process.

D. Taking notes while reading

Writers use different ways to take notes while reading sources. They may write an annotated reference, direct quotations, paraphrases and/or summaries depending on the purpose and use in the research paper. Annotating, quoting, paraphrasing and summarizing are also good strategies to avoid plagiarism.

Plagiarism is considered theft of the work of others. Plagiarism is taken very seriously in academic work and most universities have a plagiarism policy that lists the consequences of using other writers' work without attribution. Plagiarism is easily identified. Sometimes a simple Google search of a student's text leads to the original source. Software available to most instructors identifies texts that have been copied from elsewhere. Usually, however, it is simply the discrepancy in style, fluency and accuracy between the student's own writing and the plagiarized text that is the giveaway.

As most academic work is built on other authors' writing, a writer must take great care to acknowledge all sources used by citing them explicitly in the text. When reading sources and deciding to use information from them as evidence, writing down the source and whether the information is a quote, paraphrase or summary is essential. This will facilitate incorporating the information into the paper in the appropriate way. Strategies to annotate are introduced next.

> *Reflection*
> *What risks do students take by plagiarizing? How likely are students to get away with plagiarism when most instructors have access to programs that allow them to identify in a few seconds where a plagiarized item comes from? What is the policy on plagiarism at your university?*

1. Annotation

An annotated bibliography is a list of sources that provides publication information and a short description of each source, called an *annotation*. Some annotations merely describe the content of the source, while others include an evaluation of the source's relevance to a researcher's thesis. An annotated reference helps the writer evaluate later in the research process whether a source is relevant to the topic. Annotations are usually about 150 words long (or four to six sentences) and may include some or all of the following information:

- the main focus of the work
- the intended audience
- relevance to the research topic
- reliability and expertise of the author
- conclusions
- your observations
- all the bibliographic information for the reference list.

> *Relevance*
> Practicing writing an annotated reference helps students understand the relevance of the sources they are reading to their topic, and it practices drawing out main points in a text. Because literature reviews can take a long time, annotations are useful to help the writer remember the content of sources read weeks before.

a. *Examining annotation*

Below are two examples of an annotated reference. The first one is rather short, while the second one is more detailed.

Example 1:

The National Archives (1998). *Women in Industry: World War 2*. Kendall/Hunt Publishing Co.

This book contains letters, pictures, cartoons, pamphlets, memoranda, and an executive order concerning the role of women in industry. The main focus is on the individual experiences of women at home during WW2. It is written for the public, but also for historians. The National Archives is a reliable government agency. Sections on document analysis and use of National Archives might lead to other sources.

Adapted from: <https://www.archives.gov/research/alic/reference/women.html>

Example 2:

Clendon, S. A., & Erickson, K. A. (2008). The vocabulary of beginning writers: Implications for children with complex communication needs. *Augmentative and Alternative Communication, 24*, 281–293. doi:10.1080/07434610802463999

The purpose of this study was to examine the vocabulary that typically developing early-elementary school children use when they write about self-selected topics. Across seven schools (K-3), 125 children in the US and 113 in New Zealand wrote about self-selected topics at least 3 times per week for 6 weeks. A total of 2,721 writing samples with 85,759 total words and 5,724 different words were analyzed to determine which words were used most frequently. The set of 163 words accounted for 70% of the total words used, with 39 of those words accounting for 50% of the total words used. While this study focused on written language, it adds to our understanding that a small set of words comprises the vast majority of the total words used in oral and written language.

Adapted from: <http://www.project-core.com/core-vocabulary/>

b. *An annotated reference*

Practice: Writing an annotation

Write an annotation of two of the sources you are reading.
1. The annotations should be no more than 100–150 words (or four to six sentences) each.
2. The annotation and bibliographic information should be written in APA format.

2. Quoting, paraphrasing and summarizing

Strategies to quote, paraphrase, and summarize primary sources for the case study are practiced in Chapter 8. These rules apply to secondary sources as well.

a. *Strategies for quoting secondary sources*

Quotations should be kept to a minimum in a research paper and must be identical to the original and attributed to the author. Use quotes only when they illustrate or enhance the thesis. Quotes should be short unless they need to be longer than two to three lines for comprehension or effect. Short quotes should be incorporated into the text in quotation marks.

Example: Mary Jones said, "The Red Cross will save the day, again" (2020, p. 74).

When a quotation contains 40 words or more it is treated as a block quotation. Bloc quotations do not use quotation marks; the entire block is indented from the margin. Place a period at the end of the quotation with the parenthetical citation directly after the text.

Example:

From the beginning of modern psychology, dream researchers have maintained that dreams cannot predict the future:

> To be sure the ancient belief that the dream reveals the future is not entirely devoid of truth. By representing to us a wish as fulfilled the dream certainly leads us into the future; but this future, taken by the dreamer as present, has been formed into the likeness of that past by the indestructible wish. (Freud, 1920, p. 89)

See Chapter 8 for further guidelines about using direct quotes.

b. *Strategies for paraphrasing secondary sources*

Paraphrasing academic text means rewording essential information and ideas expressed by someone else, usually an expert. It is not a summary of ideas but a rephrasing of short passages, conclusions, or opinions. A paraphrase must also be attributed to the original source. In order to paraphrase effectively, remember to:

1. Read the original passage carefully.
2. Without looking at the original text, write down your paraphrase.
3. Mark the note as a paraphrase.
4. Write the key words on the side to remind you where the content of the paraphrase belongs in your paper.
5. Check your paraphrase against the original to make sure it is accurate.
6. Use quotation marks if you decide to use words or phrases verbatim.
7. Write down the author, title, year, and page number.

See Chapter 8 for more strategies to paraphrase. Below, strategies for summarizing academic text are presented.

c. *Strategies for summarizing secondary sources*

Writing summaries is an excellent way to understand the main points in a secondary source and to practice writing. Summarizing involves retelling the main idea(s) in your own words. Always attribute summarized ideas to the original source/author.

Try these strategies when writing a short summary of an article or chapter:

1. Write the author's name, title of article and purpose for writing the article.
2. Use the present tense.
3. Write one sentence for each idea the author has presented.
4. Use connectors to join the ideas together.
5. Find the main point, the supporting points and finally the conclusion.

A summary varies in length depending on the length of the original text. A good rule of thumb is to keep the summary approximately 1/3 of the length of the original text and restate only the main points without giving examples or details. See Chapter 8 for further details on summarizing.

Use the checklists below for quoting, paraphrasing and summarizing while working with secondary sources for possible inclusion in your paper.

Practice: Writing quotations

> Choose two to three quotes from your sources that you might be able to use in your paper.
> 1. Write a sentence that introduces the quotation.
> 2. Format the quotation according to APA style. Include an appropriate APA in-text citation.
> 3. Write a sentence that explains how each quote will advance your thesis.

Practice: Writing paraphrase

> Paraphrase 3–4 lines from one of your sources that are relevant to your topic.
> 1. Read the original passage carefully.
> 2. Without looking at the original text, write down your paraphrase.
> 3. Mark the note as a paraphrase.
> 4. Write the key words on the side to remind you where the content of the paraphrase belongs in your essay.
> 5. Check your paraphrase against the original to make sure it is accurate.
> 6. Use quotation marks if you decide to use words or phrases verbatim.
> 7. Write down the author, title, year, and page number.

Practice: Writing summaries

1. Find the topic sentence.
2. Find the main ideas that support the topic sentence.
3. Rewrite the topic sentence in your own words.
4. Present the author's main supporting ideas in 2–3 sentences, using your own words.
5. Use discourse connectors where appropriate.
6. Place key words in the margins that indicate where you might use this information in your paper.
7. Record the information necessary for citations and reference list.
8. Be sure to note the page number of source.

Writers can use summaries, paraphrases, and quotations in the same text. A writer can summarize a report, paraphrase conclusions and quote passages from interviews or diaries. It is important that they are relevant and that they advance the thesis.

E. Organizing sources for inclusion in the paper

Writing a research paper requires connecting ideas and relating them to a working thesis. At the beginning of this chapter, you wrote up a "working thesis". The working thesis guided the data collection and helped identify possible sources for this paper. Perhaps the review did not yield data to support what seemed to be a strong idea or research may have uncovered new or contradictory evidence. When this happens, the writer may reevaluate and change the working thesis to reflect the actual data as they emerge.

This process begins with the writer organizing the data into logical categories that will become evidence for the thesis. The categories (themes) will provide the basis for paragraph development later in the writing process. The new sources should be organized so that the writer can evaluate their relevance to the working thesis and decide whether there is enough information to support a thesis statement.

The next sections focus on strategies to help students limit the sources to those relevant to the research question/working thesis. This includes establishing the themes that are most pertinent to the topic and examining the categories of ideas that support or challenge those themes and eliminating others. The mind map/cluster diagram about John's grandmother as a businesswoman created earlier is used as an example in the next section. You can work with your mind map from p. 243.

1. Strategies for organizing sources according to themes

Regardless of how clear, focused, and insightful a thesis statement may be, the paper will not succeed unless the ideas in the body of the paper are organized logically, and unless all the evidence directly supports the topic and point of view of the thesis statement. The writer must therefore choose the themes that relate to a thesis and integrate into the paper only the secondary sources that will adequately support the thesis.

Organization of sources begins with the writer reviewing all the sources looking for:

- evidence to support main themes or ideas from previous brainstorming points
- logical connections among ideas
- new main ideas that sources have revealed.

This section reexamines basic strategies for organizing and evaluating data and applies them to the sample social history paper where John's grandmother is the main subject. In this example, John writes about how his grandmother saved the family business and how the grandmother's experiences reflect changes in opportunities for women at the time. Using a cluster diagram, he outlined ideas that appear to support the following thesis:

> World War 2 brought about social changes that changed the lives of women like my grandmother.

a. *Examining ideas that support John's thesis*

The diagram below shows some of the supporting ideas that John believed would serve as evidence to support the thesis and provide the necessary historical background. The ideas on the cluster map are the topics that the writer investigated. However, research did not uncover data to support all of these ideas. Therefore, after collecting data in each of these areas, John needed to determine if:

- the data provide sufficient evidence for each of the supporting ideas
- the supporting ideas establish the validity of the thesis
- more research is required
- the thesis needs to be modified based on research.

John found ample evidence to show how the Second World War brought about social changes in the lives of women in the United Kingdom, including his grandmother's life, and that led to a movement that affected many women around the world. He was not able to find as many sources supporting other themes.

A possible new working thesis might be:

> World War 2 brought about social changes that led to financial independence for women like my grandmother.

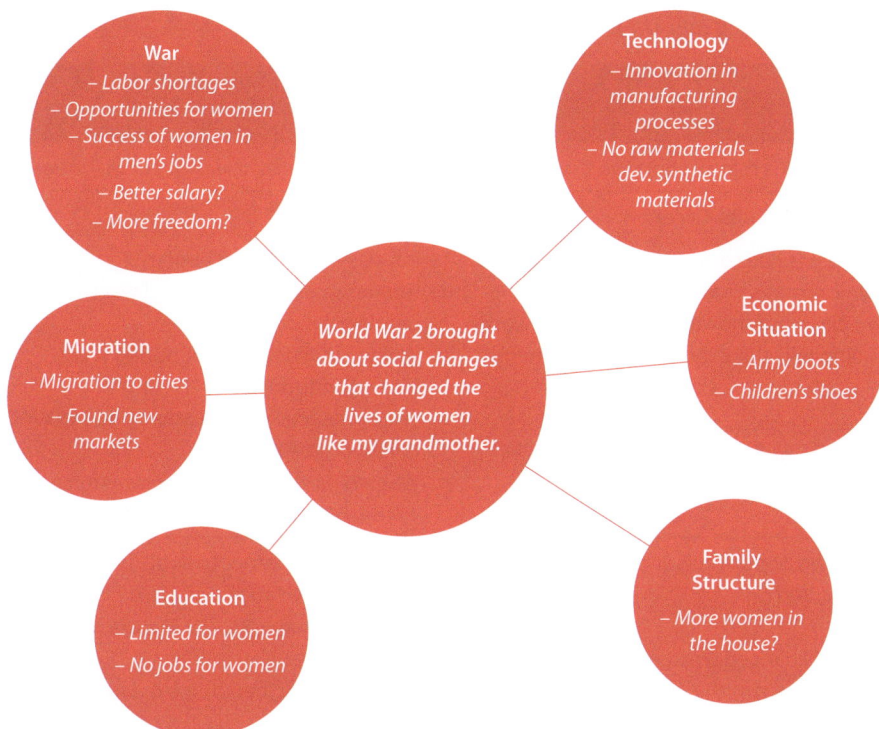

Using this model, the writer's conclusions should provide evidence for what will become the final thesis. The author begins the evaluation process by listing sources that appear to support some of the themes they identified for their paper. One way to accomplish this and organize the data at the same time is to use a T chart, as shown below.

b. *T chart*

The two-column outline, or T chart, was introduced in Chapter 5 and is a useful framework that helps the writer organize data. It creates a visual representation of the types and amount of data available. The steps for creating a T chart are given below:

- begin by listing in column A, the original main ideas from the cluster map
- add any new concepts or ideas that emerged during data collection to column A
- review all of the data carefully several times to find evidence to support ideas
- note evidence in column B, next to corresponding main idea.

Example for the paper on John's grandmother.

Thesis: *World War 2 brought about social changes that led to financial independence for women like my grandmother.*	
A. Main ideas that support the thesis	B. Evidence to support validity of main ideas
I. Failing business – economy	
Businesses had to adjust to changing economic climate. Women brought in innovative ideas and showed they could do work traditionally done by men (management)	1. Interview aunt (army boots) 2. Gender roles during times of war (www.genderroles.com) 3. Women in management during WW2 (Brown and Jones, 2017) 4. The home fires – the economy during WW2. (Smith et al.,1999) 5. Women participating in the workforce 1918–1944 (Jordan et al., 1972)
II. limited opportunity for career for women prior to WW The war changed western society's views about women in the workforce	1. Letter, grandmother to aunt 2. Interview with aunt 3. Job advertisements. The Manchester Examiner 4. The Women's Liberation Movement (Brown, 2009) 5. Gender roles during times of war <www.genderroles.com> 6. History of labor participation (book, Smith 2012) 7. Statistics, www.laborstatistics.org, Ministry of Labor
Opportunities during WW2 Changes in workforce	1. Statistics <www.laborstatistics.org> Minister of Labor 2. History of labor participation (book, Smith 2012) The road to women's financial independence (article, Aug., 2001)
Migration	Census 1944 <www.census.org>
Technology (move to failing business/economy) Changes in manufacturing Innovation	The history of manufacturing in the UK and US <www.hmus.org>
Family Structure	
Education	

Developing the T chart revealed that there were not enough sources to support an inclusion of the themes of education, family structure and migration. These were therefore eliminated. The theme of technology was incorporated into the theme of the failing business under a new heading, economy.

2. Organizing new information for inclusion in the research paper

Below is a T chart for you to evaluate the themes you might use as evidence to support your working thesis along with the sources that support those themes.

Practice: Organizing the evidence using a T chart

Your working thesis:

A. Main themes or ideas that support the thesis	B. Evidence to support validity of main ideas (remember to cite)
I	1.
	2.
	3.
	4.
II	1.
	2.
	3.
	4.
III	1.
	2.
	3.
	4.

Strategies for reviewing the themes (ideas) and evidence

Review the data on the T chart outline you created.
1. Does each main idea support the thesis statement directly? Put a line through the ideas that do not relate to the thesis.
2. Are there a sufficient number of main ideas to support the thesis?
3. Is each main idea supported by at least three pieces of evidence? Circle the main ideas that need more evidence.
4. Does the evidence support the main idea directly? Put a line through the evidence that does not support the main idea.
5. Does the research suggest any modifications to the working thesis?
6. Eliminate any main ideas that do not relate to the thesis statement.
7. Is additional research needed for the main ideas that do not have sufficient evidence?

3. Reevaluating the strength and relevance of the new information

Once the sources have been organized according to themes, the writer needs to evaluate again the quality and quantity of the evidence. Is there enough reliable data to support each theme? Themes with weak or insufficient support and themes that do not directly support the thesis weaken the research paper and must be eliminated, no matter how interesting they are.

Triangulation

Triangulation is the process of using multiple sources and types of data to validate the credibility of an idea. For this paper at least five sources of different types (a book, two articles and two websites) are needed. One point or idea is discussed in one paragraph using multiple sources. Remember that presenting data from a single source limits credibility. Below is an example of how one point is presented in a paragraph with several sources.

Data triangulation framework for a paragraph based on one idea
Examine the example below:

> Working thesis: *World War 2 brought about social changes that led to financial independence for women like my grandmother.*
> Main idea #2: Opportunities for women were limited prior to WW2.

The data from John's T chart outline shows that there are four sources of data to support the main idea. Moreover, the data comes from four types of sources: an interview and letter, a book (Brown, 2009), a website <www.ww2genderroles.com>, and an article, (Jordan, Kowalski & Yang, 1972).

*Note that these are all fictitious sources created for this example.

Main idea: opportunities for women were limited prior to WW2				
Source 1	Source 2	Source 3	Source 4	Source 5
Interview with aunt	Letter from grand-mother to aunt	Precursors to the Women's Liberation Movement (Brown, 2009)	Gender roles during times of war <www.ww2genderroles.com>	Women's participation in the work force from 1918–1944 (Jordan, Kowalski & Yang, 1972)
Primary source	Primary source	Secondary source – book	Secondary source – website	Secondary source – article

Practice: Data triangulation for a paragraph

Using the chart below, triangulate the sources you have identified to support each of the ideas you will present as evidence to support your thesis. A chart for one paragraph is provided.

Main idea:					
	Source 1	Source 2	Source 3	Source 4	Source 5
Type of source					

If you need more data to support an idea, this is the time to conduct a follow-up search for the sources that will provide the missing data. The search is more focused than the previous one as this time the search criteria are more specific.

F. Expanding language

Researchers in most disciplines use a specific way of reporting their findings. Their choice of vocabulary is an indication of the strength or weakness of their results or the certainty of their claim.

Sometimes it is difficult for a reader to interpret how confident the experts are in their findings. For instance, researchers in the humanities and social sciences avoid using the verb *prove* but prefer to use words like *support* or *validate* as it is difficult to prove anything that has to do with human behavior. However, proving hypotheses is common in the natural sciences.

The following words indicate weaknesses in findings or express caution about their implications: *would* (most frequently used), *may, suggest, indicate, assume, possible/possibly, could*.

Words that suggest strength in research findings are: *show (that)* (most frequently used), *find (that), determine, will, it is clear/clearly, the fact that, demonstrate (that), confirm, support*.

These examples show the strength of claim from weak to strong:

The findings may indicate that climate change is a threat. (weak)
The findings suggest that climate change is a threat. (stronger)
The findings confirm that climate change is a threat. (strongest)

Exercise:

Arrange the following sentences according to the strength of the claim made from strongest to weakest.

I.
1. The results of our study could possibly help to develop appropriate interventions.
2. The results of our study will help to develop appropriate interventions.
3. The results of our study may help to develop appropriate interventions.
4. The results of our study should help to develop appropriate interventions.

II.
1. Based on the results of our study, we assume that teachers should help to develop appropriate interventions.
2. It is clear from the results of our study that teachers should help to develop appropriate interventions.
3. The results of our study demonstrate that teachers should help to develop appropriate interventions.
4. The results of our study suggest that teachers should help to develop appropriate interventions.

Chapter 12

Writing the research paper

In the last chapter, students developed a working thesis, read and organized their sources and grouped them into themes. This chapter begins by establishing a thesis statement to guide the final stages of writing the research paper. Students examine and practice synthesizing information which is essential to writing clear body paragraphs. Students are led through writing the first draft of the research paper based on a detailed outline of its architecture and a blueprint of its content. As with previous writing assignments, the body paragraphs are written before the introduction and the conclusion. The chapter concludes as students assess the quality and quantity of evidence they provide to support the thesis statement and finally, revise and edit the paper.

In this chapter, students will:

- develop the thesis statement for the research paper,
- synthesize and organize the evidence that supports the thesis statement,
- write body paragraphs appropriate for a research paper,
- write topic sentences as guideposts for each paragraph,
- write concluding sentences for each paragraph,
- write an introduction and a conclusion appropriate for a research paper,
- develop strategies to combine paragraphs into a coherent whole,
- assess the content of the paper for quantity and quality.

A. Examining the thesis statement

After sources have been identified that will provide the evidence for the thesis, the next step is to sharpen the working thesis into a thesis statement that will guide the writing of the paper. The new thesis statement is based on the reviewed sources and should reflect the writer's findings.

1. From working thesis to thesis statement

Below is the evolution of the thesis statement from the previous sample case study on John's grandmother to a new thesis statement that will guide the writing of his research paper:

> **John's original working thesis from the case study:** My grandmother's leadership, keen insight and wartime economics propelled her to create a shoe empire during WW2.

The thesis was revised in Chapter 10 as seen below:

> **Revised thesis:** By turning a failing factory into a thriving business with innovative ideas and insightful leadership, Sarah Woodward's remarkable entrepreneurship demonstrated that women were as capable as men.
>
> <u>Presents</u> the topic: Sarah Woodward
>
> <u>Informs</u> the reader of a claim about the topic: demonstrated that women were as capable as men.

Based on the old thesis and additional readings, John created a possible new working thesis for the research paper:

> *World War 2 brought about social changes that led to financial independence for hard-working and creative women like my grandmother.*
>
> <u>Presents</u> the topic: *Hard-working and creative women like my grandmother*
>
> <u>Informs</u> the reader of a claim about the topic: *World War 2 brought about social changes that led to financial independence for hard working and creative women.*

In these examples, the thesis statement controls the paper by showing how WW2 brought about changes that made the grandmother a successful businesswoman. But the grandmother also had certain characteristics such as being hard working and creative. The *content* of the paper will examine the factors that led to the grandmother's success (changes in women's careers during WW2, failing business, in addition to innovation and hard work). The *evidence* will illustrate and describe how the onset of WW2 opened up opportunities for women by presenting statistics and historical accounts, and add to points about the hard work, and creativity which led to the grandmother's success. The evidence is based on support from the secondary and primary sources.

The paper must contain clear and sufficient evidence to convince the reader why the grandmother became successful. The new thesis statement summarizes the claim or point of view John will present. The thesis statement:

- determines content and structure of the essay
- is a roadmap for the research paper
- usually refers to the topic + the writer's point of view about it + and reasons for the point of view
- tells the reader what to expect
- is usually in the introductory paragraph
- is supported by evidence.

Use this description as a model for developing a new thesis statement for your research paper in the next section.

B. AWARE: Arranging to write the thesis statement and outline

The thesis statement will guide the development of a detailed outline of the evidence that supports the thesis. First the thesis is developed.

1. The thesis statement

Use the chart below to develop a thesis statement for your research paper. Consider the T chart and triangulation from the previous chapter. As the thesis statement needs to provide a unified claim, use the discourse connectors as seen in the guidelines below to make your thesis statement unified.

From working thesis to thesis statement for the research paper

The General Topic: The socio-historical context of a remarkable person I know
Current working thesis:
New thesis:

> What is the topic of the thesis statement?
>
>
>
> What is the claim about the topic (point of view)?
>
>
>
> Use discourse connectors:
>
> If the thesis can be divided into two or more claims, try to connect them with a coordinating conjunction (like *and, but, for, nor, or, so, yet*). Or, if appropriate, try to connect the two statements with a subordinating conjunction (such as *through, although, because, since*) to show the relationship between the two statements.
>
> Write up the new revised thesis:

The new thesis will now drive the organization of the research paper. The next step is to make a detailed outline of the architecture of the research paper based on the new thesis statement and the sources you have selected.

2. The detailed outline

An outline helps the writer maximize the impact of the data by arranging it effectively. The outline serves as a framework for organizing ideas and finding new connections in the data. It also helps the writer identify and remove redundant and overly detailed material. The outline is not a draft, but helps the writer determine whether the body of the paper:

- supports the thesis
- presents the ideas in logical order
- shows the relationship of the main ideas
- demonstrates the relationship between the main ideas (topic sentences) and support (evidence).

The following is a model of an outline for the social history research paper. It should be familiar already and is placed here for review. Review the outline.

Notice that the outline and the models presented in this book contain three body paragraphs. This is for demonstration only as the guidelines call for more than three body paragraphs to fulfil the assignment.

Introduction	
Thesis:	
Body Paragraphs	
A. Main ideas that support the thesis	B. Evidence to support validity of main ideas
I. Idea	1. Evidence
	2. Evidence
	3.
II. Idea	1. Evidence
	2. Evidence
	3. Evidence
	4.
III. Idea	1. Evidence
	2.
IV. Idea	1. Evidence
	2. Evidence
	3.
V. Idea	1. Evidence
	2.
Conclusions	
Restated thesis	

The outline gives a sense of the organization of the evidence for the thesis statement. The next sections focus on writing the body paragraphs.

C. Examining the body paragraphs of a research paper

The development of the body paragraphs in a research paper follows the same principles as writing the paper itself. Each paragraph discusses one theme or discussion point, supported by relevant sources. Each paragraph begins with a topic sentence that informs the reader of the main theme and the nature of the support for the general thesis. This is followed by synthesized evidence uncovered in the review of the literature that demonstrates the validity of the topic sentence. The final sentence of the paragraph summarizes or offers concluding remarks about the content of the paragraph.

> **Relevance**
> Understanding the basic structure of body paragraphs of a research paper provides novice writers with a blueprint from which they can develop their individual style of writing.

1. Synthesizing sources for body paragraphs

Previous chapters introduced ways to report findings of experts for a research paper. The process began when the evidence chosen for possible inclusion in the research paper was summarized, paraphrased and quoted. Then the sources were grouped according to themes. The themes were then organized in an outline to examine their relevance and relationship to one another and to the topic. The next step is to write a synthesis of the sources by themes for incorporation into the body paragraphs of the research paper.

A synthesis involves combining two or more sources to support the thesis. The synthesis is more than presenting summaries of material. To some extent, all research papers are synthesis papers because they combine the evidence (facts, statistics, examples, and quotes from experts, etc.) to show the reader a new perspective on the topic.

The themes also provide the basis for paragraph development. One theme is discussed in each paragraph in most literature review papers. This is shown below in the example of an outline of the second paragraph of the sample paper about the grandmother: The theme of the paragraph is the limited opportunities for women before the war.

> Thesis statement for the whole paper: *World War 2 brought about social changes that led to financial independence for creative and hard-working women like my grandmother.*
>
> Theme of the 2nd body paragraph in the body of the paper: *Limited opportunities for women before the war.*

Topic sentence of the paragraph:

Until the forties, women of my grandmother's generation were frustrated by the limited opportunities for them to seek employment outside of the home.

Supporting evidence:

> In a letter to her sister, my grandmother described years of frustration when she tried to find employment in local factories before the war (primary source: letters from grandmother to her sister, 1941).
>
> My grandmother went on to explain that two years after the war began "the factories actively recruited women workers." She was hired and continued to work until the end of the war (primary source: interview with grandmother).
>
> Prior to 1941, newspapers contained virtually no advertisements for work considered suitable for women. After 1941 advertisements aimed at female workers began to appear and continued steadily until the end of the war (primary source, Daily News, National News; secondary source, Smith, 2012).
>
> Labor statistics from the war period demonstrate the growing number of women in the work force during the war years. By 1945, the number of women employed increased to 25,000 from 5,000 in 1940 in her area (secondary source: Statistics from Ministry of Labor, www.laborstatistics.org).

> **Relevance**
> Novice writers often write summaries of their secondary sources author by author rather than synthesize their findings point by point to support the thesis of their research paper. Being able to synthesize sources and identify the difference between synthesis and summary are essential academic skills.

The example below demonstrates how to develop a synthesis of the work of four expert sources and examples from the primary sources to support the writer's point of view expressed in the topic sentence and the thesis statement. These are six sources in all. At the end of these guidelines there is a sample draft essay that illustrates all the points in the instructions.

Please take the time to go over the following assignments carefully as understanding and practicing synthesis develops skills that are important to academic writing across all disciplines.

Note that even though many of the examples in this chapter include only three body paragraphs, your research paper will include more paragraphs depending on the length of the paper, number of sources and themes.

Synthesis

> **Example:** Body paragraphs
>
> In the example below, the author takes a position on a topic which is stated in the thesis. The writer supports the thesis by synthesizing evidence from different sources.
>
> A synthesis involves combining two or more summaries to support the thesis.
>
> In the example below, evidence is provided by synthesizing the work of four expert sources and drawing on the writer's own observations and experience to make a point about a particular aspect of sleep. The example shows how the information from one source relates to the other sources and how they work together to support the thesis.
>
> The body of the sample paper consists of three paragraphs. Each body paragraph states a position clearly in a topic sentence. The topic sentence opens the paragraph and previews the evidence that will support the position (thesis). The rest of the paragraph gives details that convince the reader. The structure follows the same outline provided earlier in the chapter.
>
> Body Paragraph 1: Topic sentence + Evidence from article 1 and 2
>
> Body Paragraph 2: Topic Sentence + Evidence from book and article 2
>
> Body Paragraph 3: Topic Sentence + Relevant personal experience

	Synthesis	
Introduction	Includes a thesis statement that makes a clear, concise point about sleep.	According to scientists, sleep deprivation is as debilitating as intoxication and poses a serious threat to public safety.
Body Paragraph 1	Uses one idea in the paragraph. 1. Includes a topic sentence that indicates the support that the paragraph will provide for the thesis. 2. Summarizes the information in the topic sentence. 3. Uses reliable sources (no popular media) 4. Presents all relevant information about the sources. (author, date, reference at end)	Everything is in this paragraph relates to **driving**. In his comprehensive overview of the sleep process, Epstein (2011) highlights the deadly results of sleep deprivation on drivers. For instance, findings from a 2006 study conducted by the Institute of Medicine of the National Academy of Science revealed that driver sleepiness was a factor in 20% of all serious car accidents and 57% of fatal accidents (Institute of Medicine of the National Academy of Science, 2006). Moreover, Epstein (2011) demonstrated that the effects of sleep deprivation on hand-eye coordination and reaction time are similar to being intoxicated. Clearly, public safety on the roads is linked to adequate sleep for drivers of cars and public transport.

Body Paragraph 2	Uses one main idea in the paragraph. 1. Includes a topic sentence that indicates the support that the paragraph will provide for the thesis. 2. Summarizes the information in the topic sentence. 3. Uses reliable sources (no popular media) 4. Presents all relevant information about the sources. (author, date, reference at end)	Everything in this paragraph relates to **transportation disasters** According to the research of Dement and Vaughn (2011), sleep deprivation was a major factor in some of the greatest transportation disasters in modern history. Sleep deprivation contributed to the 1989 environmental disaster caused when the oil tanker, Exxon Valdez, ran aground, spilling millions of gallons of crude oil into Prince William Sound in Alaska. The authors attribute the accident's cause to the accumulated sleep deprivation of the third mate who was piloting the ship. The man had slept fewer than six of the previous 48 hours. Similarly, Johnson and Smith (2008) report that a year-long investigation found sleep deprivation played a major role in the disaster of the space shuttle Challenger. The study cited an error in judgment attributed to the sleep deprivation of the managers who decided to launch the Challenger despite a lack of evidence that the shuttle was safe in cold temperatures. Dangers to public safety only increase when sleep deprived professionals make decisions involving huge and powerful craft. _{Content from Epstein and Dement & Vaughn republished in Behrens, L. & Rosen, J. (2011).}
Body Paragraph 3	Uses one idea in the paragraph. 1. Includes a topic sentence that indicates a personal experience that supports the thesis. 2. Summarizes the event with relevant details (evidence)	Everything is in this paragraph relates to **a personal example.** Most people have been touched by a tragedy caused by sleep deprivation. The 20-year-old son of my neighbor fell asleep at the wheel one night on the way home from a late class at the university. He died the next day in the hospital, leaving his family heartbroken. His mother explained that he had stayed up the previous night in order to complete a paper for his course. By the time he was driving home from class, he had not slept for more than 40 hours.
Conclusion	1. Paraphrases the thesis. (According to scientists, sleep deprivation is as debilitating as intoxication and poses a serious threat to the public safety.) 2. Restates the main points.	Public safety is threatened as much by sleep deprivation as by intoxication. Research has shown that a lack of sleep impairs the cognitive functions required to navigate any vehicle, aircraft, or watercraft safely. The Exxon Valdez and Challenger disasters illustrate that even highly trained professionals lose the ability to function effectively when they lack sleep. Public safety depends on a good night's sleep and the good judgment of all citizens.

Practice: Synthesis

> Examine three reviews of a recent film online or in newspapers. Use the example of synthesis presented above as a model.
>
> Examine the critics' views about two of the following aspects of the film such as the direction, cinematography, acting, costumes, score, plot, etc.
>
> Synthesize the three critics' views about two of the aspects of the film listed above.
>
> Each paragraph should synthesize the critics' views on one aspect of the film. For example, if the choice is cinematography and acting, the three critics' views about the cinematography should be discussed in one paragraph, and their views about the acting in another paragraph.
>
> For each paragraph:
>
> 1. Write a topic sentence that introduces the topic and point of view presented in the paragraph.
> 2. Write the evidence to support the topic sentence point by point (not critic by critic).
> 3. Write a short concluding sentence summarizing the findings.

The next step is to create a blueprint for the content of each of the body paragraphs for the research paper. Each paragraph sketches the synthesized evidence, point by point as seen in the sample and practice above.

2. A blueprint for incorporating synthesis into a research paper

The purpose of the chart below will be to serve as a guide in preparation for writing the content of each paragraph.

The chart will serve as a guide for creating the blueprint for the synthesized information/data you have gathered. Fill in the chart using your own data. This will guide you in the development of your body paragraphs, introduction, and conclusion in later sections.

	Section	Content/Evidence	Your notes
INTRODUCTION	Subject	Write a brief description of your remarkable person.	
	Time and place	Describe the person in relation to his or her times.	
	Causes: A dilemma, problem, crisis, predicament, situation, etc.	Summarize the relation of the personal situation to the public context. Summarize the factors that make this person remarkable.	

	Section	Content/Evidence	Your notes
BODY PARAGRAPHS	Ideas: Decisions, actions, help, hindrances, challenges, setbacks, good luck, etc. in their socio-historical context.	List each important idea within its socio-historical context that contributed to the outcome. Idea 1 Idea 2 Idea 3 Idea 4, 5, 6 (if relevant)	
CONCLUSION	Outcome	Summarize the most important events Describe the significance of the outcome to the person and his or her times.	

D. AWARE: Arranging to write body paragraphs

You now have a blueprint for the content of the whole research paper including the sources that provide the evidence for the thesis. In this section the focus will be on creating a detailed outline for each of the body paragraphs. Good body paragraphs organize presentations of ideas for both the writer to write them and for the reader to read and understand them.

The following guidelines review the organization and content of effective body paragraphs:

1. Each paragraph has unity and cohesion: Unity means confining the paragraph to a single topic or idea. Cohesion means using a controlling idea or logical division of ideas. If you change the topic, start a new paragraph.
2. Each paragraph has a topic sentence: The topic sentence tells the reader what the paragraph is about and what aspect of an idea will be developed. It is usually the first sentence of the paragraph.
3. Supporting sentences help to develop the topic or present evidence for the claim presented in that paragraph.
4. Each paragraph has a concluding sentence: The concluding sentence sums up the information given in the paragraph. It may be introduced by a signaling phrase such as "In conclusion" or "To sum up" or "Finally". It usually restates the topic sentence in different words or sums up the evidence in the supporting sentences.
5. The paragraphs are connected by transition words or sentences that signal to the reader the relationship between the ideas that each paragraph presents.

The detailed outline of each of the body paragraphs of the research paper on a remarkable person can now be drafted, including how the ideas relate to one another and to the thesis statement.

A detailed outline for the body paragraphs

> Use the chart below to write out the outline for each of the body paragraphs in your paper on a remarkable person.
>
> Introduction
>
> **Thesis statement:**
>
> Body Paragraphs
>
> **Topic sentence: Main Idea 1**
> evidence in support of the topic sentence (source)
> evidence in support of the topic sentence (source)
> evidence in support of the topic sentence (source)
> Transition
>
> **Topic sentence: Main Idea 2**
> evidence in support of the topic sentence (source)
> evidence in support of the topic sentence (source)
> evidence in support of the topic sentence (source)
> Transition
>
> **Topic sentence: Main Idea 3**
> evidence in support of the topic sentence (source)
> evidence in support of the topic sentence (source)
> evidence in support of the topic sentence (source)
> Transition
>
> **Conclusion**
> Restated thesis:

E. AWARE: Writing the body paragraphs

You are now ready to write up the body paragraphs. The introduction and the conclusion are written later. This is because there may be a slight change or adjustment of the thesis statement during the writing of the paper itself. As the introductory and concluding paragraphs contain a reference to the overall thesis, it is wise to leave them until last.

Now write the first draft of the body of the research paper using the outline created above and the guidelines below.

> Writing the body paragraphs
> 1. Write the first draft of the body paragraphs of the paper.
> 2. Use the outline to guide you as you compose each paragraph.
> 3. Each paragraph should discuss only one idea that is introduced in a topic sentence.
> 4. Each topic sentence must be followed by supporting sentences and finally a concluding sentence.
> 5. Include two or more sources to support the theme.
> 6. Include at least one quote and one paraphrase in the text.
> 7. Use transition words to create cohesion within and between paragraphs.

The first full draft of the body of the paper is now ready. In the next section, you will write an introduction that provides the context for the research before presenting the significance of the findings in the conclusion.

Research papers vary in terms of expectations about what should be included in introductions and conclusions. A research report on a quantitative study in the natural sciences has a different structure than a position paper in history. Always check with your instructor for any specific guidelines about what to include in your introduction or conclusion.

F. Examining introductions to research papers

Strategies for writing introductions have been practiced in previous chapters. This section will review the strategies briefly and then introduce new strategies for writing introductions to research papers. The introduction is a crucial part of a research paper and contains specific information or moves that will be expected by the reader. An effective introduction contains a move which situates the topic in its research context. A good introduction indicates to the reader where the paper fits in the ongoing discussion in the field. The introduction also informs the reader about the writer's message and how it will be presented. It is the road map for the content of the paper. Whereas the introduction to the previous essay was only one paragraph, the introduction to the research paper can be longer, even two to three paragraphs. This is because a research paper that reviews what experts have said about the topic tends to be more complex and may require a more detailed orientation for the reader than a paper based on primary sources.

1. Strategies for writing effective introductions to a research paper

The most widely used approach to writing an introduction is to begin with a general statement or establishing a territory for the topic. Effective introductions to papers based on secondary sources demonstrate that the writer has reviewed what the most reliable experts have said about the topic. The second purpose is to give the reader enough background knowledge to understand the thesis. This is followed by the writer's view on the topic. The writer's view can be in the form of short concluding remarks in a sentence or two that inform the reader about the findings based on the review of the literature. The introduction also informs the reader why this is an interesting topic and the paper is therefore worth reading. This part should then lead into the thesis statement. A good introduction outlines the structure of the paper. This is the model presented here. An effective introduction will:

- attract the reader's interest,
- introduce the general topic/problem/territory,
- define key terms if necessary,
- develop sufficient background to understand the thesis,
- present a clear and concise thesis,
- reveal the type of evidence that will be used to support the thesis and the organizational structure.

Additionally, an introduction to a research paper based on secondary sources may:

- place the study into its larger context by indicating the major influences (sources) when appropriate,
- indicate the writer's understanding of the problem,
- point out why this review is worth conducting and therefore also worth reading or why the research question is interesting.

Clearly, all this information cannot be conveyed in a few sentences, so the introduction may need to be two to three paragraphs long. The general strategies in writing good introductions presented in Chapter 10 still apply and should be reviewed when writing the introduction to this paper. However, the focus of the following sections will be on adding information to introductions that place the paper into the current discussion in the field citing secondary sources and explain why this review/study is worth conducting.

Below is an example of an introduction to a research paper. The key aspects are identified in the right-hand column.

Introductions

An introduction to a research paper should:

1. Attract the reader's interest.
2. Introduce the general topic/problem.
3. Define key terms if necessary.
4. Develop sufficient background to understand the thesis.
5. Present a clear and concise thesis.
6. Reveal the type of evidence that will be used to support the thesis and the organizational structure.

Sample Research Paper Introduction 1

Vast public funds are spent on subsidizing industry. In Australia, the extent of assistance, via both direct financial assistance and protection, varies greatly between industries and between specific sectors of industries. In its broadest sense assistance is given to industries in order to attempt to stabilize the industry during difficult periods or to enable the industry to adapt to long term changes in the economy. Due to changes in agriculture world-wide, caused by the price squeeze and volatile world export markets, assistance has been given to Australian agriculture. During the period 1982–83 the direct cost of this assistance was just under $500 million (Johnson et al., 1983).	**Attracts readers' interest** *General* *Background and context* *Indicator of specific focus and understanding of the problem* *Identification of source*
In this essay, the forms of agricultural assistance will be discussed in terms of the type of assistance, the rates of assistance to agriculture in comparison with those of other industries, the effects of assistance, and finally, whether assistance can be justified. It will be argued throughout the paper that, despite the problems associated with assistance and despite the complex nature of the issue, there should be assistance of several kinds so that the agricultural sector is able to maintain its economic viability (Jones, 1997). <u>In particular, it will be argued that this assistance is at its most effective when it is target specific</u>.	*Issues which will be covered and indication of the order* **Major source/influence** Thesis statement Indication of conclusion

Adapted from an original idea from:
http://www.services.unimelb.edu.au/asu/download/Writing-

G. AWARE: Arranging to write an introduction

Use the guidelines and strategies presented above to write an introduction to a research paper.

Arranging to write: An outline of an introduction to a research paper

Write a three-paragraph introduction to your research paper using the detailed outline below. Address each topic in one to two sentences to avoid an overly long introduction. Remember to:

- introduce the general topic/problem and attract the reader's interest,
- define key terms only if necessary,
- develop sufficient background information for the reader to understand the thesis,
- place the study into its research context by indicating the major influences (sources),
- say why this study is worth conducting or why this is an interesting question,
- present a clear and concise thesis,
- reveal the type of evidence that will be used to support the thesis and the organizational structure.

Paragraph 1	(1) Attract interest and introduce the general topic/problem to provide sufficient background
	(3) define key terms only if necessary
Paragraph 2	(4) place the study into its theoretical context by indicating the major (sources)
	(5) say why this study is worth conducting or why this is an interesting question
Paragraph 3	(6) present a clear and concise thesis
	(7) reveal the evidence used to support the thesis and the organizational structure

H. AWARE: Writing an introduction

Writing an introduction to a research paper

Write a full draft of the introduction using the guidelines presented above.

The introduction can now be added to the body paragraphs. The next step is to write the conclusion. This will be the focus of the next section.

I. Examining conclusions to research papers

In some ways a conclusion is the opposite to a good introduction. If the introduction presents the content of the paper, the flow of ideas naturally leads to the conclusion. Readers expect certain information to be present in the conclusion. A conclusion reminds the reader what was said in the paper. It brings together different parts of the argument presented and discusses the larger implications of the findings. A conclusion paraphrases the thesis and how it was supported. A conclusion should not offer any new material.

As with introductions, the length of the conclusion should be in proportion to the length of the essay. For this paper, a two to three paragraph conclusion may be appropriate.

1. Strategies for writing effective conclusions to research papers

One strategy for writing conclusions is to reverse the order of items presented in the introduction. Instead of moving from general to specific statements, start by paraphrasing the thesis statement and summing up the information in the paper, allowing the statements to become more and more general (view sample below). Remember, the conclusion should remind the reader of the points that have been made in the paper.

Reflect upon the significance of the writing. What might be some of the larger implications of the argument? How might the results affect the general public? What are the consequences of one course of action or another, or no action at all? Remind the reader why this was an important topic to study.

No single study will answer all questions or solve a problem for all time. Sometimes a writer must omit important information or not follow an important lead in the review. Usually, the writer explains in the conclusion why he or she chose to follow some leads and not others or to omit information. The common reasons given are that they were beyond the scope of the paper (not directly relevant to the thesis), time or length limits. It is also possible that data or sources could not be accessed or were not available for some other reason.

It is customary in a research paper to indicate to the reader what questions arose during the study that were not answered or what further research might be undertaken.
Use phrases like:

This study raised an interesting question…
One (two, three) question(s) remains unanswered…
A further examination of… might reveal ….

> **Relevance**
> If the student does not point out the limitations of the paper, the teacher will do it, sometimes resulting in a lower grade.

A good final sentence leaves the reader with something to think about, perhaps a new way of looking at a concept presented in the paper. This could be a quotation or statistics to emphasize a point or an expert opinion to lend authority to the conclusion. This is also a good time to insert a writer's own experiences or views, if appropriate. Return to an anecdote, example, or quotation that may have been used in the introduction but add further insight that derives from the evidence presented in the body of the paper.

Previous chapters presented the following general strategies for writing conclusions. They were:

1. Paraphrase the thesis.
2. Synthesize the major ideas.
3. Explain the significance of the findings.

These strategies also apply to a research paper. But a conclusion to a research paper should also include:

4. A description of limitations or unanswered questions.
5. A final sentence pulling the findings together and explaining their significance and implications.

Below are two examples of conclusions. The first has only one paragraph and the second has two paragraphs. Both have all the components that characterize an effective conclusion presented at the beginning of this section.

Practice: Reading to write 1: conclusions

The following is a conclusion that matches the sample introduction presented above with its key aspects identified in the right-hand column.

Sample research paper conclusion 1:

The comparative analysis across the industry sectors offered in this essay therefore indicates that for the agricultural sector in particular, (1) economic viability can only be maintained when assistance is offered at a variety of levels. Further, as the economic crisis of 82/83 shows, (2) targeting specific assistance is an extremely successful crisis management tool. (3) To claim that industry assistance should be abandoned because it is 'complex' and 'problematic' therefore, fails to (4) acknowledge the substantial benefits that the scheme has delivered over the last decade. (5) This study has not addressed all the relevant questions concerning industry assistance; indeed, (6) more needs to be done to address the complex problems associated with various assistance initiatives. But the advantages of targeting specific measures are a promising benchmark for future enterprise. (7) These will benefit industry and ultimately the public at large who fund the initiatives.	1. Revisiting major themes of the paper 2. Restatement of the thesis 3. Restatement of support 4. Explains the significance of the findings 5. Points out any limitations or unanswered questions that perhaps were beyond the scope of the study 6. Suggests further research 7. Final summarizing sentence

Adapted from: <http://www.services.unimelb.edu.au/asu/download/Writing->

Practice: Reading to write 2: conclusions

Sample research paper conclusion 2 (a two paragraph conclusion)

The use of English as a medium of instruction in universities around the world is increasing. (1) Very little is known about the effect this trend has on the nature of learning, especially when students' native language is not the same as the language used for assessment and for communicating their knowledge. (2) The studies reviewed in this paper showed that at least a third of international students have some difficulty in comprehending English academic texts. (2) This review also showed that even though students, in general, are content with their English skills and their English language preparation, they acknowledge that working in English increases their workload and that they must employ different strategies to access the curriculum. (3) The fact that they have informal, receptive skills with little practice in formal productive language constrains the learning process. (4 These constraints are added to the general challenges all students face to when encountering new concepts, constructs and terminology in a new field of academic study. (5) The results of the study presented above pose further questions. (6) The first has to do with the depth of students' acquisition of new knowledge (Prosser et al. 1994) when a good deal of their cognitive and memory capacity is spent on linguistic processing. (7) Also, to what extent students are able to master the academic discourse of their particular linguistic domain when the input is largely in a different language than the output. (7) These questions for further research have implications for educational policy. They become increasingly important as the use of English spreads in academia at the same time as the population of university students increases and becomes more linguistically and educationally heterogeneous.

1. Restate the thesis
2. Synthesize the major ideas
3. Explains the significance of topic and thesis
4. Explains the significance of findings
5. Points out any limitations or unanswered questions that perhaps were beyond the scope of the study
6. Suggests further research
7. Ends with a final sentence pulling the findings together

J. AWARE: Arranging to write a conclusion

Use the guidelines below to give a sense of the overall content and focus of the paper in the conclusion.
1. Paraphrase the thesis and support from the introduction for use in the conclusion to the research paper. Restate the thesis, summarize, and paraphrase the main points. Remember to use one or more of the strategies presented in Chapter 10.
2. Write your restated thesis from the previous practice.
   a. Write the restated first supporting idea.
   b. Write the restated second supporting idea.
   c. Write any subsequent restated supporting idea/s.
3. Write a statement that shows the significance of your topic.
4. Write a statement indicating the significance of your findings.
5. Write a statement indicating any weaknesses, unanswered or interesting questions raised by your study.
6. Write a statement suggesting further research.
7. Write any final words you would like to leave your readers with.
8. Add discourse connectors to indicate the relationship between the ideas expressed in the sentences.

K. AWARE: Writing a conclusion to a research paper

Writing a conclusion to the research paper

Write up the first full draft of your conclusion based on your work from the previous practice.

Once the conclusion is added to the introduction and body paragraphs, the first full draft of the research paper is completed.

L. AWARE: Assessing the research paper

The purpose of assessment is to determine whether the thesis statement is credible and whether there is enough reliable evidence to support the thesis statement including whether the quantity and quality of the sources are adequate. Refer to Chapter 9 for examples.

Use the reverse outline strategy to assess your evidence by creating a single paragraph that contains:

- the thesis statement in full,
- the topic sentences for each paragraph.
    1. Does each topic sentence in a new paragraph relate directly to the thesis statement? Underline any topic sentences that do not relate directly. These need to be changed or revised.
    2. Does the thesis accurately reflect the supporting points in the reverse outline? If it does, you have a viable thesis statement. If the relationship between the working thesis and topic sentences are not clear and direct, what changes can you make to more accurately reflect the supporting evidence?
    3. Are there a sufficient number of main ideas to support the thesis?
    4. Are the quantity and quality of the evidence sufficient to support the topic sentence in each body paragraph?
        a. Is each main idea supported by at least three pieces of evidence? Circle main ideas that need more evidence.
        b. Is the evidence convincing?
        c. Are there two or more sources for the evidence provided in each paragraph?
        d. Do you use at least five sources; a book, two articles and two websites?
        e. Is additional research needed for the main ideas that do not have sufficient evidence?

The next step is to revise and edit the draft.

M. AWARE: Revising

1. Parallelism and cohesion

Parallel structure refers to the use of the same pattern of words to show that ideas are of equal importance. Parallelism is an important cohesive element that keeps the reader focused on ideas rather than language. Faulty parallelism interrupts the reader's flow and blunts the writer's message. Parallel structures can occur at the word, phrase, or clause level.

A common way to join parallel structures is with the use of coordinating conjunctions such as *and* or *or*.

In the example below, note that the writer uses two different grammatical constructions to describe the actors. Read the sentences out loud and notice which is more fluent.

Not parallel: *The playwright hired actors with clear voices and who project strong emotions on stage.*

Parallel: *The playwright hired actors who have clear voices and who project strong emotions on stage.*

Parallel: *The playwright hired actors who project clear voices and strong emotions on stage.*

2. Parallel words and phrases

The following sentence has faulty parallelism at the word and phrase level. The writer has mixed word forms within the same sentence. Read the sentence aloud and notice how awkward it sounds.

Not parallel: *Dr. Smith likes to travel internationally, classical music, and he spends quality time with his family.*

The sentences below show several different ways of correcting the faulty parallelism.

Parallel:
Dr. Smith likes international travel, classical music and time with his grandchildren. (nouns)

Dr. Smith likes to travel internationally, to attend classical music concerts, and to spend time with his grandchildren. (infinitive verbs)

Dr. Smith likes traveling internationally, attending classical music concerts, and spending time with his grandchildren. (gerunds)

Faulty parallelism is not only awkward but makes it hard for the reader to take meaning from your sentence and obscures the sharpness of your message.

Practice: Revising for parallelism

> Read your draft for parallelism.
>
> When editors are marking a paper for revisions, they use a pair of slanting lines in the margin (//) to indicate a faulty parallel structure in the sentence.
>
> 1. Read your paper out loud, paragraph by paragraph. Notice any places that sound awkward.
> 2. Place a // mark in the margin next to any sentences that sound as if they may have faulty parallelism.
> 3. Revise the sentences so that all structures are parallel.

Below are checklists based on the revision and editing practiced in earlier chapters.

Checklist for revising and editing

		Yes	No	Comments
Assignment Chapter 11	1. The paper fulfills the requirements of the assignment in terms of topic, sources, length and format			
Introduction Chapter 2,7,10,12	2. The introductory paragraph presents necessary contextual information to establish the significance of the topic 3. The information goes from general to specific 4. The introduction includes a thesis statement 5. The thesis statement includes a topic and a point of view 6. The thesis statement previews the direction of the paper			
Body Paragraphs Chapter 2,5,10,12	7. The body paragraphs are of similar length 8. Paragraphs are organized thematically and support the thesis/message of the paper 9. Paragraphs are logically organized according to the strength, depth, importance of the evidence 10. Each paragraph discusses an element of the thesis statement 11. Each paragraph contains a topic sentence 12. Each paragraph presents properly cited supporting evidence 13. Evidence relates directly to the topic sentence and the thesis/message 14. Each paragraph contains a final summary sentence 15. A variety of discourse connectors/transition words link paragraphs to show how ideas are connected 16. The paper contains quotes and paraphrases in accordance with the assignment			
Conclusion Chapter 7,10,12	17. The conclusion restates the author's position (re-worded thesis) 18. The content ties into the introduction and summarizes the main points 19. Limitations and further questions are included if appropriate 20. The conclusion includes the author's final thoughts on the topic 21. No new information is introduced in the conclusions			

		Yes	No	Comments
Format Chapter 10,12	22. The required formatting style is used throughout the text and in the bibliography/reference list 23. Your name and the title of the paper is included and in the correct format 24. The font, font size, line spacing, and margins conform to the guidelines 25. All in-text citations are appropriately cited 26. All in-text citations are included in the bibliography/reference list 27. Each page has a running-head (if applicable)			
Quotes and Paraph. Chapter 8	28. Number of direct quotes and their length is limited 29. All quotes, paraphrases, and/or summaries in the text are attributed to the author 30. Quotes and paraphrases are reported according to the require format			
Language Chapter 10,12	31. Academic language is used throughout the text 32. The text does not include slang, contractions, clichés or colloquial language 33. A neutral tone is used throughout 34. Sentences are not overly long nor embedded. 35. Structures are parallel			
Vocabulary Chapter 2	36. Vocabulary is varied, academic and clearly relates to topic 37. Terminology specific to the topic or discipline is used 38. Synonyms are used to avoid repetition 39. Precise and specific vocabulary is used 40. Commonly confused word pairs e.g. affect or effect are appropriately used 41. Pronoun references are clear and consistent			
Discourse conn. Chapters. 5,10	42. Discourse connectors and transition words are varied and clearly signal relationships between sentences (and paragraphs)			

		Yes	No	Comments
Grammar Chapter 3	43. Consistent standard usage and spelling is used 44. Past tense is used consistently for reporting data 45. Subjects and verbs agree in number 46. Apostrophes are used according to convention 47. Articles and determiners are used according to conventions especially non-count nouns			
Punctuation Chapter 2	48. The text does not have sentence fragments, comma splices or run-on sentences? 49. Punctuation for discourse connectors and introductory words and phrases are according to convention 50. All quotes, paraphrases, and/or summaries in the text are punctuated according to convention 51. English conventions are used for capitalization			

References

Ardley, B., & Ardley, N. (1989). *The Random House book of 1001 questions and answers*. Random House.
Behrens, L., & Rosen, J. (2011). *Writing and reading across the curriculum (11th ed.)*. Pearson.
Clendon, S. A., & Erickson, K. A. (2008). The vocabulary of beginning writers: Implications for children with complex communication needs. *Augmentative and Alternative Communication*, 24 (4), 281–293.
Connor, U. (1996). *Contrastive rhetoric: Cross-cultural aspects of second-language writing*. Cambridge University Press.
Coxhead, A. (2000). A new academic word list. *TESOL Quarterly*, 34(2), 213–238.
Cresswell, J. W. (2007). *Qualitative inquiry and research design: Choosing among five approaches* (2nd ed.). Sage.
Graff, G., & Birkenstein, C. (2012). *They say, I say: The moves that matter in academic writing*. W.W. Norton.
Holden, C. (1980). Identical twins reared apart. *Science*, 210, 1323–1327.
Hyland, K. (2007). Genre pedagogy: Language, literacy and L2 writing instruction. *Journal of Second Language Writing*, 16, 148–164.
Kaplan, R. (1966). Cultural thought patterns in intercultural education. *Language Learning*, 16, 1–20. https://doi.org/10.1111/j.1467-1770.1966.tb00804.x
Lave, J., & Wenger, E. (1991) *Situated learning: Legitimate peripheral participation*. Cambridge University Press. https://doi.org/10.1017/CBO9780511815355
Lichtman, M. (2006). *Qualitative research in education: a user's guide*. Sage.
Link, F., & Almquist, S. (1997). *Thinking to write: A work journal program*. Curriculum Development Associates.
Nesi, H., & Gardner, H. (2012). *Genres across the disciplines: Student writing in higher education*. Cambridge University Press.
Saldana, J. (2009). *The coding manual for qualitative researchers*. Sage.
Wolcott, H. F. (1994). *Transforming qualitative data: Description, analysis, and interpretation*. Sage.
Swales, J. (1990). *Genre analysis: English in academic and research settings*. Cambridge University Press.
Yavorsky, J. E., Dush, C. M., & Schoppe-Sullivan, S. J. (2015). The production of inequality: The gender division of labor across the transition to parenthood. *Journal of Marriage and the Family*, 77(3), 662–679. https://doi.org/10.1111/jomf.12189

Index

A

academic communication   8
academic discourse   8, 12, 18, 138
academic discourse
   community   8
academic genres   6, 90, 245
academic language   11, 18
academic research   51, 160
academic texts   10, 20
academic vocabulary   9, 12–15,
   20–21
academic voice   1, 14, 23
academic word families   20
Academic Word List   12, 20
academic writing   3–5, 11, 17–19,
   23–24, 45–46, 51, 58–61, 89,
   137, 159–160, 163, 211, 216, 237,
   273–274
adjective   41–42, 71, 123–124
adjectives   42, 71, 79, 123, 233
adverb   20, 42, 63, 106, 124
adverbial clauses   62–63, 66
adverbs   41–42, 105, 123
analysis   27, 31, 117, 127, 160, 183,
   188–195, 203, 216, 224
analyze   37, 47, 67, 86, 98–99, 120,
   132, 161, 187, 192, 195, 204, 238
analyzing the data   203
annotated   254–256
annotation   255–256
APA   17, 79, 153, 155, 164, 167, 169,
   177, 183, 216–219, 231–235, 240,
   252, 254, 256
architecture   3, 23–24, 59–60, 67,
   80, 89, 113, 116, 127, 154
argument   26–27, 31, 89, 161, 176,
   238, 283
arranging to write (AWARE)   3,
   46–47, 75, 82, 98, 102, 119–120,
   132, 144, 150, 199, 226, 242, 243,
   247, 249, 251, 254, 263, 265, 269,
   277, 278, 282, 286

art   3, 14, 59
article   4, 14, 118, 138, 173, 174–177,
   188, 234–235, 244, 248–249,
   251–254, 258, 264, 274
articles   8, 138, 162, 197, 202, 218,
   233, 241, 244–246, 248, 251–253,
   264, 287
assess   13, 36, 37, 55, 58, 67, 78,
   101–102, 145, 151, 186, 202, 229,
   267, 286
assessing (AWARE)   3, 46, 55–58,
   59, 78, 83, 101–102, 111, 121, 134,
   145, 151, 229, 286
assessing strategy   101, 102, 121,
   229
assessment   23, 59–60, 78, 122,
   203, 286
assessment checklist   58
assignment   4, 17, 19, 36, 38, 47,
   51, 54–56, 67, 74–75, 82–83, 85,
   153, 155, 159, 161, 182–183, 216,
   219, 231, 238, 240, 244, 248,
   271, 289
assignments   4, 6, 16, 18, 38, 51,
   55–56, 127, 154–155, 159–160,
   182, 211, 238, 267
author (authors)   16–17, 29–32,
   163–174, 176–179, 216–219,
   233–235, 252–254
AWARE   3–4, 45–67, 74, 82, 111,
   131, 137, 144, 154, 183, 207, 209
AWARE Approach   45, 67

B

background information   25, 36,
   140–141, 144–145, 152, 220, 222,
   245, 282
background questions   140
blueprint   28, 272, 276–277
body paragraph   25, 31, 34–35, 54,
   78, 92, 121, 128, 213, 282, 289

body paragraphs   23, 25–26,
   28–29, 31–32, 34–35, 53–54,
   56–57, 60, 75, 77, 89–90, 92–94,
   96–97, 100–101, 111, 113–115,
   118, 120–121, 128–131, 134, 140,
   152–155, 207, 209, 211, 227, 267,
   271, 272–275, 276–279, 282,
   286, 289
brainstorm   50, 53, 67, 75
brainstorming   47, 49–50, 75–77,
   82, 98–99, 120, 132, 242
building blocks   3, 23, 25, 59–60,
   80, 90, 183, 232–233

C

case studies   7, 90, 160, 181–184,
   220
case study   46, 159–163, 181–205,
   207–266, 268
case study research question
   181, 187
case study research questions
   176, 186–187
causal language   111, 127, 130–131,
   134, 231
cause (see cause/effect, cause
   and effect)   63–64, 127–134,
   154–155
cause and effect   29, 127, 131–135,
   154–155
cause/effect   26–28, 30, 89, 111,
   127, 137, 148, 154
checklist   58, 78, 79, 84, 123, 125,
   134, 135, 152, 153, 179, 227, 231,
   289
Chicago   17, 153, 191
citation   16–17, 162–164, 167, 177,
   191, 207, 209, 216–220, 230, 232–
   233, 240, 243, 252–253, 257–258
citations   211, 213, 216–218, 220,
   231–233, 240, 246, 253, 254,
   259, 290

cite   216, 218, 227, 237, 251–252, 263
citing   16, 159, 163, 216, 232, 252, 255, 280
clause (clauses)   10, 39, 62–66, 79, 84, 105–106, 126
cluster   47, 98, 241–242, 259–261
clustering   47, 98, 100, 132, 201
code (codes)   192–195, 203–204
code index   194, 203
coding   193–195, 203
cohesion   67, 95, 105, 211–212, 215, 230, 277, 279, 287
collect   189, 202–203
collection   172, 183, 185, 188–191, 201–203, 261
comma splices   125–126, 135, 153, 179, 291
comma usage   79, 84
commonly confused words   124
communicate   8, 23–24
communication   4–6, 18–19, 28, 39, 137–138, 218–220, 231–232
communities   5, 8, 237
community   4–6, 8, 17–18, 23–24, 26, 28, 162
community of practice   6
compare (*see* compare and contrast, compare/contrast) 12, 25, 27–28, 30, 34, 36
compare and contrast   30, 111
compare/contrast   26–28, 31, 37, 89, 111–113, 115, 118, 120, 137, 143–145, 148, 151
concluding sentence   74, 185, 212, 214, 227, 239, 276, 277, 279
concluding sentences   89, 212, 214–215, 230, 267
conclusions   137, 146–152, 252, 257, 271, 283, 284–286, 289
conducting research   47, 51, 60, 161, 181, 183, 207, 237
conjunction   63–64, 124, 270
conjunctions   63, 79, 227, 287
connectors (*see* discourse connectors)
contrast (*see* compare and contrast, compare/contrast) 26–27, 30, 63, 112–115, 116, 118–121, 124, 144–145, 150–153

contrasts   212
counterpoint   144–145
Coxhead   12, 13

D

data (*see* primary data, *see* secondary data sources) 13, 134, 160–162, 172, 181–205, 207–213, 216, 229–230, 245, 259–261, 263–264, 265, 270, 276, 291
data collection   172, 183, 185, 189–191, 197–198, 200–203, 207, 209, 261
data triangulation   198, 264, 265
date of publication   165, 176, 234–235, 248, 252, 254
description   19, 26, 27, 28, 30, 38, 69–78, 85, 153, 155, 83, 240, 255–269, 276, 284
description in thesis-driven writing   70
description to support a thesis   74, 78
detailed outline   269–270, 277–278, 282
direct quotations   17, 163–164, 169, 172, 254
directives   36–38
disciplinary literacy   245
discipline   5, 7, 13, 23, 55, 159, 162, 170, 178, 240, 245–246, 290
disciplines   3, 5, 14, 70, 161, 181–182, 237, 241, 244–246, 265, 273
discourse   4–5, 8–10, 12, 18, 138, 160, 237, 245–246
discourse connectors   9, 12, 14–15, 80–81, 84, 95–96, 105–108, 115–116, 128–129, 212, 269, 290–291
documenting   191, 243–244, 250, 252, 254
draft   49, 53–55, 59, 76–77, 83, 97, 100–103, 120–122, 134, 145, 151–153, 198, 213, 270, 278–279, 282, 286–288
drafting   49, 53–54, 59, 210–211

E

edit   67, 146, 152, 179, 252
editing (AWARE)   3, 46, 59, 61, 84, 105, 124, 146, 152–153, 179, 231, 288
editing checklist   79, 84, 125, 135, 153
effect (*see* cause/effect, cause and effect)   27, 29, 124, 127–133, 135, 290
effects   28, 50, 127–129, 131–133, 135, 155
email   19, 75, 77
enumeration   27–29, 32, 89, 93, 95–97, 107–108, 148, 154–155
essay assignment   36, 141, 185
essays   7, 25, 28–29, 90, 146, 154, 207
evaluate   37, 89, 237
   evidence   229, 263–265
   quantity and quality of data   195–198, 204–205
   sources   192, 248–249, 251
   thesis statement   148
   working thesis statement   241
evaluating   121, 203
evaluation matrix   197–198, 205
evidence
   assessing evidence   55–59
   evaluating evidence   229, 264–265, 287, 289
   evidence and conclusions   146, 223, 225, 284
   evidence and introductions   138, 282
   evidence in a case study   209, 210–214
   evidence in a research paper   238, 241–245
   evidence to support cause and effect   127–134
   evidence to support compare and contrast   113–123
   evidence to support a thesis   24–32, 34–37, 74–75, 97, 207, 241, 267
   evidence to support a topic sentence   92–94
   establishing and organizing evidence   51–55, 90, 98–103, 107–109, 111, 117–123, 227, 259–263, 271–278

description as evidence   70
narrative as evidence   82
revising evidence   60
evidence evaluation matrix   197–198, 205
evidence to support a thesis   35, 74, 97, 207
expert sources   51, 55–56, 92–93, 97, 101, 240, 273–274
explanation   70, 76
expository   24, 37, 74, 151, 237
expository essay   23, 24, 25, 69, 154, 207
expository genres   6–8, 10
expository thesis   18, 26, 28, 112
expository writing   7, 24, 26, 69, 74, 82, 185

F

formal language   11, 18–19, 77, 152, 172, 231
format   153–155, 177, 183, 216–218, 231–232, 234–235, 240–244, 252, 254, 258, 289–290
formatting   79, 191, 216, 231–232, 234, 243, 290
formulating a research question   183, 201
fragment (fragments)   20, 39–43, 44, 63–66, 291
free writing   47, 132, 201

G

general to specific organization   140, 142–143, 147, 222, 227–228, 289
general topic   47, 49–51, 57, 99–100, 108, 142, 240, 269, 281–282
generating ideas   75, 98, 100, 119, 200–201
genre (genres)   6–8, 10, 23, 80, 90, 104, 146, 181, 245
gerund   20, 39, 41–43
graphic organizer   52, 81, 83
graphic organizers   52, 132

H

Hyland   6
hypothesis   160

I

illustration   70
incorporating direct quotations   169
infinitive phrases   41–43
informal language   8, 11–12, 152, 231
informational directives   36–38
informed consent   184
instructions   36, 38, 154
interpretive directives   37
interview (interviews)   164, 177–179, 188–191, 202–203, 218–220
in-text citation   164, 169, 177, 216, 218–219, 230, 253, 258
in-text citations   164, 173, 211, 216, 218–220, 230–232, 240, 253–254, 290
introduction (introductions)   25, 32–33, 35, 45–46, 75–77, 90, 93, 100, 114–115, 117–118, 133, 137–146, 154, 155, 220–224, 227–228, 238, 240, 246, 271, 274, 276, 278–284, 289
introductory words   84, 291

L

Lave & Wenger   6
listing   47, 75, 98, 100, 132
literary   6–8, 16, 51
literary genres   6
literary texts   6
literature review   45, 51, 56, 237–240, 244, 246–248, 252
long quotations   167–168
long summaries   176

M

methods   160, 182, 187, 190, 198, 218, 233
mind map   47, 98, 241–243
MLA   17, 79, 153
move (moves)   138–140, 139, 142, 146–147, 151, 154, 279
multiple authors   217, 233
multiple causes   127, 129, 131–133, 155
multiple effects   127–129, 131–133, 155
multiple sources   4, 31, 56–57, 95, 130, 229, 248, 264

N

narrative in thesis-driven writing   69
narrative to support a thesis   80, 82
narrowed topic   49, 50, 99–100
narrowing the topic   222
Nesi & Gardner   6, 23, 159
non-count nouns   61, 84, 291
noun   39, 41–42, 124, 135
noun clause   62, 64–66
nouns   41–42, 61, 122–123, 160, 288

O

observation   70, 161, 187, 191–192
observations   35, 101, 161, 188, 191–193, 197, 203, 255
organizational patterns   28, 37, 113, 127, 138
organize   24, 52, 132, 176, 181, 190, 192–193, 195, 198, 203–204, 211, 228, 237–238, 261, 267, 277
organized   8, 24, 26, 113, 141, 195, 198, 211, 230, 238, 260, 289
organizing   3, 7, 47, 52–53, 100, 193, 199, 238, 259, 260, 263, 270
organizing sources   259–260
organizing the data   193, 203, 259
outline   35, 52–54, 83, 100–102, 120–121, 128–129, 132–134, 198–199, 205, 210, 214, 226–230, 263–264, 269–274, 278–279, 282, 286–287
outlining   52, 100, 120

P

paragraph (paragraphs)   24–25, 28–32, 34–35, 54, 56–57, 60, 74, 78, 83, 89–96, 101–103, 107–108, 113–114, 118, 120–121, 128–130, 134–135, 222, 227–231, 239–240, 264–265, 272–277, 289, 290
paragraph unity   67, 102–103, 231
parallel   107–108, 287–288, 290
parallelism   287–288
paraphrase   16–18, 163, 169–173, 178–179, 225, 257–258, 284, 286
paraphrased   149, 163–164, 171, 173, 177, 219, 272

paraphrases 169–171, 259, 275, 283, 289–291
paraphrasing 164, 169–170, 172–173, 256–257, 283
paraphrasing direct quotations 172
paraphrasing secondary sources 257
participants 184–186, 197, 202, 219
past tense 172, 211, 227, 230, 291
personal communication 177, 218–220, 231–232
phrases 8–10, 38–42, 62, 84–85, 105, 150, 168, 176–177, 212, 214–215, 283, 288, 291
plagiarism 16–18, 159, 163, 173–179, 209, 254
planning 47, 83, 183, 189, 202
point of view 7, 24–26, 28–29, 47, 49–50, 54–55, 59, 67, 99–100, 107–108, 112, 127–129, 132, 142–143, 145, 147–149, 151, 208–209, 222–224, 227, 230, 241–243, 257, 269, 276, 289
point-by-point organization 113–114, 116–118, 120
precise language 11, 71, 123
precise vocabulary 70–72, 122–123
precision 12, 20, 78, 84
preposition (prepositions) 39–40, 124
prepositional phrases 39–40, 43, 62
present tense 211, 258
presenting 108, 132, 148–149, 163, 173, 207, 272, 279
  evidence 37, 209, 230
  data 193, 197, 264
  information 10, 23, 28
  quotations 164
  results 245
  primary 159–163, 187–190, 202, 211, 216, 219, 230, 264, 273
  data 187–188, 202, 208, 213, 227, 230
  data sources 187, 202
  research 161, 163, 211, 230
  sources 160–161, 181, 183, 187–190, 197, 202, 216, 218–219, 252, 273
private writing 5

production 196, 210–214, 225
pronoun (pronouns) 39, 65, 233, 290
public writing 4–6
published sources 237, 244, 248, 250
punctuation 79, 86, 106, 167, 291
  punctuation for discourse connectors 105, 125, 135, 291

Q

qualitative research 160, 182, 185, 202
quality of evidence 55, 121
quantitative research 160
quantity of sources 56
quotation (quotations) 17, 163–170, 172–173, 177, 188, 217–219, 257–259, 284
quote 101, 164–165, 167, 178, 188, 192, 252–256, 258–259
quotes 34–35, 163, 191, 193, 252, 257, 289–291
quoting 164, 256–257
  quoting secondary sources 257

R

reading to write 32, 72, 81, 92, 96, 116, 118, 129, 130, 139, 142, 148, 149, 162, 213, 221, 225, 239, 284, 285
reference list 191, 216, 218–220, 231–233, 236, 252, 254–255, 259, 290
references 17, 51, 164, 194, 216, 218, 231–234, 236–237, 240, 244, 246, 252, 254, 290, 293
reflection 55, 59, 223
relative pronouns 65
relevance 96, 138, 146–147, 150–151, 161, 192, 200, 249, 251, 255, 259, 264–265, 272
reliability of sources 237
rephrase 101, 146, 228
  rephrase the thesis 148, 151, 164, 223, 228
rephrasing 148, 169, 223–224
report (reports) 6–7, 23, 90, 159, 160–161, 166, 174, 177, 186, 202,

211, 218, 234–235, 237, 244, 258, 259, 272, 279
reporting verbs 165–166, 177, 179, 211
research 159–163, 182–197, 202–205, 208–209, 211, 216, 225, 226, 229, 238, 241, 244–246, 250, 252, 259–260, 263–265
research paper 159, 160, 200, 211, 218, 220, 237–238, 240, 243, 245, 250, 252, 257, 259, 263–264, 268–270, 272, 276–286
research question 162, 181, 183, 185–189, 192–198, 201–205, 207, 208, 226, 238, 241, 248, 251–252
research to support a thesis 159
results 30, 37, 160, 211, 225, 245–246, 265–266
reverse outline 101–102, 121, 134, 229–230, 286–287
review 8, 37, 45, 146, 154, 163, 174, 179, 187, 189–190, 192–195, 204, 228, 237–242, 244–248, 251–252, 254, 261, 263, 277, 279–280, 283
review of the literature 237, 239, 241–242, 244, 272, 280
reviewing 161, 190, 192, 203, 243, 254, 260, 263
revise 59–60, 67, 84–85, 123, 134, 151, 210, 227, 230, 287–288
revising (AWARE) 3, 46, 59–60, 78, 84–85, 102–103, 122–123, 134, 146, 151–152, 179, 207, 230, 231, 288–289
revising strategy 58, 102, 122
revision 58–59, 120–121, 229, 288

S

sample draft essay 273
sample reference list 236
scholarly sources 244, 248
secondary 159–162, 211, 264, 268
secondary data sources 162, 211, 216, 230
secondary research 159–162, 245–246
secondary sources 46, 160–162, 188, 200, 216, 237–238, 241, 243, 244, 248, 250, 252–253, 256–258, 264, 280

Index 299

sentence (sentences)   39–44,
    62–66, 83–85, 102, 105–106,
    125–135, 166, 169, 171–174, 179,
    284, 288, 289, 291
sentence fragments   8, 23–24, 39,
    41–44, 62–64, 291
short summaries   174
short quotations   164
single cause   129, 132, 133, 155
single effect   129, 133, 155
social context of writing   4
source (sources)   15–17, 51, 56–58,
    94, 134, 160–165, 169–171, 173,
    176, 177, 183–190, 192–195, 197,
    202–205, 209, 216–220, 231–235,
    237–252, 254–255, 257–259,
    264–265, 272–278, 279–280,
    282, 286–288, 289
spelling   13, 86–87, 291
statement (statements)   143, 145,
    154, 164, 194, 222, 226–228,
    280, 286
strategies   4, 46, 47, 78, 111, 140,
    147, 163, 171, 172, 174, 186, 189,
    191, 192, 193, 196, 221, 223, 227,
    246, 248, 280, 283, 284, 286
strategy   54, 58, 67, 71, 72, 73, 99,
    100, 101, 102, 105, 121, 122, 140,
    142, 148, 149, 150, 193, 197, 222,
    223, 225, 229
style (styles)   8, 11, 14, 15, 17, 20,
    59, 153, 164, 169, 177, 191, 216,
    231–233, 252, 255, 290
subject   39–43, 62–66, 81,
    90–91, 111–115, 174, 181–185, 187,
    190–193, 199–203, 208, 220, 222,
    225–227, 238, 291
subject-by-subject organization
    113–114
subordinate clauses   10, 39, 62
subordinate phrases   39, 62
summaries   173–174, 254, 258–
    259, 272–274, 290–291
summarize   17, 32, 34, 37, 163, 259,
    276–277, 286
summarizing   177–178, 209, 240,
    254, 256–258, 284
    summarizing interviews   177
    summarizing secondary sources
        258

summary   17, 45, 56, 67, 102, 150,
    163, 173–179, 234, 248, 255,
    257–258, 289
Swales   6, 138
synthesis   146, 186, 216, 225, 228,
    272–274, 276
synthesizing sources   272

T
T chart   100, 117–118, 120, 261,
    263, 264, 279
thematic analysis   216
thematic coding   193–194
theme (themes)   192, 194–199,
    203–208, 210–211, 213–214, 216,
    225–230, 237–239, 241–242, 245,
    248, 259–261, 263–264, 272, 279
thesis (see thesis statement)
    24, 28, 35, 45, 54, 55, 58, 67, 74,
    75, 78, 82, 101, 114, 140, 143,
    148–150, 174, 220, 237, 241–243,
    248, 250–251, 259–261, 263, 265,
    267–275, 277–278, 280–287, 289
thesis and organizational patterns
    28
thesis statement   3, 24–35, 47,
    49–52, 54, 58–61, 74, 78, 82–83,
    90, 102, 112–115, 121–122, 127–
    129, 132, 138, 142, 144, 146–148,
    151, 185, 187, 208, 210, 223–224,
    226–227, 251, 267–274, 286–287,
    289
thesis-driven writing   45, 51, 70
topic   4, 11, 24–29, 31–32, 35–37,
    47, 49–50, 55, 58, 81–83, 91,
    97–103, 107–109, 112, 113, 121,
    127, 132–133, 138, 140–142,
    145–149, 183, 185–186, 194, 208,
    212, 222, 238, 240, 242–243, 247,
    251, 260, 268–270, 274, 277, 281,
    286, 289–290
chosing a writing topic   47
topic sentence   25, 31, 35, 54–57,
    60, 81–82, 90–94, 100–104,
    107–109, 114–115, 117, 121,
    129–130, 134, 176, 214–215, 227,
    229, 251, 259, 272–279, 287, 289
triangulation   197–198, 204,
    264–265
two-column graphic organizer   52

U
UK spelling   13, 86–87
understanding the assignment
    75, 82, 240
US spelling   13, 86–87

V
Venn diagram   119–120
verb (verbs)   10, 20, 36, 39, 41–43,
    61–66, 86, 124, 128, 130–131, 135,
    165–166, 172, 186–187, 202, 211,
    288, 291
verb endings   86
verbal phrases   41–42
visualization   71–73, 78
visualize   52, 78, 132–133
voice   3–4, 14–16, 18, 67, 97, 107,
    119, 122–123, 164

W
Web   162–163, 209, 233, 235, 244,
    249–250, 253
word families   20
word precision   78
working thesis   47, 49, 53, 55, 58,
    60, 67, 100, 120–122, 131–132,
    138, 185, 226, 241–243, 246–247,
    259–260, 263–264, 268–269
working thesis statement   47,
    50, 54, 59, 76, 99–100, 122, 132,
    208–210, 226–227, 229–230
writing (AWARE)   46, 53, 74,
    76, 82, 97, 101, 118, 120, 131, 134,
    144, 150, 154, 178, 199, 227, 278,
    282, 286
writing assignment   17, 36, 38,
    47, 51
writing assignments   154